The Job Search
Your Guide to Success

Second Edition

The Job Search
Your Guide to Success

Second Edition

Barbara Zarna

Director of Education
Sawyer School of Business

GLENCOE
McGraw-Hill

New York, New York   Columbus, Ohio   Woodland Hills, California   Peoria, Illinois

Library of Congress Cataloging-in-Publication Data

Zarna, Barbara.
  The job search : your guide to success / Barbara Zarna. – 2nd ed.
     p.   cm.
  Includes index.
  ISBN 0-256-14449-4
  1. Job hunting. 2. Job hunting–Data processing.   I. Title.
  HF5382 7.Z37   1996
  650.14—dc20   96–18084

Send all inquiries to:
Glencoe/McGraw-Hill
8787 Orion Place
Columbus, Ohio 43240-4027

Printed in the United States of America.

0256-14449-4

5 6 7 8 9 10   079/055   03 02 01 00

PREFACE

I am grateful that many thousands of students have benefited from the first edition of *The Job Search: Your Guide to Success*. My objective in preparing the second edition is to preserve the basic structure, approach, and features of the the first edition, while adding important new coverage and updating existing material. Some of the changes you will find in the new edition are as follows:

- The Internet is such a widely used method of advertising job openings throughout the country and I felt it important to include this resource to facilitate the job search process. I have given specific Web sites that should prove useful to students.

- To make my directions for producing resumés, reference sheets, and cover letters more universal, I have added a separate appendix for each of the leading software programs in use today—WordPerfect 6.0 (DOS), WordPerfect 6.1 (Windows), and Microsoft Word 6.0.

- I have included an appendix covering how to use the mail merge feature from all three of the programs above to produce envelopes to accompany cover letters.

- Casual dress is becoming more and more accepted in the workplace today and I felt it important to address this issue in Chapter 9. It is necessary to understand what is acceptable casual dress in the workplace.

- I have changed some of the resumé formats and broadened the scope of the career objectives to touch a wider cross-section of career paths.

Whether we like it or not, it's a fact that most people will change jobs, and even careers, several times. Gone are the days when people would be employed by the same company in their hometowns and retire with 30–40 years of service. Today's graduates will likely extend their job search nationally through the internet and face possible relocation. Evolving technology, advances in manufacturing processes and computer applications, and corporate restructuring are just some of the factors influencing the trend toward job and career mobility.

In my 28 years of teaching experience, I've never found a book that offers concrete, realistic guidance which truly prepares students for the job search that lies ahead. Many courses and career preparation programs rely heavily on lectures and handouts in a worthy effort to bring this important aspect of education into a student's academic experience. However, after just a few months, students may forget the specific job search skills that were covered in seminars or in class. Too often the emphasis is placed only on resumé preparation. This made me realize that trusting such a crucial set of skills to short-term memory is neither the most reliable nor effective way to master the job search process.

On completion of *The Job Search: Your Guide to Success*, students will be equipped with the essential skills necessary to get a job, and more important, to secure the jobs that are right for them.

Furthermore, they will learn that effective job search skills are important in the long term—not just for landing the initial job but for a lifetime of career satisfaction in a work world that will change and change again with the passing of time. Students will gain important insights that will aid them in keeping their job and advancing within a company.

■ ORGANIZATION AND METHOD

Chapter 1 emphasizes the value of taking a personal skills assessment, completing interest evaluation exercises, overcoming obstacles to employment , and exploring a wide range of job options.

Chapter 2 covers effective portfolio preparation to present one's abilities to a prospective employer. Whenever you see this portfolio symbol, it indicates information relevant to your portfolio. My students tell me that their carefully developed portfolios are what moved them ahead of other candidates and helped win the job. Portfolio preparation includes specific directions on preparing a resumé and reference sheet using WordPerfect and Microsoft Word, along with 10 sample resumés and 2 sample reference sheets illustrating different styles and formats. As letters of recommendation enhance any portfolio, I have included a sample. Often my students are told by their busy employers to write their own letter, and the employer then signs it.

Chapter 3 offers suggestions and alternatives for exploring job leads, through various sources—including the internet. Chapter 3 also details researching companies and planning a job search strategy. A handy Activity Log will help students become more organized in their searches.

Creating a basic cover letter and completing an application form are covered in Chapter 4. Various letters with specific directions for preparation using WordPerfect and Microsoft Word are included.

Chapter 5 addresses the importance of personal appearance, preparation, and practice for the initial interview to make an immediate good impression.

Chapter 6 is a good example of what sets this book apart from others because it prepares students to respond effectively to over 50 questions most commonly asked during employment interviews. Concrete sample responses are provided that get at the heart of the interviewer's reason for asking certain questions. Students are also shown how to ask the right questions themselves to make the interview successful.

In Chapter 7, students learn the importance of prompt interview followup, as well as how to evaluate job offers, negotiate salaries, write letters to decline or accept job offers, and handle rejection constructively. Again, a variety of sample letters is provided.

The job search process doesn't end with a job offer—keeping a good job is what counts. Chapter 8 examines the critical first year, including adapting to the workplace, maintaining personal ethics, handling sexual harassment, and dealing with stress.

Chapter 9 looks beyond the initial job to review networking strategies, job trends, casual workplace dress, total quality management concepts, and what to expect in the changing world of work. At some point in one's career, it may be necessary to write a letter or resignation. A sample letter is provided to help end a job on a good note.

APPENDIXES

The Job Search: Your Guide to Success, includes eight appendixes that provide detailed, explicit, step-by-step instructions on using WordPerfect and Microsoft Word to type resumés, reference sheets, and cover letters as well as merging primary and secondary files to create both the letters and envelopes. These help students create professional job search materials *and* give them practical word processing experience. Other appendixes cover job testing procedures and useful internet sites to enhance the job search process.

ACKNOWLEDGEMENTS

I thank Bunny Barr of Richard D. Irwin for her encouragement, David Helmstadter and Carla Tishler of Mirror Press for their support and direction, Clare Wulker for her skilled editing of my manuscript, Jim Labeots and Crispin Prebys of Richard D. Irwin for their production and design expertise, and Gail Coates of Montgomery and Associates for her help in developing the illustrations. I am most grateful to my students, past and present, for sharing their job search experiences, and to my colleagues at Sawyer School of Business. In addition, I'd like to acknowledge the following individuals for their guidance and feedback:

Marilyn Chernoff, Sawyer School, Pennsylvania

Jewell Linville, Northeastern Oklahoma State University, Oklahoma

Miki McKenzie, Four-C Business College, Texas

Thomas L. Means, Louisiana Tech University, Louisiana

John Payne, Ohio Valley Business College, Ohio

Jean Rohrer, Hagerstown College of Business, Maryland

Candyce Skimin, Metropolitan Business College, Illinois

Marlene Stys. Barnes Business College, Colorado

Esther Tremblay, Duff's Business Institute, Pennsylvania

John Turpin, Phillips Jr. College, Utah

Elizabeth Zorn, McLennan Community College, Texas

Finally, I'd like to thank my family—Bill, Stacy, and Brian—for their support and encouragement.

Barbara Zarna

CONTENTS

INTRODUCTION

*A*s you near the end of your formal training and education, you may feel a variety of emotions toward the prospect of beginning a new career. While you may feel excited, confident, and enthusiastic, it is normal to feel anxious at the idea of leaving your somewhat "safe" educational environment. Soon you will be facing the "real" business world.

But remember that you have worked hard to attain the skills and knowledge necessary to make your future success a possibility. From this point on, your full-time efforts must be geared toward finding the job that is right for you. This is hard work and will require your total effort, learning to deal with emotional extremes, acquiring new job-seeking skills, and applying organizational techniques and effective work habits. Also, a good sense of humor is invaluable. Now it is time to present your qualifications in a way that will turn your job search into a success.

You need a job, and somewhere an employer has the job you want. You will enhance your chances of getting that job by marketing your job talents and showing employers you have the skills they need. Today's job market is very competitive, and only those who are well prepared will succeed.

Now is the time to begin that search while your skill levels are at their highest. So often students say, "I'm going to take a vacation when I finish school, and then I'll look for a job. After all, I've worked hard, and I deserve a little rest and relaxation." Taking this approach would be a big mistake because the added edge you've worked so hard to achieve would be lost. Instead, get a job, and let the company pay you for that week's rest and relaxation.

An honest, realistic, direct approach to your job search is the aim of this book. So let's get started! Together we will work toward your ultimate goal of obtaining and keeping your first job on your new career path. Make this the first of a long list of successes.

Don't delay—get started today!

TIME OUT

How do you feel right now as you are about to begin your job search?

_____

_____

_____

_____

_____

_____

_____

_____

_____

_____

_____

_____

_____

_____

_____

_____

_____

_____

_____

_____

_____

_____

_____

CHAPTER **1** ASSESSING YOUR SKILLS
AND EXPLORING YOUR
OPTIONS

Evaluating Your Interests and Skills

*B*efore you begin to look for a job, take some time to determine where your interests lie, at what you excel, and why you are good at certain things. You have to know and understand yourself before you can expect to sell an employer on your strengths. You need to take a close, objective, and honest look at yourself. It doesn't matter how other people see you. What's important is how you see yourself because *you* are the most important person in your job search effort.

What are your interests? What activities do you naturally like to do? For example, do you like to work with your hands? Do you like to work alone, or do you prefer to work as part of a team? Do you like to solve puzzles, or do you need to have tasks clearly defined? The more your interests match the position you choose, the more likely you are to succeed.

Listing your accomplishments helps you realize what you can do based on what you have already done. Your past accomplishments give you clues about what you are good at and what you should consider doing. Once your interests match your skills, preparing accomplishment statements is an excellent way to present your "can do" abilities to future employers. When you sum up what you have done for others, you can easily convince new employers you can do the same things for them.

Skills, knowledge, abilities, and talents relate to the technical aspect of a job. Do skills you now have match those needed for the job you want? One way to find out is to prepare an inventory of your skills so that you will be ready to discuss your capabilities with an employer.

Personal preferences will help you determine what job qualities or factors will be ideal for you.

These are just some of the questions you need to answer before you begin job hunting. Remember, your goal is not only to sell the employer on your strengths but also to make sure the job you accept is right for you. Check with your school's counseling or career development center to see if they have the *Holland Self-Directed Search* career assessment which explores careers by looking at the kinds of activities and preferences that you have and matching them with Holland's six personality types. Also, *SIGI Plus & Focus II* are user-friendly computer programs designed to help you make informed career decisions and plans.

To help you begin to determine the direction your job search will take, fill in the Self-Assessment Chart on page 12 after reading the following directions and reviewing the sample on page 11. Give this a great deal of thought, and don't sell yourself short. Although from the time you were little you were told not to be a braggart, now it is time to toot your own horn. If you don't, no one else will.

Begin by listing your specific skills and abilities. Usually these are things that can be measured or tested. For example:

- Typing or shorthand speed.

- Beginning, intermediate, or advanced-level use of any software.

- Composition and records management skill.

- Telephone techniques.

- Bookkeeping.

▲ For those who have never worked before or have no recent experience, you must realize that you still have many skills and abilities that are not work related. One example is that you might have the ability to run a household. Perhaps you successfully operated your household within a budget.

Next fill in the knowledge section. Generally this would involve the specific training or experience gained that allows you to use your skills and abilities to their fullest potential. For example:

- Cortez Peters Championship typing methods.

- Mastery of Gregg shorthand principles.

- Competency with various software packages.

- Business communications and records management courses.

- Specific telephone system knowledge.

- Accounting principles and computerized accounting programs.

▲ Running a household within a budget requires knowledge of time management, communication skills, accurate record-keeping and attention to detail.

Fill in the talents section. This is an area that usually cannot be tested as easily. The criteria are more vague. For example:

- Organizational ability.

▲ Indicates information for students who have never worked before or have no recent experience.

- Ability to prioritize tasks.

- Ability to perform under pressure.

- Ability to solve problems.

Now put down all of the things that you are interested in. For example:

- Computers.

- Travel.

- Sports.

- Outdoor activities.

- Dancing.

- Current events.

- Advertising.

- Public speaking

List your personal preferences regarding your job search. For example:

- Do you want to work close to home?

- What are your job expectations?

- Where do you want to live?

- Do you mind commuting and traveling?

- What is an adequate income level?

- Would you mind relocating?

- What benefits are essential in your total compensation package?

- Do you need health benefits or are you covered under someone else's policy?

- Would you prefer to work for a large, medium-size, or small company?

- Do you prefer a very professional working atmosphere or a more relaxed setting?

- Would you like a variety of responsibilities and challenges or prefer a more routine, defined role?

Finally, complete the accomplishments section. For example:

- Completed an educational training program.

- Worked part time while going to school and raising a family.

- Two years' previous experience in the field.

- Supervised five employees.

- Implemented cost-saving plan.

▲ Operated household within a budget.

To help you get started, look at the sample Self-Assessment Chart on page 11. This chart has been completed for our fictitious office worker, Mary Stadnika.

Obviously, no two people would fill out this form in the same way. Each of you is an individual with unique interests, skills, abilities, preferences, talents, and accomplishments. Look inward as you complete this chart to reveal a true picture of yourself.

TIME OUT

What kind of job environment would best fit your personality?

_____

_____

_____

_____

_____

_____

_____

_____

_____

_____

_____

EXERCISE 1.1	SELF-ASSESSMENT CHART

SAMPLE FORM FOR MARY STADNIKA

SKILLS AND ABILITIES

Typing 60 wpm

Shorthand 100 wpm

WordPerfect 5.0/5.1/6.0

Lotus, Version 2.4

dBase **III** Plus

Bookkeeping

10 Key machine

Filing

Dictaphone

KNOWLEDGE

Electronic typewriter

IBM 486, Dos 6.0, Windows

Advanced word processing concepts

Accounting Principles

Records management

Gregg shorthand system

Business composition

TALENTS

Creative writing

Playing flute

Organizational techniques

Juggling a busy schedule

Human relations

Public speaking

INTERESTS

Like working with people

Like to work on computers

Like all sports

Enjoy the outdoors

Enjoy writing short stories

PERSONAL PREFERENCES

Variety and challenge in my work

Work close to home

Work for large company with room for

advancement

Relaxed but professional atmosphere

ACCOMPLISHMENTS

Handled variety of assignments for temporary

placement agency

Organized new filing system

Completed advanced word processing training

Maintained perfect attendance in school;

graduated with honors

EXERCISE 1.1	**SELF-ASSESSMENT CHART (CONCLUDED)**

SKILLS AND ABILITIES

_____

_____

_____

_____

_____

_____

_____

KNOWLEDGE

_____

_____

_____

_____

_____

_____

TALENTS

_____

_____

_____

_____

_____

_____

_____

INTERESTS

_____

_____

_____

_____

_____

_____

_____

PERSONAL PREFERENCES

_____

_____

_____

_____

_____

_____

ACCOMPLISHMENTS

_____

_____

_____

_____

_____

_____

_____

■ MASTERING THE OBSTACLE COURSE

Experiencing obstacles or barriers is a natural part of job hunting. Learning to hurdle each and every obstacle that gets in your path is also essential.

You have to make a prospective employer believe that there isn't anything you can't do. Convince him or her that your training, education, and past experiences make you perfect for the job. Stress your desire and ability to learn new methods and your adaptability to changing conditions. Self-confidence is the key!

By acknowledging your shortcomings or the negative factors in your background to yourself, you can address each specific issue head-on and deal with it. Anticipate any factors in your past that might concern a prospective employer and decide how you could overcome those objections.

Being well prepared requires a lot of practice. Listed in Exercise 1.2 on page 14 are obstacles that may prevent you from finding satisfaction in employment. Recognizing a problem is the first step toward overcoming it. But remember that not all of your concerns will concern your potential employer. Be honest with yourself and put a check mark next to any statements that cause you serious concern.

After you have identified any barriers, you'll need to work on eliminating them. Face the obstacle head-on, and decide what specific steps you can take to overcome each barrier. These obstacles did not appear overnight; likewise, it will take planning, thought, and time to arrive at the best solutions.

Some obstacles, such as "I lack reliable transportation," can be overcome more easily than other obstacles. In this example, possible solutions are getting a bus schedule from your house to possible job locations; looking for a job within walking distance of your house; asking a family member or friend to drive you to interviews or a job; or joining a ride pool.

Other obstacles are more difficult and deep rooted. One such obstacle is "I don't have enough self-confidence." This is a common response, so if you checked it, you are not alone. Often students say that family members and friends are always putting them down. Remind yourself constantly that what you think of yourself is what is important. If you like yourself, others will too. Refer to your list on page 12 and note all of the skills, knowledge, talents, and abilities you have to offer. Stress these strong points. Being prepared for any task you undertake increases your self-confidence. Finally, the self-doubt you may be feeling right now should lessen if not disappear by the time you complete all the exercises in this book.

Unfortunately, there are some obstacles that we can do nothing about. The obstacle "I am too old" is one example. Unless you find the Fountain of Youth, age is something we will all need to deal with

continued on page 15

| EXERCISE 1.2 | **IDENTIFYING OBSTACLES** |

_____ I don't have a high school diploma or GED.[1]

_____ I have health problems.

_____ I don't have reliable transportation.

_____ I have sick family members for whom I must care.

_____ I don't have adequate child care.

_____ I need to improve my appearance.

_____ I have housing problems.

_____ I have a poor scholastic record.

_____ I have no work experience.

_____ I don't handle stress well.

_____ I need to improve my attitude.

_____ I lack job-related skills.

_____ I don't have enough self-confidence.

_____ I am unwilling to start at the bottom.

_____ I have poor references.

_____ I am too lazy.

_____ I am afraid of rejection.

_____ I am too old.

_____ I procrastinate too much.

_____ I am too young.

_____ I choke on tests.

_____ I don't use proper grammar.

_____ I have no realistic goals.

_____ I have a police record.

_____ I am superior to most other people.

_____ I am not good in English or spelling.

[1]Refer to the paragraph following the list for clarification.

EXERCISE 1.2	(CONCLUDED)

_____ I am handicapped.

_____ I have no enthusiasm for my chosen career field.

Today if you do not have a high school diploma or a GED, it is almost impossible to find a job. So don't delay. Talk to your teacher or counselor to find out how to apply for the GED test in your community. These tests are given only periodically throughout the year at set locations. The cost varies, but can be as high as $35. Test results take approximately four weeks, and certificates are mailed even later. You may see the importance of not waiting until the last minute.

In addition, list below any obstacles you may be facing that were not enumerated above.

_____

_____

_____

_____

_____

_____

_____

_____

_____

_____

at some point in our careers. Does it have to be an obstacle, however? Or could it be considered a plus? The trick is to make an employer view your age as an advantage because you are more mature, dependable, and experienced.

For each obstacle you checked or listed on page 14 and this page, state in Exercise 1.3 on page 16 what steps you can take to overcome these barriers. Be specific. Consider these obstacles carefully. You owe it to yourself to be honest and thorough in your approach to this section. If you get stuck, discuss the problem with your teacher, a counselor, a family member, or a close friend. Sometimes an objective outlook can open the door to additional or more realistic solutions. Even so, some of your tougher obstacles may become ongoing projects as you strive to find workable solutions.

EXERCISE 1.3	**MASTERING THE OBSTACLE COURSE**

OBSTACLE

Steps for Overcoming Obstacle

_____

_____

_____

_____

_____

OBSTACLE

Steps for Overcoming Obstacle

_____

_____

_____

_____

_____

OBSTACLE

Steps for Overcoming Obstacle

_____

_____

_____

_____

_____

OBSTACLE

Steps for Overcoming Obstacle

_____

_____

_____

_____

_____

OBSTACLE

Steps for Overcoming Obstacle

_____

_____

_____

_____

_____

OBSTACLE

Steps for Overcoming Obstacle

_____

_____

_____

_____

_____

■ EXPLORING THE JOB FIELD

Now that you have done a thorough self-evaluation—realizing your interests, skills, abilities, talents, accomplishments, knowledge, and personal preferences—it is time to discover what is available in the job field. Remember, the key to finding the right job is to do your best to match your strengths and interests to an employer's requirements. So you may want to begin by finding out what most employers require for the position you want. What are typical duties and responsibilities? Find out whether prior on-the-job experience is required. If it is required, how much is required? Would certain skills be accepted in place of job experience? Make sure that you are prepared for the search that lies ahead.

One place to start is at your local library. In addition, talk to friends, relatives, teachers, or workers already in your field. Get their insights and opinions. Read the classified ads, taking specific note of job requirements. Call up employment agencies and ask questions relevant to your situation.

Surfing the Internet is becoming one of the most up-to-date resources for employer information, job opportunities, and career research. The Internet's World Wide Web contains thousands of sites which grow and change daily. Because of constant changes, the Internet offers no central directory; this means you have to learn to surf the net yourself to find the information you are seeking. Netscape is one program you can use to browse the World Wide Web. If you click on Net Search from the menu bar, you will be given an explanation of and access to popular search methods referred to as search engines. The easiest way to search is by using key words. Recommended key words might begin with: employment, jobs, careers, business, companies, and various specific fields such as engineering, pharmaceutical, and so on. As you access a site, you'll find additional links to sites with more information. Once in a site, you simply click on any highlighted or underlined words that are of interest to you to jump to another site. The more you jump, the wider the web of information you create. Don't worry about losing your place. The back and forward options at the top of your screen conveniently allow you to retrace your steps. See Appendix J for a list of books and magazines that contain Internet information to help you become a master at surfing the net. In addition, specific Web site addresses are provided for you to start your career search.

Helpful Hints

1. If possible, use the Internet either before or after normal business hours when connections are not so busy.

2. When connecting to a site takes more than one minute, click on the Stop button at the top of your screen and try again

later. The server is probably too busy to handle your connection.

3. Use a wide variety of key words in your searches to find the most resources.

4. Be patient. Sometimes the graphics at different sites take a while to load.

5. Beware of downloading files—some may have viruses. Download to floppy disks only and then have disks scanned for viruses before using them again.

6. Keep a journal of helpful sites you've visited and their addresses so that you can quickly access them again in the future.[2]

Keep in mind your personal preferences. You have a responsibility to yourself to make sure that the job is right for you. Examine the four classified ads on page 19 for the position of administrative assistant taken from a recent newspaper. Look closely to see that even though they all are ads for the same job title, they are really quite different in content. The skills and experience required can vary widely based on the office environment and industry in which you work.

Also, you need to get some idea of what the starting salary range is for an entry-level position in your area. Knowing the range for someone with one to two years' experience and the range for someone with quite a bit of experience is also useful. This information gives you a realistic picture of what you can expect from a job now and what you can look forward to in the future.

Try to find out what the typical compensation package is for someone in your field of work. Are health, dental, optical, and prescription coverage offered at no cost to the employee? Or will the employee have a deduction taken from each paycheck? Is there a waiting period before the coverage takes effect? Is this coverage only for the employee or for the entire family? Is life insurance protection offered? If so, how much? Is disability insurance offered, what does it cover, and when does it go into effect? Are there provisions for paid sick, personal, and vacation days? Is there a plan for tuition reimbursement? Is there mileage reimbursement when using your personal car for business purposes?

The more information you can gather now, the better prepared you will be for what lies ahead. With preparedness comes self-confidence.

---

[2]This information was obtained from the Career Development Center at Michigan State University, "Cruising for Careers on the Internet," 1995.

Administrative Assistant
Excellent communication and
organizational skills required.
Typing, Word Processing, 50wpm
required; WordPerfect 6.1 and
Lotus 1-2-3 helpful. Windows,
Excel, PageMaker, Corel Draw,
Novell. Please send résumé to
MCAFC, Attn: Dan Wells, 560
Kirts, Ste 120, Troy, MI 48084

Administrative Assistant
Full-time with a nonprofit
organization requires a
flexible, positive team player
with good communication, word
processing and database
skills. Bookkeeping a plus.
Start $8 an hour. Call MSI,
9A.M.-5P.M., 737-0044

Administrative Assistant
Excellent opportunities with
Farmington Hills corporation.
Both short- and long-term
assignments for candidates with
WordPerfect 6.1, Lotus, Harvard
Graphics, or Draw Perfect a
plus. Call Sue 473-2931

Administrative Assistant
Uniforce Temporary Services
Small Southfield CPA firm seeks
individual with computer
experience. Secretarial and
organizational skills required.
Knowledge of accounting
software helpful. 358-0300

CHAPTER **2** DEVELOPING YOUR
PROFESSIONAL PORTFOLIO

■ ORGANIZING YOUR PORTFOLIO

Before you begin your job search, set aside some time to develop a professional portfolio. A portfolio is a binder in which you will put a copy of your resumé, reference sheet, diplomas, certificates, awards, and samples of past work performance. Your portfolio should highlight your abilities, experiences, and accomplishments. It can be an impressive aid in obtaining a good position, but only if everything in it is perfect. Start by purchasing an attractive, thin three-ring binder with pockets and several plastic cover sheets. The plastic cover sheets will protect your portfolio contents, and the binder will store them.[1]

Organize your portfolio in the following manner:

- An original copy of your resumé.

- An original copy of your reference sheet.

- Any letters of recommendation that you have.

- Your diploma from the last school you attended. If you have diplomas from more than one school, you may include all of them if you wish.

- Your final transcript from your last school attended—if you had good grades.

- Any special certificates you may have received that exemplify your accomplishments. Perfect attendance records are good to include.

- Samples of your work. For example, in the secretarial field, you should include documents produced with word processing software, spreadsheet software, and database software; documents illustrating your composition ability; and documents showing your typing ability, such as purchase orders, news releases, ruled or boxed tables, agendas, or itineraries. Exactly how many examples to include will be up to you. Remember, the portfolio can be very impressive, so make your choices wisely. Quality, not quantity, is most important.

- Two or three extra copies of your resumé and reference sheet in the back pocket of your portfolio. You never know when you may need an extra copy. For example, if a potential employer is interested in you he or she may send you to someone else for a second interview. Then, you would want to leave a copy of your resumé with the second person.

---

[1]The portfolio symbol above always indicates something relevant to your portfolio.

Start now to prepare the actual documents you wish to include. Make sure they are error free and eye pleasing in format. Remember, you are about to begin on your professional career, and your portfolio must present that image of you! This will take time and will be an ongoing process.

■ PREPARING YOUR PORTFOLIO

You will prepare your portfolio contents over a period of time. Right now you are ready to build the foundation of your portfolio—your resumé and reference sheet.

DEVELOPING A RESUMÉ

Now that you have taken a personal assessment of your skills and determined what qualifications you have for the type of job you want, it is time to develop a resumé. A resumé summarizes your past education, work experience, and accomplishments. Your resumé should reflect your special mix of skills that can help employers meet their goals. Its purpose is to advertise your ability to do the job. You don't need to tell potential employers everything about you because, if you did, there would be no reason to call you in for an interview. Instead, highlight your important accomplishments and make employers want to know more about you.

Because you will send your resumé to many different companies, it must be general enough to meet various employer needs. Although each company is looking for something unique in a prospective employee, you can customize your response to each individual want ad through a cover letter, which we discuss in Chapter 4. The cover letter gives you an opportunity to elaborate on important points not highlighted on your resumé but that pertain specifically to an individual job.

Establishing the Contents

The contents and order of contents usually follow a standard format. The most typical format follows.

1. *Your Career Objective.* The first step you should take in preparing your resumé is to develop a career objective. What kind of job are you looking for? The career objective should be as broad or as general as possible so that it can be applied to a number of industries or companies. For example, don't say "To obtain an executive secretarial position in the legal field." Such a statement would limit your opportunities. Your career objective should not state just what you want out of a job, but also how an employer would benefit from

EXERCISE 2.1	PREPARING EXAMPLES OF YOUR WORK

List below the work examples to be included in your portfolio. Give this careful thought and planning.

_____

_____

_____

_____

_____

_____

_____

_____

_____

_____

_____

hiring you. One example would be "To obtain an office position where my skills, work experience, and educational training will make me a valuable addition to a team-oriented staff." This is general enough to leave the door open to a wide variety of business opportunities. However, it provides the employer with an image that you have the confidence to make an immediate impact.

2. *Work Experience.* Gather the following information for each job you have held: beginning and ending dates of employment, listing month and year only; company name, complete address, and telephone number; job title; and a short description of your job duties. Use descriptive, action words to identify your job responsibilities and successes. These words can be divided into three categories: transferable skills, self-management skills, and special knowledge skills. *Transferable skills* are aptitude related and are transferable from one activity to another. They are enhanced through learning and are usually recognized as action verbs that end in either "-ed" or "-ing." On page 26 is a list of some transferable skills. *Self-management skills* are consistent and characteristic ways you adapt to demands made on you. These skills are acquired through early learning and reinforced through your experiences.

A list of self-management skills is found on page 27. *Special knowledge skills* reflect specific knowledge and mastery of content. Usually they are developed through learning, memorization, and on-the-job training. Examples of special knowledge skills are knowing how to rebuild a fuel-injected carburetor, knowing how to use WordPerfect software, and knowing how to take someone's blood pressure.

List your employment history in reverse order providing the information for your most recent job first. In general, don't go back more than 10 years. Any experience before then that you feel is important can be mentioned in your cover letter. If you are a recent high school graduate or have been out of the workforce for a period of time while caring for your home and family, it is possible that you will have little or no work experience to list. If you have volunteered your time to work, for example, at a hospital, in your local library, for a school PTA group, as a school classroom aide, for a fund-raising event or a charity, list this as work experience.

3. *Education.* Gather the following education information: name and complete address of school; dates attended, listing month and year; degree or diploma received, or credits earned toward a degree; scholastic honors and awards. Begin with your most recent education. It is not necessary to list your high school if you have had education beyond high school. If you have limited work experience, you may wish to provide your educational background second and list your work experience here.

4. *Activities/Honors/Skills/Accomplishments.* Activities or honors may be included on the resumé if space allows. List all major activities, awards, and accomplishments, as well as any abilities relevant to your career objective. These can show leadership, organization, critical thinking, teamwork, self-management, initiative, or influencing others. Skills refer to an area of expertise that can be tested. Knowledge of software, typing, shorthand, office machines, accounting, and machine transcription are just some skill examples that you could list if you were entering the office field. Accomplishments can be used to identify areas where you have excelled in your work performance. Created company newsletter and implemented a database records management system are two examples of accomplishment statements.

5. *References.* The last section of your resumé is a statement indicating that you are willing to provide references. The standard line is "Available upon Request." Then list your actual work, educational, and personal references on a separate reference sheet as discussed on page 44.

Never include irrelevant personal information such as height, weight, age, or marital status in your resumé. Do not give your salary expectations. If an advertisement asks for salary history or salary

EXERCISE 2.2	**PREPARING YOUR CAREER OBJECTIVE**

Prepare your career objective statement.

_____

_____

_____

_____

Second attempt at sentence construction.

_____

_____

_____

_____

Third attempt at sentence construction.

_____

_____

_____

_____

requirements, you should answer this request in your cover letter.

Preparing the Document

Most resumés should be no longer than one page, although those with extensive experience or advanced degrees may need two pages. In today's job market, it is not uncommon for an employer to receive more than 100 responses to an individual advertisement. Therefore, most human resources personnel will make up their minds about your resumé in less than 60 seconds.

To make your resumé stand out, use good quality, 100 percent cotton fiber bond paper in white, off-white, or ivory. Catchy colors or

EXERCISE 2.3	**EXPERIENCE INDICATOR CHART**

Review the skill word list on this page and page 27 and the sample Experience Indicator Chart on page 28.[2] Then complete an Experience Indicator Chart for each job you have held. Use the descriptive action words found on the skill word lists to identify your job responsibilities and successes. Next, rank your skills as shown on page 28, giving top priority to those activities you prefer and skills at which you excel.

By completing an Experience Indicator Chart for each job you have held, you will be able to concisely describe on your resumé the highlights and accomplishments you have achieved through previous work experience.

TRANSFERABLE SKILLS

accomplished	built	defined	expanded	incorporated
accounted for	calculated	delegated	expedited	increased
achieved	cataloged	delivered	explained	indicated
acquired	caused	demonstrated		initiated
adjusted	changed	designed	familiarized	innovated
administered	checked	determined	filed	inspected
advised	chose	developed	financed	instructed
aided	classified	devised	foresaw	interviewed
analyzed	closed	did	formulated	introduced
anticipated	combined	diminished	forwarded	
applied	communicated	directed	fostered	joined
appointed	compared	discovered	found	
appraised	completed	drafted		kept
arranged	composed	dramatized	gained	
assessed	conceived		gathered	labored
assisted	concluded	earned	gave	launched
assumed	conducted	edited	graded	lectured
assured	constructed	educated	greeted	led
attended	continued	elected	grossed	licensed
authored	controlled	employed	guided	located
authorized	convinced	encouraged		looked
awarded	coordinated	enjoyed	handled	
	corrected	enlarged	helped	made
began	counseled	ensured	highlighted	maintained
boosted	counted	entered	housed	managed
bought	created	established	hunted	maximized
briefed	critiqued	evaluated		met
brought		excelled	identified	modified
budgeted	decided	executed	implemented	monitored
			improved	motivated
			included	moved

[2]Reprinted from the 1992–93 *CPC Annual*, Special Two Year College Edition, with the permission of the College Placement Council, Inc., copyright holder.

Transferable Skills (*concluded*)

negotiated
netted

observed
opened
operated
ordered
organized
oversaw

paid
participated
perceived
performed
persuaded
pioneered
placed
planned
played
prepared

presented
processed
produced
profited
programmed
projected
promoted
proved
purchased

qualified
quickened

ran
rated
realized
received
recognized
recommended
reduced

reported
researched
returned
revealed
reviewed
revised

said
saved
screened
scrutinized
selected
sent
served
shipped
showed
sifted
simplified
smothered

solved
sought
spearheaded
specified
spoke
started
stated
stopped
streamlined
strengthened
stripped
studied
submitted
suggested
summarized
supervised
supported
surveyed

target
taught
tested
took over
toured
tracked
trained
transformed
translated
traveled
tutored
typed

uncovered
updated

won
wrote

SELF-MANAGEMENT SKILLS

adventuresome
alert
assertive
astute
attention to detail
authentic
aware

brave

calm
candor
cheerful
concentration
concern for others
cooperative
courageous
curious

decisive
dependable

eager
easygoing

emotional stability
enthusiasm

firm
flexible
friendly

generous
good judgment

helpful
honest

initiative
integrity

kind

loyal

open-minded
optimistic
orderly

patient
perform under pressure
persistent

poised
polite
potential for growth
punctual

reliable
resourceful
reverent

self-confident
self-controlled
self-expression
self-reliant
sense of humor
sincere
spontaneous

tactful
thorough
thrift
tolerance
trustworthy

versatile

EXPERIENCE INDICATOR CHART

Company Name   *Lundy International*

Company Street Address   *50134 Las Olas Blvd.*

Company City, State, Zip Code   *Ft Lauderdale, FL 33321*

Company Telephone   *(305) 734-1202*

Job Title   *Secretary*

Transferable Skills

2   Assisted sales manager with monthly reports

3   Maintained filing system

4   Monitored travel-expense reports for all salespeople

6   Attended conference on sexual harassment

5   Awarded Employee-of-the-Month in sales dept.

1   Tracked sales growth

Self-Management Skills

4   Optimistic

6   Outgoing

3   Self-confident

5   Loyal

1   Honest

2   Cooperative

Special Knowledge Skills

4   Fluent in Spanish

2   Mastered advanced WordPerfect concepts

1   Take shorthand at 100 wpm

3   Know desktop publishing concepts and features

EXPERIENCE INDICATOR CHART

Company Name _____

Company Street Address _____

Company City, State, Zip Code _____

Company Telephone _____

Job Title _____

Transferable Skills

_____

_____

_____

_____

_____

_____

Self-Management Skills

_____

_____

_____

_____

_____

_____

Special Knowledge Skills

_____

_____

_____

_____

_____

_____

EXPERIENCE INDICATOR CHART

Company Name _____

Company Street Address _____

Company City, State, Zip Code _____

Company Telephone _____

Job Title _____

Transferable Skills

_____

_____

_____

_____

_____

_____

Self-Management Skills

_____

_____

_____

_____

_____

_____

Special Knowledge Skills

_____

_____

_____

_____

_____

_____

EXPERIENCE INDICATOR CHART

Company Name _____

Company Street Address _____

Company City, State, Zip Code _____

Company Telephone _____

Job Title _____

Transferable Skills

_____

_____

_____

_____

_____

_____

Self-Management Skills

_____

_____

_____

_____

_____

_____

Special Knowledge Skills

_____

_____

_____

_____

_____

_____

TIME

OUT

Based on your self-evaluation so far, what do you believe are you strongest traits?

_____

_____

_____

_____

_____

_____

sizes other than 8.5 × 11 inches are unprofessional. Have your copies printed on a high-quality photocopier or with a letter-quality printer.

For visual effect, use full capitalization for major headings and company/school names only. For further emphasis, use boldface for your job titles. Use strong action verbs and eliminate most abbreviations except those that are well known. Choose a format that puts your strongest, most salable points first. Be completely honest because false statements are grounds for dismissal.

Use one-inch side and top/bottom margins if your resumé is less than a page. In general, triple-space before each major heading (typed in bold and all capitals) and double-space after each one. Double-space between each item under a specific heading. Turn justification off.

Type your resumé using a word processing program and then save it to a personal disk. As updates are needed, then, you won't constantly have to retype your resumé. Because WordPerfect and Microsoft Word are the most widely used software programs in the country, you will be given step-by-step instructions on creating a resumé using these programs. If you follow these instructions, your resumé will look exactly like those in this book (See Appendixes A through C.)

On pages 34–43 are examples of different resumé styles. Examine each one carefully and choose the style that you prefer and that best matches your experience and background. You can combine styles or alter spacing to keep your resumé to one page. Just remember that your resumé has to be complete, concise, correct, attractive, and interesting enough to make the employer want to meet you and learn more about you.

EXERCISE 2.4	**PREPARING YOUR RESUMÉ**

Using the guidelines and examples on the following pages, prepare your resumé. If possible, use a computer.

PREPARING A LETTER OF RECOMMENDATION

Many times the person you ask to write a letter of recommendation for you will be either too busy or not know how to write one. Therefore, he or she may say, "Why don't your write your own letter, and then I'll sign it." If this situation happens to you, ask the person for a couple of sheets of company letterhead on which you can type the letter. In writing the letter, try to state in what capacity this person has known you, the length of time, your strong points, and his or her endorsement for your future career endeavors. One example of a letter of recommendation follows.

SAMPLE LETTER OF RECOMMENDATION

Date

To Whom It May Concern:

It is with great pleasure that I write a letter of recommendation for JoAnn Doherty.

As JoAnn's supervisor for the past six years, I have found her to be an extremely capable, bright individual. I can always depend on JoAnn to be here daily, on time, and ready to give total effort. Her sense of humor, organizational skills, professional attitude, and ability to get along well with everyone in the office are what I appreciate most.

I would have no hesitation in recommending JoAnn Doherty for any position for which she might be considered. We will really miss JoAnn but wish her all the best in her new career.

If you have any questions or require further information, please feel free to contact me at (give company telephone number).

Sincerely,

Name of Reference

FERNANDO SUAREZ

30045 Schoenherr Road
Warren, MI 48090
(810) 555-9876

CAREER OBJECTIVE

To obtain a position where my experience in numerical control technology and management background will benefit a growth-oriented organization.

EDUCATION

1/94 - Present	**Franklin Technical Institute** 26051 Hoover Road, Warren, MI 48089 *Numerical Control Technology Course* Diploma will be awarded September 1996
8/91 - 5/93	**Malcott Community College** 14500 Twelve Mile Road, Warren, MI 48089 *Liberal Arts* Earned 32 credits

AREAS OF SKILLS

- Operation of mills and lathes
- Numerical control programming
- Machinery process knowledge
- Loss and scrap control
- Quality control

EXPERIENCE

1/93 - Present	**Bartlett Machining Corporation** 456 Oak Park Drive, Livonia, MI 48021 *Millwright Apprentice* • Operate a LaBlonde lathe • Operate a Bridgeport mill
5/90 - 9/92	**K & B Auto Parts** 3978 Jefferson, Detroit, MI 48028 *Assistant Manager* • Conducted bank transactions • Prepared payroll • Trained new employees • Assumed all purchasing duties • Implemented computer inventory program

REFERENCES

Available upon Request

SAMPLE RESUME No. 2

KAREN RAAB

34909 Veronica
Falls Church, VA 22041
(703) 758-3300

CAREER OBJECTIVE	An administrative assistant position that will utilize my computer skills to enhance your office staff.
EDUCATION	Draper Business School 27500 Dequindre, Falls Church, VA 22041 **Administrative Assistant** Diploma awarded June 1995 County Line High School 36849 Arsenal, Falls Church, VA 22041 **General Courses** Diploma Awarded

AREAS OF SKILLS

Typing 65 wpm	Computer Accounting
Shorthand 100 wpm	Accounting Principles
WordPerfect 6.0 Windows	Business Communications
Microsoft Word	Records Management
Lotus 4.0	Pegboard Payroll Systems
Excel 5.0	Business Machines

EXPERIENCE

2/93 - Present

Rinker Lumber
93876 Gratiot, Falls Church, VA 22041
Cashier: Handle cash transactions, tabulate inventory, prepare sale displays, and stock shelves.

10/91 - 9/92

El Diablo Restaurant
39387 Hoover, Falls Church, VA 22041
Waitress/Cashier: Served customers, accepted payments, balanced cash drawer.

9/89 - 6/90

Van Dyke School District
49478 Automobile, Falls Church, VA 22041
Co-op Office Assistant: Provided clerical support, answered telephones, typed correspondence, and kept accurate records.

REFERENCES   Provided upon Request

SAMPLE RESUMÉ NO. 3

MARCO GARAVAGLIA

20419 Malibu Street
Springfield, OH 45503
(513) 881-2204

CAREER OBJECTIVE

To obtain an engineering position with a company that will benefit from my design and purchasing experience and offer room for professional growth.

EXPERIENCE	**Blount Corporation**
	12345 Mason Street, Springfield, OH 45503
1991 - Present	*Designer*

◆ Design automotive brake tubes using CAD
◆ Attend design meetings
◆ Responsible for developing a cost-saving design for an assembly clip

Jostin, Inc.
9943 Buckley Avenue, Springfield, OH 45503

1988 - 1990   *Purchasing Assistant*

◆ Inventory control of plant materials
◆ Responsible for purchasing all prototype materials

Summit Design and Engineering
12311 Ridge Road, Springfield, OH 45503

1983 - 1987   *Draftsman/Minor Layout*

◆ Operated the blue print machine
◆ Filed drawings
◆ Made checker changes on board
◆ Drew detail and minor layout schemes

EDUCATION   **Drayton School of Engineering Design**
14500 Springmount Avenue, Springfield, OH 45503

1994 - 1996   *Associate Degree in Autobody Design - 3.6 GPA*
Dean's List Honors

AFFILIATIONS

◆ Society of Manufacturing Engineers
◆ Soceity of Automotive Engineers
◆ Engineering Society of Ohio

References Available upon Request

SAMPLE RESUMÉ No. 4

MARY BRAY
32100 Hayward Place
Denver, CO 80211
(303) 555-9876

CAREER OBJECTIVE

An administrative office position that will benefit from my word processing and accounting experience.

WORK EXPERIENCE

3/93 - Present   C.P.C. INTERNATIONAL
139 Harvard Avenue, Denver, CO 80223
Secretary/Accounts Payable Supervisor
Operate IBM-PC inputting current data for customer files, expedit credit memos to offset deductions taken by our accounts, and compile month-end reports.

7/89 - 2/93   NOVATRON CORPORATION
13900 Irving Street, Denver, CO 80219
Accounts Payable Clerk
Supported company CPA, handled all payables, and forecasted monthly cash flow.

9/86 - 7/89   PSI INTERNATIONAL
139 Kidder Drive, Denver, CO 80221
Receptionist/Accounts Payable
Directed all incoming calls, messages, and appointments. Promoted to accounts payable because of exceptional work performance.

EDUCATION

1/93 - 1/96   WELCH COLLEGE OF BUSINESS
21890 Lombardy, Denver, CO 80215
Associate Degree in Office Administration
Diploma awarded with Honors January 1996

AREAS OF SKILLS

Typing 70 wpm	Desktop Publishing	Records Management
WordPerfect 6.0	Computer Accounting	Telephone Techniques
Quattro Pro	Principles of Accounting	Human Relations
dBase III Plus	Pegboard Payroll Systems	Dictaphone
Microsoft Word	Business Machines	Business Communications

REFERENCES

Available upon Request

PHILLIS FISHER

980 Madison Place
Fremont, CA 94539
(415) 431-1000

CAREER OBJECTIVE

To become a medical assistant in a hospital, clinic, or doctor's office.

EDUCATION

Kent Junior College
90087 Kaiser Road
Fremont, CA 94539
Medical Assistant Associate Degree
Diploma will be awarded August 1996

Fremont High School
23190 Fremont Avenue
Fremont, CA 94539
Medical Career Course/College Prep
Diploma awarded June 1994

EXPERIENCE

Tri-County Medical Center
98712 Alameda Avenue
Freemont, CA 94539
Receptionist
7/94 - 8/95

Cherrywood Nursing Home
345 Stadler Road
Fremont, CA 94539
Patient Aide - Co-Op Program
9/93 - 6/94

AFFILIATIONS

➤ Student Organization of Medical Assistants
➤ California Medical Association

AWARDS/HONORS

➤ Kent Junior College Honors List - 3.7 GPA
➤ Outstanding Medical Assistant for 1995-96
➤ High School Perfect Attendance 1992-94

REFERENCES

Available upon Request

SAMPLE RESUMÉ No. 6

LINDA KAY

Home Address:
23400 Stadler Road
Sterling Heights, MI 48313
(810) 555-7800

School Address:
233 Shaw Lane
Lansing, MI 48823
(517) 355-8899

CAREER OBJECTIVE

To obtain an entry-level position where I can utilize my culinary and creative talents.

EDUCATION

1994 - 1996   **ISI SCHOOL OF CULINARY ARTS**
890 Lansing Road, Lansing, MI 48823
Diploma will be awarded December 1996

EXPERIENCE

1995 - Present   **BAKER'S SQUARE**
39021 Holt Avenue, Okemos, MI 48022
Pastry Chef: Prepare and bake all desserts.

1992 - 1994   **KEN'S COUNTRY KITCHEN**
12003 E. Grand River Road, East Lansing, MI 48824
Short-Order Cook: Prepared breakfast and lunch grill orders
at this very busy establishment.

1989 - 1990   **LONG'S BANQUET CENTER**
23000 Garfield Road, Clinton Township, MI 48044
Waitress: Served family-style meals at large banquets;
developed good customer-relations skills.

ACTIVITIES

- Volunteered to deliver Meals on Wheels - 1995
- Varsity Basketball - 3 years
- Secretary, Student Council - 1 year
- Member of SADD - 2 years

REFERENCES

Available upon Request

SAMPLE RESUME No. 7

GARY DELISO

School Address
321 Bogue Street, Apt. 226
East Lansing, MI 48823
(517) 337-4471

Home Address
14360 Eastland Road
Utica, MI 48084
(810) 979-3451

OBJECTIVE
To obtain a full-time position in the marketing field offering professional growth potential based on job performance.

EDUCATION

MICHIGAN STATE UNIVERSITY, EAST LANSING, MI 48824
➤ College of Business - 3.6 GPA   ➤ Overall - 3.2 GPA
➤ Marketing Courses - 4.0 GPA   ➤ Graduation - May 1996

EXPERIENCE

CARDALE CORPORATION, ROCHESTER HILLS, MI 48309
Marketing Intern (May-August, 1995)
➤ Only marketing person employed by Cardale
➤ Reorganized past sales projection data
➤ Arranged and implemented new sales projection layout
➤ Assisted with slide presentations to customers
➤ Responsible for all MAC computer applications
➤ Developed brochure page layout

Quality Control Inspector (May-August, 1994)
➤ In-process inspection of anti-lock brake and plastic components
➤ Operation of Acu-Gage, calipers, force tester, and micrometers
➤ Generated and plotted data for SPC charts

KENTUCKY FRIED CHICKEN, CLINTON TOWNSHIP, MI 48044
Counter Help/Cook (May 1990 - January 1994)
➤ KFC "All Star" for excellence in job performance
➤ Responsible for customer service, cash accountability, computer operations, inventory, food preparation, sanitation, and new employee training.

AFFILIATIONS

MSU MARKETING ASSOCIATION - VICE PRESIDENT - 1995
➤ Responsible for publicity, advertising, and communications
➤ Business College Student Senate Representative
➤ American Cancer Society Volunteer
➤ Executive Board Member of the Month for February

SOCIETY OF AUTOMOTIVE ENGINEERS - 1995
➤ Management/Marketing Committee for Formula Team SAE

AMERICAN MARKETING ASSOCIATION - 1994/95

QUALIFICATIONS
➤ Dean's List Honors
➤ Attended MSU Leadership Conference in January 1995
➤ WordPerfect, Word, Excel, PageMaker, Photoshop, E-mail, and DeskScan
➤ Pascal and Fortran computer programming background
➤ Conscientious work ethic and willingness to learn
➤ Strong organizational skills and attention to detail

REFERENCES AVAILABLE UPON REQUEST

SAMPLE RESUMÉ No. 8

JOSEPH BELLIOTTI

776 Beach Street
Mt. Vernon, NY 10550
(914) 468-9000

OBJECTIVE

To obtain an entry-level position in retail management with advancement potential.

EDUCATION

Oakhill Community College
11111 Fulton Avenue
Mt. Vernon, NY 10550
Associate Degree in Retail Management, 1996

EXPERIENCE

Retail Clerk
Aco Hardware
11122 Euclid Avenue
Mt. Vernon, NY 10552
1994-1996

Electrician's Assistant
Rite-Way Electrical
30303 Edison Avenue
Mt. Vernon, NY 10550
Summer, 1993

ACCOMPLISHMENTS

■ Received merchandise, stocked shelves, cleaned store, verified inventory, and assisted customers

■ Contributed toward a 3 percent increase in store productivity

■ Professionally handled customer complaints in a helpful and polite manner

■ Developed specific job performance quotas

REFERENCES

Available upon Request

SAMPLE RESUMÉ NO. 9

SHARON LEBELT
3838 MacKenzie Lane
Metamora, Michigan 48455
(313) 411-8890

CAREER OBJECTIVE: To use my accounting skills in commercial banking to bene-fit a progressive company.

QUALIFICATIONS:
- Work well with people at all levels
- Thrive in a competitive and challenging environment
- Adept at developing strong working relationships

EDUCATION: **Bacon School of Finance**
Troy, Michigan 48084
Associate Degree in Accounting - March 1994

EXPERIENCE:

3/94 - Present
S & B Savings and Loan Association
Detroit, Michigan 48236
Branch Management Trainee
Responsible for generating customers' account statements, arranging trust funds, and organizing new safety deposit box system.

2/92 - 6/94
Troy Vocational Instruction & Placement
Troy, Michigan 48084
Job Development Representative (Internship)
Introduced prospective employers to the services of Troy VIP through outside consultations, phone solicitation, and mass advertising.

10/90 - 3/92
One on One Athletic Club
West Bloomfield, Michigan 49077
Tennis Instructor

ACCOMPLISHMENTS:
- Led a simulated corporate profitability program
- Taught elementary economics for Junior Achievement

REFERENCES: Available upon Request

SAMPLE RESUMÉ NO. 10

VERONICA LETSCHER

33090 El Mar Drive
Lauderdale-By-The-Sea, FL 33308
(305) 776-4421

CAREER OBJECTIVE: To pursue a prosperous career in the travel industry where my computer and organizational skills would be an asset.

QUALIFICATIONS:

- Detail-oriented, organized, and enthusiastic
- Skilled in human relations
- Enjoy fast-paced office atmosphere
- Able to prioritize work and meet deadlines

SKILLS:

- WordPerfect 6.0
- Lotus 1-2-3
- SabrePars
- ApolloFiling
- dBase IV
- Rolm Telephone System

EDUCATION:

DISANTO SCHOOL OF TRAVEL
11100 Las Olas Boulevard
Fort Lauderdale, FL 33306
Certified Travel Agent/1994

EXPERIENCE:

CARLTON CORPORATE TRAVEL
3249 Commercial Boulevard
Fort Lauderdale, FL 39098
Corporate Travel Agent (1994-Present)

HORIZON AIRLINES
Miami, FL 48236
Reservationist (1992-1994)

REFERENCES: Available upon Request

person has known you, the length of time, your strong points, and his or her endorsement for your future career endeavors. One example of a letter of recommendation follows.

DEVELOPING A REFERENCE SHEET

After you have prepared an effective resumé, prepare a reference sheet of people who can attest to your qualities. Unless asked for, the reference sheet is not submitted with your cover letter and resumé. Keep copies in the back of your portfolio, however, so they are always available. There are three types of references: work, educational, and personal.

Work References

Consider people who would give you a good recommendation at your current and past jobs. Three work references are usually sufficient. Of course, if your present supervisor does not know that you are looking for another job, don't list him or her as a reference.

After you have established yourself in a profession, colleagues and people who have worked for you may be used as references.

Once you have chosen work references, contact each and ask permission to use his or her name as a reference. You might ask if the person would be willing to write a letter of recommendation, addressed as "To Whom it May Concern," for your portfolio. Work references should be listed on your reference sheet in the same order as on your resumé. They should contain: person's full name and title; company name; full business address, including city, state, and zip code; and correct business telephone number.

Educational References

Next list any educational references. References can be teachers or a counselor, principal, placement director, or co-op coordinator. Include each person's full name and title; school name, full school address, including city, state, and zip code; and school telephone number.

Personal References

List personal references last. These should not be relatives or former employers. Always list three personal references. You should include: person's full name; full home address, including city, state, and zip code; and home and work telephone numbers.

| EXERCISE 2.5 | **PREPARING YOUR REFERENCE SHEET** |

Prepare your reference sheet, referring to the examples on this page and page 46. Center each line horizontally, and center the entire page vertically. (Refer to Appendix D for specific directions on typing a reference sheet in WordPerfect and Microsoft Word.)

SAMPLE REFERENCE SHEET NO. 1

CHRISTINE POKRYWKA

Work References

Ms. Tracy Scholke
Manager
Hudson's, Lakeside Mall
14200 Lakeside Circle
Sterling Heights, MI 48043
(810) 555–3232, Ext. 202

Mr. James Tropea
Comptroller
Ford Motor Company
14002 Michigan Avenue
Dearborn, MI 48009
(810) 576–4009

Educational References

Mrs. Mary Crawford
Co-Op Coordinator
Macomb Community College
14500 Twelve Mile Road
Warren, MI 48099
(810) 758–3000

Personal References

Ms. JoAnn Williams
38897 Fairfield Drive
Warren, MI 48089
(810) 555–7765

Mr. John Berkley
24356 Spalding Court
Warren, MI 48089
(810) 574–3000

Ms. Carol Newhouse
100 Lakeshore Drive
St. Clair Shores, MI 48236
(810) 882–5680

Below is an alternate example in which the headings are omitted. Because of the type of information provided on the reference sheet, the reader should be able to differentiate among your three types of references. Also, it is standard practice to list work first, education second, and personal last.

SAMPLE REFERENCE SHEET NO. 2

CHRISTINE POKRYWKA

Ms. Tracy Scholke
Manager
Hudson's, Lakeside Mall
14200 Lakeside Circle
Sterling Heights, MI 48043
(810) 555–3232, Ext. 202

Mr. James Tropea
Comptroller
Ford Motor Company
14002 Michigan Avenue
Dearborn, MI 48009
(810) 576–4009

Mrs. Mary Crawford
Co-Op Coordinator
Macomb Community College
14500 Twelve Mile Road
Warren, MI 48099
(810) 758–3000

Ms. JoAnn Williams
38897 Fairfield Drive
Warren, MI 48089
(810) 555–7765

Mr. John Berkley
24356 Spalding Court
Warren, MI 48089
(810) 574–3000

Ms. Carol Newhouse
100 Lakeshore Drive
St. Clair Shores, MI 48236
(810) 882–5680

■ PRESENTING YOUR PORTFOLIO

Although your portfolio is developed over a period of time, once you have completed a resumé and reference sheet, you may interview and present your portfolio. You must be sure to present your portfolio at the proper time during the interview. Perhaps when asked about your educational or work background, you can say something like "I really enjoyed my training at Foster Business School because it taught me to do so many realistic office jobs. As a matter of fact, I've brought my portfolio, which contains some samples of my work. Would you care to take a look at it?" Then you can use your portfolio as a means of generating further discussion.

If the samples of your work are taken from actual jobs you've performed, that's even better. Then you should present your portfolio when asked about the responsibilities of the jobs you have held.

If, throughout the entire interview, you cannot find the right opportunity to present your portfolio, try these two ideas: First, if you are told that you are going to be tested, ask if the interviewer would like to look at your portfolio while you are taking the test. Second, if the interviewer asks if you have any questions, ask your questions and then say something like "This position sounds very interesting to me and one for which I am well qualified. If you'd care to look at my portfolio, you will be able to see the kind of work I am capable of doing."

This portfolio adds a professional touch to your job search. It is essential that you find some way to present it to the interviewer during the course of the conversation. In many instances, a good portfolio has been responsible for securing the job for an individual. Take pride in your portfolio preparation and let this valuable tool be a deciding factor in your job search success.

CHAPTER *3* FINDING A JOB

■ WHERE TO GET INFORMATION

In today's job market, it is essential to have a competitive edge in your job search. Those who learn how the job-hunting game is played and who are well prepared for the competition are the ones who get the jobs. There are many ways to locate a job:

- Networking/personal contacts.

- Your school's placement department.

- Classified ads.

- The Internet.

- State employment services.

- Telephone directory.

- Company visits.

- Employment agencies.

- Libraries.

But don't limit yourself to just one method. Investigate and explore all avenues available to you.

NETWORKING/PERSONAL CONTACTS

Networking is an important component of any job strategy. It is an information-gathering technique utilizing family, friends, business associates, teachers, and community members as sources of information. Most employers prefer to hire someone they know or a person who has been referred by someone they know. Because networking can account for 60 to 80 percent of all job offers, it is essential that you expand your network of personal and professional contacts. This will put you in touch with less common sources of information such as trade associations, other companies, and organizations. Your understanding of the field you wish to enter will grow as your network expands. Remember, the more people you talk to, the better your chances become of finding a viable job lead.

Begin by making a list of relatives, friends, neighbors, business associates, or anyone else who can give you information about possible job openings. It is extremely important to be courteous and respectful when conducting your networking campaign. Don't bombard people with desperate pleas for job leads or bluntly ask them for a job over the telephone. Treat your networking contacts as you would a potential employer in a businesslike fashion. It is a good idea to provide them with a copy of your resumé and maintain fairly regular contact so they will not stop thinking about you. You should contact networking sources at least once a month to update them on your job search and ask them about any new job leads, networking contacts, or career information. Maintaining a positive relationship with your networking contacts builds their confidence in you and makes it easier for them to recommend you to potential employers.

When you initially contact each person, try to get inside information that will lead you to a job opening. Here is a list of potential questions to ask of someone in your chosen field:

1. What is a typical workday like for you?

2. What skills are required of you on a regular basis?

3. What about your job challenges you? What do you enjoy?

4. Is there anything dangerous that I should be aware of?

5. How often do you work past 6 PM and on the weekends?

6. What is the toughest season of the year in your job?

7. Would it be possible for me to walk through and observe a typical workday?

8. How much is the field growing, and is there room in it for someone like me?

9. How many people are entering this field?

10. What rising developments do you see affecting future developments?

11. What changes in the industry have you seen through your company?

12. How frequently do layoffs occur, and how do they affect the morale of the employees?

13. What reasons do you see for people leaving this field or your company?

14. Who are the most important people in the industry today?

15. What does your track record look like for promoting women and minorities?

16. Is there an opportunity for self-employment in your field? If so, where?

17. What would my earnings potentially be if I entered this field?

18. Is job-hopping necessary to receive a promotion?

19. How did you get your job?

20. If given the opportunity to start all over again, would you choose the same career path? Why?

21. How long does it take for managers to rise to the top?

22. What is the background of most senior-level executives?

23. What educational preparations would you recommend for someone who wants to advance in this field?

24. What qualifications do you seek in a new employee?

25. How do most people enter this profession?

26. Do you find any of my skills to be strong in comparison to other job hunters in this field?

27. What do you think about the experiences I've had so far? For what types of positions would they qualify me?

28. What do you think of my resumé? How would you suggest I change it?

29. Can you recommend any courses that I should take before proceeding further with my job search?

30. What companies might be interested in hiring someone with my background?

31. Considering my background, how well do you think I would fit in this company and/or profession?

32. How does your company compare with others we've discussed?

33. Would the work involve any lifestyle change such as travel or late night business meetings?

34. Considering all the people you've met in your line of work, what personal attributes are essential for success?

35. While taking my skills, education, and experience into account, what other fields would you suggest I explore before making my final decision?

36. What personality traits are required?

37. Where should I write to obtain updated information on salaries, employers, and industry issues?

38. What professional organizations or journals should I be familiar with?

39. Is there anything else you think I need to know?

40. Who else might you recommend I speak with? Would you mind if I used your name when I call?

Remember to tailor your questions to your own personal situation and speaking style. So that you don't wear out your welcome, avoid asking too many questions. Prepare your agenda, know what you are going to say, and decide exactly what you would like to know before your meeting begins with your networking contact.

By asking questions that get people talking about things or situations with which they are familiar, you can learn valuable information that may assist you with your job search. Listen carefully and take notes. If you contact five friends and each one refers you to just two other people, you will have increased your job network to 15 people who can give you job-related information.

TIME OUT

Make a list of people to include in your network.

After contacting your network leads, go back to your sources and let them know what happened. People like to know you made good use of their referrals, and they may think of others who may help you.

If you left a company on good terms, former employers or co-workers are an especially good source. Contact them and ask if they are aware of any openings for which you may be qualified. Perhaps a former co-worker knows of an opening with a competitor.

In addition, it is always important to join professional organizations in your field and to maintain active membership. Through monthly meetings with people in the same profession, you will be able to add greatly to your networking list. Who will know better about openings in your field than the people who are presently working in it! See if there are any networking clubs in your area. There may be an initial fee to join and then monthly dues.

YOUR SCHOOL'S PLACEMENT DEPARTMENT

A month or two before you complete your educational training, register with your placement department. Discuss with the counselors your responsibilities in using their services and what they can do for you. Find out their procedure for listing job openings, providing resource information about companies, arranging interviews on campus, and entering your resumé onto the school's database. Your credentials (transcripts of grades and resumé) are available to potential employers when requested. Therefore, it is

TIME OUT

Make a list of all the local newpapers that may contain classified ads geared to your job search.

important to keep an updated resumé on file in your school's database. Most placement departments offer lifetime placement services at no charge.

CLASSIFIED ADS

Employment ads are a quick way to look at a variety of jobs. Although most jobs are not advertised, ads do point to general industries and specific companies where employment activity is taking place. If there were several ads for mortgage closers, you might consider sending your resumé to all the mortgage companies in your area. These ads can give you ideas about where else to look. Often there will be a classified ad announcing a Job Fair. It will state the date, time, location, and sometimes even the companies that will be represented. Read the classifieds every day! Follow the directions in the ad—a phone call, a letter, a fax, and so on. Small local newspapers and professional journals carry classified ads. Some employers advertise through local cable television networks and on radio stations.

THE INTERNET

Many companies are now looking for job candidates on the their World Wide Web home pages. A home page can provide all sorts of valuable data to job seekers. A job posting on a company's home page typically contains more detail about a position than a classified ad. You can get information from mission statements, product descriptions, and recent press releases. Most pages also offer details about employee benefits—though not usually about salary. One reason advertising on the Internet is becoming so popular is cost—recruiting via a home page is about as close to free as one can get. Companies seeking technical expertise find the quality of the applicants on the home pages to be superior. The logic is that if a person can use the Internet to send a resumé through E-mail, then to some degree they have the right experience. At this point, sales and service industries are not attracting many resumés via the Internet. Refer to Appendix J for specific Internet addresses that may be of value to you in your job search.

STATE EMPLOYMENT SERVICES

Register with the job counselors at your local State Employment Security Commission. They can be a lucrative source of job leads. Counselors will give you an ID card allowing you to stop in at any time to look over the job openings in the Job Bank. Some major corporations do all their hiring through this commission. There is no fee charged. In addition, classes on resumé preparation and interviewing techniques are sometimes offered. Most state government job openings are listed with the commission; and the majority of city, county, state, and federal openings require a civil service examination. Civil service examinations are different at the city, state, and federal levels. Also, there are different tests for different occupations. Generally civil service tests cover basic math and English skills, logic and reasoning powers, and specific skill areas pertaining to the job. Ask your school counselor for information about the next testing date. If you have already taken and passed this test, then you are ahead of the majority of people who may be interested in an ad. Be sure to mention that you have passed the civil service examination in your cover letter.

TELEPHONE DIRECTORY

Particular areas of interest can be pursued by mailing resumés and cover letters to individuals or companies that offer work in your field of study. For example, if you knew you wanted to work for an advertising company, you would look under "Advertising" in the Yellow Pages. Find out as much as possible so that when you write your letter of application, you will be able to customize your letter to fit the particular company.

TIME OUT

Pick five companies from the Yellow Pages that you might like to work for. List their names, addresses, and phone numbers.

You never know where or when there may be a job opportunity. There may be a current opening that needs to be filled immediately. Perhaps there is a newly created position that only human resources people know about and for which you may qualify.

COMPANY VISITS

Particular areas of job interest can be pursued by going directly to the personnel office at a company. Fill out an application and leave a copy of your resumé. Remember, be prepared to treat this just as you would an employment interview. You never know with whom you will be speaking. Timing and luck are important. You may just find that the company has an opening in your field and is interested in interviewing you on the spot.

EMPLOYMENT AGENCIES

Private employment agencies earn money only when an applicant is hired. Make sure that the company, not you, pays the fee. To determine if a particular employment agency suits your needs, telephone first and ask if the agency deals with the industry or specific company you are pursuing. Ask if the job listings in your area meet the

TIME OUT

Make a list of five companies that you can visit directly. Give their addresses and phone numbers.

salary level you desire. Find out if further training is offered to make you more marketable. Make sure that you do not have to sign an exclusive contract to work with that one agency only.

Employers contact a private employment agency and describe the available position and what qualifications that applicant must have. Then the agency reviews all resumés, pulls as many as possible that fit the requirements, and submits them to the employer. The agency's loyalty is to the employer, not to you. Therefore, register with as many private agencies as possible to learn about more job openings.

Some employment agencies place people in temporary jobs that offer benefits for both the employer and the employee. Employers can see how their business operates with a larger staff, get an unexpected surge in work completed without making a long-term commitment, and audition an employee before making an offer of permanent employment. Employees gain the chance to stay current in their field, generate at least some income, gain experience, and get a foot in the door. A temporary job can act as a bridge to full-time employment by providing training and on-the-job experience in skills that are in demand in the workplace. It is also an opportunity for workers to showcase their talents to prospective employers. Temporary work offers relief from psychological stress and the financial pressures that often make workers accept mediocre job offers out of desperation.

To turn a temporary job into a permanent position, let your intentions be known, be confident, learn everything you can about the company, use this time to brush up your skills and develop new ones, avoid office politics, volunteer for extra assignments, network as much as possible, and keep focused on the future. Don't abandon your search for permanent employment just because you find a temporary job. Before signing with a temporary-placement agency, be sure to ask if you would be allowed to accept a full-time position offered by a company for which you are working on a temporary assignment. If you want to keep busy on these temporary assignments, register with more than one agency. If an employment agency ever tells you that you will have to pay a fee, you are not dealing with a desirable company. Don't get involved in a situation such as this because you will be the loser.

LIBRARIES

Libraries have books on occupations and often post local job announcements. Sometimes libraries offer employment-seeking seminars to review resumés, cover letters, and interviewing techniques. Usually the fee is nominal. In addition, other books and manuals are available to help an individual find a job. *The Consumer Resource Handbook*, *National Aid Search*, and *National Employment*

Weekly are just a few of the resources. The library also can supply lists of major employers in each city.

■ HOW TO RESEARCH A COMPANY

Because of the time needed to research a company, it's best to delay your research until after you have an interview appointment. Then you should make the time to go to the library and do the research necessary to prepare you for the interview.

However, for those companies you contact cold, meaning that you have no idea whether they have any openings, it is best to gather any information about that company beforehand so that it may be used in your cover letter with great effect. Because there will be no urgency to respond, you will be able to take the time to do the proper research before contacting the company.

Employers are impressed with an applicant who has taken the initiative to research their company. The research shows interest and enthusiasm on the part of the prospective employee. It also says that you know what direction you want to take with your career and that you have certain ideas about the type of firm for which you would like to work.

Basically you should try to find out the number of years the company has been in business; what services it performs or products it produces; who are its biggest competitors; what its reputation is within the industry; its location; whether it has divisions or subsidiaries; the number of employees; and its sales, assets, and earnings. To find this information, start with your local library, which may have the company's annual report on file. Some of the most useful publications are:

- *Million Dollar Directory* by Dun & Bradstreet

- *Ward's Business Directory* by Information Access Company.

- *Standard & Poor's Register of Corporations, Directors, and Executives.*

- *Thomas Register of American Manufacturers.*

- *Moody's Manuals.*

Beyond these, ask your librarian for help in finding specialized single-industry directories. In addition, check with your school's placement department and ask friends or relatives if they have heard of the company.

If all else fails, call the company directly and explain to the receptionist that you have applied to the company and would like to know a little more about it. Perhaps he could take a moment to answer just a few basic questions for you.

■ PLANNING YOUR STRATEGY

Success in your job search will occur as the result of creating a strong foundation on which to build. The cornerstones of this foundation have been laid through the preparation of your portfolio, including your resumé and reference sheet, which you have already successfully completed.

Now it is time to organize your job search to maximize your efforts. You must learn to manage your time wisely to get the best results from your efforts. You have concluded all the preliminary work by deciding what type of position you are interested in and qualified for, and you have resolved any obstacles in your path. In addition, you are ready to take advantage of all your resources to find good job leads.

When the time comes to actively and vigorously pursue your job search, keep all your letters and replies in a folder. You must be organized. Complete an Activity Log form similar to the one shown on page 61 for each company you contact; then attach the form to the want ad and any future correspondence. This form will help you keep track of the date of your first contact with a company and all pertinent information regarding that company, such as: the name of the people you talked with and their titles, what was discussed, and how the conversation ended. This will make your follow-up contact much easier. Make sure you have a good supply of stamps and envelopes. Make a plan, and stick to it. One possible plan is illustrated below and on page 60.

WEEKLY PLANNER

SUNDAY—THE MOST IMPORTANT DAY OF THE WEEK

1. Cut out the want ads that interest you from the newspapers in your area. Separate ads into those that need a cover letter and those that need a telephone call.
2. Assuming you have access to a computer, prepare a secondary file listing each of the addresses to which you want to send your resumé. See Appendix E for step-by-step instructions to create a secondary file. You will be merging these addresses with your cover letter, which will be discussed in Appendix E.
3. Then merge your primary file cover letter and secondary file addresses to the screen. (Step-by-step directions are given in Appendix E.) If you have 20 addresses in your secondary file, then you should have 20 letters on your screen.
4. Triple-check your letters to make sure that they are correct and complete, add any additional comments necessary to each letter for the specific ad, and print out two copies. To demonstrate how to customize your general cover letter to meet the requirements listed in the want ad, let's suppose the ad was for an advertising company and the position required some

accounting background. In the opening paragraph you would mention that the advertising field had always been of interest to you. Because they are looking for someone with an accounting background, you would want to make sure that being detail-oriented and having an aptitude for math are listed as some of your strengths.

5.   Staple each want ad to one copy of the appropriate letter, along with your activity log, and place it in your folder for safekeeping.

6.   Sign the other copy of each letter.

7.   Type an envelope for each response. (See Appendix F.)

8.   Stuff each envelope with the appropriate letter and one copy of your resumé. Don't staple your letter and resumé. Put the letter on top of the resumé and fold both, bringing the bottom edge up to the area of the salutation and making a crease. Then fold the top of the papers down. Place a stamp on each of the envelopes.

Monday

1.   Drop your resumé in the mailbox first thing this morning. It is imperative that your cover letter and resumé be in the mail on Monday.

2.   At 8 AM place telephone calls to each of the advertised companies listing a telephone number to call. Have a copy of your resumé in hand and be prepared to answer questions about your background and qualifications. Have a calendar, pen, and paper handy. You can expect one of two responses to your call. After asking some general questions, the company's representative may tell you to send in your resumé. The other possibility is that he or she will arrange a time for you to come in for an interview and be tested. Be sure to ask for directions if you are not familiar with the location.

3.   Once you have scheduled an appointment time, find out all you can about that company, as discussed earlier in this chapter.

4.   If you did not have access to a computer on Sunday, do your secondary file and merging as early on Monday as possible. The key is to get your letters in the mail before noon so that they will be received the next day.

Tuesday

1.   Contact both permanent- and temporary-placement employment agencies and set up appointments to fill out applications and be tested and interviewed.

Wednesday, Thursday, Friday

1.   Send out an unsolicited cover letter and resumé (this is not in response to any job lead you received through personal contacts or the classified ads). Rather it is sent to a company where you might like to work but for which you have no idea if there is an opening in your field. Unsolicited cover letters will be discussed in greater detail on pages 73–75. You never know when an opening may occur, and your timing might be perfect.

2.   Stop in and hand-deliver your resumé to any company for which you might like to work.

3.   Try calling companies listed in the Yellow Pages to see if they are taking applications. Then ask if you can drop off a resumé. If not, offer to mail it.

TRACKING YOUR PROGRESS

ACTIVITY LOG

Date	Company Name	Company Address	Company Phone	Contact Person and Title	Pertinent Names and Titles	Activity	Results and Follow-Up
6/1	Acme Mfg.	130 Main Warren MI 48089	(313) 758-2100	John Schmit Recruiter	Judy Comfort Supr of Personnel	1st Int. with Personnel Dept.	Went well. Will call me in 1 wk to arrange 2nd interview
6/10	"	"	"	Rick Moeller Head of Sales Dept	Sue, Secy	2nd Int. with Sales Dept. this time	Took & passed tests. Went well.
							Offered job at $8 hr. Will give answer by Monday

ACTIVITY LOG

Date	Company Name	Company Address	Company Phone	Contact Person and Title	Pertinent Names and Titles	Activity	Results and Follow-Up

ACTIVITY LOG

Date	Company Name	Company Address	Company Phone	Contact Person and Title	Pertinent Names and Titles	Activity	Results and Follow-Up

ACTIVITY LOG

Date	Company Name	Company Address	Company Phone	Contact Person and Title	Pertinent Names and Titles	Activity	Results and Follow-Up

NOTES

CHAPTER **4** APPLYING FOR A JOB

■ HOW TO WRITE A COVER LETTER

A cover letter accompanies your resumé when you are responding by mail or fax to an advertised job opening. The cover letter introduces you to a prospective employer. Although the letter alone probably will not secure a position for you, it will create an impression of you. A good cover letter makes a prospective employer want to talk to you. A cover letter tells how your job talents will benefit the company, shows why the employer should read your resumé, and asks for an interview. The letter also may overcome any objections the employer might have about something in your resumé.

To stand out from all other applicants, you should focus on the needs, concerns, or problems faced by the potential employer. Concentrate on the *employer's* needs, not your own. Suggest ways in which you might help the company meet those needs or concerns. Because a company may receive hundreds or thousands of responses to one ad, the key to your success in taking this approach will be your ability to have your resumé and cover letter stand apart from other applicants.

To do this, try to obtain as much information about the company as possible. In your cover letter, address every point that is mentioned in the ad. While we will later write a general cover letter to be sent to all ads, it will be necessary to customize it for each and every ad to show that you match the company's needs. Personalize your response as much as possible. The more you are in touch with the person doing the hiring through telephone contact or personal interviews, the better your chances are of getting an offer. Employers hire the people they feel comfortable with and like. While your resumé is an introduction, be sure to follow up personally to make your efforts count.

Keep the letter to one page, use short sentences and paragraphs, and proofread it carefully. Type the letter on the same quality and color paper as your resumé, and send your original.

Make every effort to send the cover letter and resumé directly to the person responsible for hiring for that position. Be sure his or her name and title are spelled correctly. A phone call to the company will give you the needed information. If you are unable to get the specific name, then use *Ladies and Gentlemen* or *Dear Sir or Madam* (used only when you send the letter to the attention of the human resources director or personnel director).

In general, set up your cover letter according to the guidelines outlined here:

1.   The *first paragraph* states the position you are seeking and how you learned about the opening. If you know anything about the company, you might state that it is the reason the particular ad caught your eye. For example, you might say, "Your ad caught my

attention because I have always wanted to work for a leader in the advertising field, where some of my creative talents would be useful."

2.   The *second paragraph* refers to the enclosed resumé, but doesn't repeat the same information. State how your training, background, and experience relate to the position offered. Include relevant work experience in a general way such as, "My five years of previous office experience in advertising have proven me to be a self-starter who is dependable and energetic and ready to give 100 percent effort on a daily basis." Your comments should coincide with the qualifications listed in the advertisement.

3.   The third paragraph points out qualities that can't be described in a resumé—personal qualities and proud accomplishments. Be positive, but not cocky.

4.   Only when asked for, use the *fourth paragraph* to address job salary. Salary history refers to current salary, whereas salary requirements refers to your desired salary. For your salary requirements, give a salary range that you feel will overlap that of the company. Always note that salary is negotiable. For example, from your research of a particular company and the marketplace in general, you might conclude that the salary range for a particular position is $7 to $10 per hour. You might then say, "With my up-to-date training from Draper Business School and my previous office experience, a salary range of $9 to $11 per hour would be an acceptable starting point. However, this is negotiable depending on other factors." When salary history is requested, don't ever state exactly what you presently earn. You could either add 10 to 20 percent to your present salary or give a figure that represents your total compensation package, including benefits. The total package adds roughly 30 percent to your base salary. Be careful, though, not to price yourself out of a job. Be realistic about market prices.

5.   The last paragraph indicates your desire for a personal interview and your telephone number during business hours. (If you work, owning an answering machine is a good idea.) Close with a statement that encourages a response, such as "The opportunity to discuss this position with you in greater detail would be appreciated. You may reach me at the above address or by telephone at (517) 555-8889. I look forward to hearing from you."

If software is available, you will be able to type your cover letter now, insert commands that will allow you to customize it later to coincide with each specific advertisement, and then merge the letter with the appropriate address for each advertisement. To use the merge feature, you will type your cover letter first; type the list of addresses second; and then merge—or join—the two documents together. (See Appendix E for specific instructions.)

EXERCISE 4.1	**PREPARING YOUR COVER LETTER**

Prepare your cover letter after referring to the examples below and on pages 70–72. However, don't just copy one of these letters. It is important that you customize your letter to fit your personality.

Refer to Appendix E for step-by-step instructions on typing a cover letter using WordPerfect or Word so that you can merge it later with the appropriate addresses.

If software is not available to set up your letter for later merging, then type the letter and address it to a fictitious company for now. Use the letter for future reference. Don't forget to sign your letter. Do not staple it to the resumé. Instead, put the letter on top of the resumé. Fold the bottom edges of the two pages up a third of the way, and fold the top edges of the two pages down to the crease. Place the folded pages in the envelope. (Directions for typing an envelope can be found in Appendix F.)

COVER LETTER NO. 1

Your Street Address
Your City, State, and Zip Code
Date

Mrs. Marilyn DeLiso, Supervisor
Norton Electronics
6543 Schoenherr Road
Warren, MI 48090

Dear Mrs. DeLiso:

The position of accounting clerk that you recently advertised in The Macomb Daily interests me a great deal. Your advertisement drew my attention because I am familiar with Norton Electronics and the quality products it produces.

The enclosed resumé outlines my experience and skills in office procedures and the accounts payable/receivable area. In addition, I am completing a training program in computer applications from Gorham Business School. This program has enabled me to expand my expertise and update my office skills in computer accounting and Lotus.

I am energetic, detail-oriented, organized, and eager to accept the challenges of a responsible position. These qualities, combined with my previous experience, make me confident that I will be an asset to your office staff.

The opportunity to meet with you to discuss how my skills would benefit Norton Electronics would be greatly appreciated. You may reach me at (313) 555-6000 most days after 2 p.m. I look forward to hearing from you.

Sincerely,

Your Name

Enclosure

COVER LETTER No. 2

Your Street Address
Your City, State, and Zip Code
Date

Ms. Deborah Osborne
Office Manager
ABC Advertising
2345 W. Big Beaver
Troy, IL 48084

Dear Ms. Osborne:

The Placement Office at Troy Community College has referred me to you for the secretarial opening in your sales department. I have a great interest in the advertising field combined with superior office skills and computer knowledge.

Please consider my qualifications noted on the enclosed resumé. Recently I completed an educational program in which I received extensive training in WordPerfect 6.0, Lotus, dBase III Plus, Microsoft Word, and desktop publishing. Additionally, I am very proud of my acquired shorthand skill and business communications ability.

By nature, I am hardworking, adaptable, punctual, and dedicated to excellence. If given the opportunity, I am confident that I would be an asset to ABC Advertising.

I am eager to discuss this secretarial position in greater detail and look forward to the opportunity for a personal interview. You may contact me at the above address or by telephone at (313) 432–1000 most days after 2 p.m. I look forward to hearing from you.

Sincerely,

Your Name

Enclosure

COVER LETTER NO. 3

Your Street Address
Your City, State, and Zip Code
Date

Personnel
P.O. Box MD 2345
San Diego, CA 48043

Ladies and Gentlemen:

This letter is in response to your recent advertisement in <u>The San Diego Press</u> for the receptionist position.

As a recent graduate of Allister School of Business, I am eager to begin my career in the office area. Through Allister's full-time training program, I gained competency in Microsoft Word, Excel, Paradox, business communications, shorthand, and office procedures.

What you cannot learn from my enclosed resumé is that I am articulate, congenial, dependable, and organized. I am confident my qualifications will allow me to make an immediate contribution to your office team.

I am interested in learning more about your company and would like to meet with you personally to discuss this receptionist position. You may contact me at (313) 256–9000 most days after 2 p.m. I look forward to hearing from you.

Sincerely,

Your Name

Enclosure

COVER LETTER No. 4

Your Street Address
Your City, State, and Zip Code
Date

Ms. Darlene Makarski, Chairman
Stanley, Jefferson and Rowe Agency
455 South State Street
Chicago, IL 60611

Dear Ms. Makarski:

Three features of the position you advertised in Sunday's <u>City Times</u> suggest that I may be the assistant account representative you are seeking. I have

- Experience in developing and implementing promotional and advertising campaigns for organizations, service groups, and business establishments.

- B.S. degree in communications with a marketing minor received from the University of Illinois, Urbana–Champaign.

- Writing and editorial background in newspapers; copywriting experience in radio.

As the former vice president of public relations for the Student Government Association, I took charge of all promotion and advertising, developed successful membership recruitment drives, and implemented original ideas in dealing with campus media.

Working part time throughout my college career, I managed several advertising campaigns for newspapers and radio, leading to an increase of 15 percent in clientele for a restaurant. I have researched extensively and drafted many recommendations based on research results during my internship in Washington. I also handled all administration necessary to keep a busy office running smoothly.

Perhaps I am the assistant account representative you need at your agency. I would be very happy to meet with you at your convenience to discuss the possibility of putting my education and experience to work for you. Thank you very much for your consideration. I look forward to hearing from you soon.

Sincerely,

Your Name

Enclosure

TIME OUT

How would you respond to an advertisement asking for your salary requirements?

_____

_____

_____

_____

_____

_____

■ HOW TO WRITER A LETTER OF APPLICATION

You should write a letter of application to accompany your resumé when you are not sure that there is a specific job opening with a company. For example, perhaps you drive by a certain company daily and think it might be a nice place to work. Or, perhaps you've always wanted to work for a lawyer, so you check the Yellow Pages for names of law firms. In either case, you have no idea whether the firm is hiring. Under these circumstances, send a letter of application.

The letter of application will differ slightly from your cover letter because the first paragraph will introduce yourself and state why you are writing, rather than tell where you heard about an opening. You will have the advantage of researching the company before writing your letter. Show that you've done some homework on the company, know what they do, their interests, and problems. Try to identify something about you that is unique or would be of interest to the employer. The last paragraph will request an interview and if possible, suggest a specific date and time that you will contact them.

On pages 74 and 75 are examples of a letter of application. Such a letter is sometimes called an _unsolicited cover letter_ because the company to which you are writing did not ask you to write or send your resumé.

EXERCISE 4:2	PREPARING YOUR LETTER OF APPLICATION

Prepare your sample letter of application, again using the method described in Appendix E if you have WordPerfect or Word. Name the letter **a:appltr.pf**. In this way, you can merge it later with the appropriate addresses. Likewise, you may type a letter of application on a typewriter using any company name for the inside address.

LETTER OF APPLICATION NO. 1

Your Street Address
Your City, State, and Zip Code
Date

Acme Products Corporation
Attention Human Resources Department
12345 East Nine Mile Road
Warren, MI 48089

Ladies and Gentlemen:

Please consider this letter an application for a drafting position with your company. I am aware that Acme is one of the leading manufacturers of automotive tubing used in brake and fuel lines. Working for a respected leader in the automotive industry and being able to contribute my expertise to support your engineering department is the opportunity for which I have been looking.

As my enclosed resumé states, I have had experience on the board as well as CAD. My experience includes work as a detailer, minor layout draftsman, designer, and checker. Upon completion of my associates degree in mechanincal engineering, I will have developed a strong background in computer-aided design.

What you cannot learn from my resumé is that I am outgoing, responsible, creative, accurate, and hardworking. I am used to working long hours to meet a deadline and find I respond well to pressure situations.

I will contact you within in a week to discuss the possibility of meeting with you regarding any present or future openings at Acme. If you wish to contact me before that time, you may reach me at (313) 431–8787. I look forward to a personal introduction at your earliest convenience.

Sincerely,

Your Name

Enclosure

LETTER OF APPLICATION NO. 2

Your Street Address
Your City, State, and Zip Code
Date

Mr. Jake T. Matula, President
Feister Corporation
1725 West Canton Street
Louisville, KY 48803

Dear Mr. Matula:

Recently I spoke with your Director of Food Services, Gordon Burger. He informed me of your intentions of implementing a more health-conscious food program at Feister and suggested I contact you. As you can see from my resumé, my credentials in the food service industry would enable me to successfully promote the growth of such a program.

In the spring of next year, I will be receiving my degree in hotel and restaurant management. In addition, I have more than two years of work experience in the field of food service. This has familiarized me with diet therapy, menu planning, and food administration.

The American Institutions Food Service Association recently recognized me for my achievements in menu planning with the Hilton Hotels Corporation. I am health conscious and enjoy working closely with others. My feelings are very positive about your organization, and I know that I could make a significant contribution to it.

Given the opportunity, I would be pleased to meet with you and discuss how I might be able to promote the growth of a nutritional food program at Feister. I will call you on Monday, January 16, to determine your interest and, if appropriate, to arrange for a personal meeting.

I look forward to meeting with you.

Sincerely,

Your Name

Enclosure

■ HOW TO COMPLETE AN APPLICATION FORM

If you have reached the point where you are filling out a job application form, then things are going well for you! You have obviously made a good first impression with your cover letter and resumé. Or, you have made a good first impression with your professional manner and appearance after walking in off the street.

The next step is to continue to make a good impression by filling out the application form neatly, completely, and error free. Your goal is to obtain an interview; or, if you already have an interview, to present yourself as the best candidate for the job. When filling out the application form, keep in mind the following points:

- Fill out everything in its entirety. Don't ever say, "See resumé." There is no guarantee that the resumé and application form will stay together.

- Follow directions. If you can't follow directions when completing an application form, the company may assume you can't follow directions on the job.

- Always use black ink when filling out an application form, unless the directions indicate to do otherwise. (An erasable pen would be great.)

- Use your neatest printing.

- Don't leave anything blank. If a question or section doesn't apply to you, write *N/A* for "not applicable."

- Read each question carefully and think before you answer. If you make a mistake, cross out your answer by putting one line through it and then neatly make the correction. You can neatly use white out, if you have any with you. If you make a major error, ask for another form. The final product must look good.

- Complete the application as quickly as possible. A prospective employer may make note of how long it takes to fill out the application.

- Be sure that all information and dates match those in your resumé. Don't leave any holes in your employment history. Make sure the information is accurate and honest. You don't want to be dismissed later because information supplied on the application was incorrect.

- Make sure your spelling and grammar are correct.

- If the application asks for salary desired, never state a dollar figure or salary. Write *Open* or *Negotiable.*

- When asked for the date you can start, answer *Upon two weeks' notice,* if you are currently employed. If you are not employed, you can answer *Immediately* or *Upon graduation.*

- Under the employment record section, never state a negative reason for leaving position. Such reasons include *was fired, personality conflict,* and *quit.* Phrases such as *Unsuitable work* or *Unsuitable working conditions* can be applied to most controversial reasons for leaving. Other common reasons for leaving a job are to further one's education, better job opportunity, career advancement, better pay, company moved, and company went out of business.

If an application form is mailed to you and you are given the option of typing or using black ink, you may want to type it—especially if you are applying for an office position. Make a photocopy of the form first, however, and practice on the photocopy to make sure all the information will fit.

At the bottom of an application form, most companies ask for your signature. Your signature on a completed employment application certifies that all of the information you have supplied is true and correct. Make sure it is!

| EXERCISE 4.3 | **COMPLETING YOUR APPLICATION FORM** |

Now fill out the application form on pages 80–82. When you have finished, your application should be as accurate, thorough, and neat as the example on pages 78 and 79. Use pencil, for our purposes only, so that you can correct any errors you make. If you do a thorough job now, you will never have to worry about filling out another application form later. When you actually apply for a job, take a photocopy of your completed form with you. Then you will basically just have to copy information from your photocopy to the application form given to you. You will have all necessary information right at your fingertips. You will be fully prepared. Bringing your completed sample application form will save time and help you make a positive impression because of your thoroughness.

PRACTICE APPLICATION FORM

FOR OFFICE USE ONLY	
Possible Work Locations	Possible Positions

APPLICATION FOR EMPLOYMENT

(PLEASE PRINT PLAINLY)

FOR OFFICE USE ONLY	
Work Location _____	Rate _____
Position _____	Date _____

To Applicant: We deeply appreciate your interest in our organization and assure you that we are sincerely interested in your qualifications. A clear understanding of your background and work history will aid us in placing you in the position that best meets your qualifications and may assist us in possible future upgrading.

PERSONAL

Date   3-15-94

Name   BOCHY   JULIA   MARIE
     Last   First   Middle

Social Security No.   366-50-1800

Present Address   123   ELM   ST. LOUIS   MO   63122
     No.   Street   City   State   Zip

Telephone No.   (314)-578-1200

Are you legally eligible for employment in the U.S.A.?   YES

State age if under 18 or over 70   N/A

What method of transportation will you use to get to work?   CAR

Position(s) applied for?   SECRETARY

Rate of pay expected $ NEGOTIABLE   per week

Would you work Full Time?   √   Part Time _____   Specify days and hours if part time?   N/A

Were you previously employed by us?   NO   If yes, when?   N/A

If your application is considered favorably, on what date will you be available for work?   UPON TWO WEEKS' NOTICE   19 —

Are there any other experiences, skills, or qualifications, which you feel would especially fit you for work with our organization?   KNOWLEDGE OF

WORDPERFECT 6.0, LOTUS, dBASE III PLUS, SHORTHAND @ 100 WPM, TYPING @ 60 WPM, SPANISH, TWO YEARS' OFFICE EXPERIENCE, PERFECT ATTENDANCE.

RECORD OF EDUCATION

School	Name and Address of School	Course of Study	Check Last Year Completed				Did You Graduate?	List Diploma or Degree
Elementary	TYRONE 30309 LITTLESTONE KANSAS CITY, MO 64123	N/A	5	⑥	7	8	[X] Yes [ ] No	N/A
High	HARPER CREEK HIGH 13960 BEACONSFIELD ST. LOUIS, MO 63122	COLLEGE PREP AND BUSINESS	1	2	3	④	[X] Yes [ ] No	H.S. DIPLOMA
College	MILLER COMMUNITY COLLEGE 13011 12 MILE ROAD ST. LOUIS, MO 63122	BUSINESS	1	②	3	4	[X] Yes [ ] No	ASSOC. DEGREE OFFICE ADMIN
Other (Specify)	SEKICH COLLEGE OF BUSINESS 26001 HOOVER ROAD ST. LOUIS, MO 63122	WORD PROCESSING	①	2	3	4	[X] Yes [ ] No	DIPLOMA WORD PROCESSING

List below all present and past employment, beginning with your most recent

I

Name and Address of Company and Type of Business	From Mo.	From Yr.	To Mo.	To Yr.	Describe the work you do	Weekly Starting Salary	Weekly Last Salary	Reason for Leaving	Name of Supervisor
ACME MANUFACTING	6	93	PRESENT		SALES SECY	$280	$320	N/A	GAYLE
1101 HALL ROAD ST. LOUIS, MO 63122									SUDDICK
AUTOMOTIVE SUPPLIER									
Telephone (314) 231-5100									

II

Name and Address of Company and Type of Business	From Mo.	From Yr.	To Mo.	To Yr.	Describe the work you do	Weekly Starting Salary	Weekly Last Salary	Reason for Leaving	Name of Supervisor
RINKY PONTIAC	1	92	5	93	RECEPTIONIST	$200	$250	BETTER OPPORTUNITY	AL
33000 GRATIOT ST. LOUIS, MO 63122									RAQUEPAU
CAR DEALERSHIP									
Telephone (314) 270-0110									

III

Name and Address of Company and Type of Business	From Mo.	From Yr.	To Mo.	To Yr.	Describe the work you do	Weekly Starting Salary	Weekly Last Salary	Reason for Leaving	Name of Supervisor
ROSE KIDD ELEM.	1	91	12	91	PTO VOLUNTEER	N/A	N/A	RELOCATED	N/A
16030 GLASDSTONE KANSAS CITY, MO 64123									
SCHOOL									
Telephone (816) 575-3400									

IV

Name and Address of Company and Type of Business	From Mo.	From Yr.	To Mo.	To Yr.	Describe the work you do	Weekly Starting Salary	Weekly Last Salary	Reason for Leaving	Name of Supervisor
SALLY WEBB	9	90	12	91	BABYSITTER	$70	$90	RELOCATED	SALLY
11201 ROUNDTREE KANSAS CITY, MO 64123									WEBB
N/A									
Telephone (816) 313-4113									

May we contact the employers listed above? _NO_ If not, indicate by No. which one(s) you do not wish us to contact? _NO. 1_

PERSONAL REFERENCES (Not Former Employees or Relatives)

Name and Occupation	Address	Phone Number
JANET PENROSE, HOMEMAKER	13098 WINONA ST. LOUIS, MO 63122	(314) 465-1310
CALVIN STEIN, FOOD BROKER	450 MAPLE ROAD ST. LOUIS, MO 63122	(314) 578-8391
KATHY BRANCH, PRINCIPAL	600 OAKHILL KANSAS CITY, MO 64123	(816) 578-2420

MILITARY SERVICE RECORD

Were you in U.S. Armed Forces? Yes _____ No _√_ If yes, what Branch? _N/A_

Dates of duty: From _N/A_ to _N/A_ Rank at discharge _N/A_
Month Day Year / Month Day Year

List duties in service including special training. _N/A_

Have you taken any training undr the G.I. Bill of Rights? _N/A_ If yes, what training did you take? _N/A_

PRACTICE APPLICATION FORM

FOR OFFICE USE ONLY	
Possible Work Locations	Possible Positions

APPLICATION FOR EMPLOYMENT

(PLEASE PRINT PLAINLY)

FOR OFFICE USE ONLY	
Work Location _____	Rate _____
Position _____	Date _____

To Applicant: We deeply appreciate your interest in our organization and assure you that we are sincerely interested in your qualifications. A clear understanding of your background and work history will aid us in placing you in the position that best meets your qualifications and may assist us in possible future upgrading.

PERSONAL

Date _____

Name _____   Social Security No. _____
　　　Last　　　　　　　First　　　　　　　Middle

Present Address _____   Telephone No. _____
　　　　　　　No.　　　Street　　　City　　State　　Zip

Are you legally eligible for employment in the U.S.A.? _____   State age if under 18 or over 70 _____

What method of transportation will you use to get to work? _____

Position(s) applied for? _____   Rate of pay expected $ _____ per week

Would you work Full Time? _____ Part Time _____   Specify days and hours if part time? _____

Were you previously employed by us? _____ If yes, when? _____

If your application is considered favorably, on what date will you be available for work? _____ 19 _____

Are there any other experiences, skills, or qualifications, which you feel would especially fit you for work with our organization? _____

_____

_____

RECORD OF EDUCATION

School	Name and Address of School	Course of Study	Check Last Year Completed				Did You Graduate?	List Diploma or Degree
Elementary			5	6	7	8	☐ Yes ☐ No	
High			1	2	3	4	☐ Yes ☐ No	
College			1	2	3	4	☐ Yes ☐ No	
Other (Specify)			1	2	3	4	☐ Yes ☐ No	

List below all present and past employment, beginning with your most recent

I

Name and Address of Company and Type of Business	From		To		Describe the work you do	Weekly Starting Salary	Weekly Last Salary	Reason for Leaving	Name of Supervisor
	Mo.	Yr.	Mo.	Yr.					
Telephone									

II

Name and Address of Company and Type of Business	From		To		Describe the work you do	Weekly Starting Salary	Weekly Last Salary	Reason for Leaving	Name of Supervisor
	Mo.	Yr.	Mo.	Yr.					
Telephone									

III

Name and Address of Company and Type of Business	From		To		Describe the work you do	Weekly Starting Salary	Weekly Last Salary	Reason for Leaving	Name of Supervisor
	Mo.	Yr.	Mo.	Yr.					
Telephone									

IV

Name and Address of Company and Type of Business	From		To		Describe the work you do	Weekly Starting Salary	Weekly Last Salary	Reason for Leaving	Name of Supervisor
	Mo.	Yr.	Mo.	Yr.					
Telephone									

V

Name and Address of Company and Type of Business	From		To		Describe the work you do	Weekly Starting Salary	Weekly Last Salary	Reason for Leaving	Name of Supervisor
	Mo.	Yr.	Mo.	Yr.					
Telephone									

VI

Name and Address of Company and Type of Business	From		To		Describe the work you do	Weekly Starting Salary	Weekly Last Salary	Reason for Leaving	Name of Supervisor
	Mo.	Yr.	Mo.	Yr.					
Telephone									

May we contact the employers listed above? _____ If not, indicate by No. which one(s) you do not wish us to contact? _____

(continued)

PERSONAL REFERENCES (Not Former Employees or Relatives)

Name and Occupation	Address	Phone Number

MILITARY SERVICE RECORD

Were you in U.S. Armed Forces? Yes _____ No _____ If yes, what Branch? _____

Dates of duty: From _____ to _____ Rank at discharge _____
               Month Day Year   Month Day Year

List duties in service including special training. _____

Have you taken any training undr the G.I. Bill of Rights? _____ If yes, what training did you take? _____

NOTES

CHAPTER **5 PREPARING FOR THE INTERVIEW**

■ ARRANGING THE INTERVIEW

Until this point the only impression a company can have of you is based on your cover letter and resumé. If the company has contacted you for an interview—either by mail or by phone—it must be interested. Therefore, you probably have the qualifications for the job.

Now you need to put your best foot forward. Conduct yourself professionally and politely when arranging for the interview.

Eliminate all background noise when talking on the phone and give the person calling your undivided attention. Your telephone manners are important. Be sure to use correct grammar, speak clearly into the mouthpiece, have a pen and paper ready to take down necessary information, and don't hesitate to ask for directions.

Sometimes this initial phone contact will take the form of an informal interview session. Have your resumé in hand to help you answer questions regarding past experience and education. Be prepared to answer questions.

Assuming an interview appointment is scheduled during this phone conversation, be sure to ask the right questions to help you prepare. For example, if you were applying for an office position, you might ask if you will be tested during your first visit. If so, in what areas will the testing be? If you will be tested on your typing speed, ask what type of equipment will be used. If you are prepared ahead of time, your stress level will be lower and you will perform much better. Fear of the unknown is always a problem, so do as much as you can to eliminate the unknown factors. Depending on the type of position for which you are applying, there may be no tests at all.

■ DRESSING THE PART

First impressions are important. Whether you realize it or not, the image you present—your attitude and your overall delivery—is affected by your clothing. The clothes you wear during an interview are an important part of how you present yourself; you should be comfortable, but professional. You need to look like you belong in the position for which you are being interviewed. So, dress the part. If you feel great about the way you look, you will convey that image. Taking time to present an attractive, professional image will add to your self-esteem and self-confidence.

Because no two interviews are alike, it is impossible to form strict guidelines for exactly what to wear for each situation. Appropriate attire will vary from one industry to the next.

FIGURE No. 5–1

"I know the ad specified a neat, polite, well-groomed person, but I can't believe you expected all that just for an interview!"

HINTS FOR WOMEN

Clothing

For a woman, a conservative business suit is always appropriate. Because styles change so quickly, a safe hem length would be just below the knee. There are no hard-and-fast rules regarding color, but most suitable is gray, black, or navy, followed by tan or camel. Both wool and linen create a professional appearance. A solid white or pale blue, long-sleeved blouse always looks nice. Pink and gray are also acceptable colors. A blouse designed to be worn with a suit, or a shell is always good for a positive impression. Another conservative option is a pleated front panel blouse that buttons down the back.

You should have two interview outfits as you will probably go on a second interview before being offered the job. A skirt and blouse or coat dress is a possible alternative, depending on the position for which you are applying. All clothes should be clean and neatly pressed.

Accessories

Accessories also should be conservative. The basic leather pump—closed toe and heel—is the most conservative choice for shoes. Make sure that your shoes are polished and match your outfit. Flat shoes or those with a heel of up to $1\frac{1}{2}$ inches are acceptable.

Select hosiery that is neutral or skin-toned. Never wear patterned stockings.

Also, make sure that your purse blends with your outfit. Because a briefcase is a symbol of authority for a woman, you may choose to carry one rather than a purse. Never carry both.

Plan the contents of your purse! Start with an empty purse. Put in your driver's license, Social Security card, a little money, an extra pair of stockings, a lipstick and blush, two pencils with erasers, two black pens, facial tissue, and your sample application form. If you are applying for an office position, you also need a typing eraser, Korrect-type, white correction fluid, a calculator, a small dictionary, and a WordPerfect/Word template and/or a command sheet.

Be careful with your jewelry selection. Never wear more than one ring on each hand. One pair of small, conservative earrings or a simple pearl or gold necklace is appropriate. A single, small bracelet is acceptable, but not an ankle bracelet. Stay away from the big, dangly hoop earrings—they're distracting. A well-tied scarf can complete an outfit and make a strong, professional statement.

Personal Grooming

Your hairstyle should complement the shape of your face. For example, if you have a long face, choose a style that creates fullness on the sides and top. Most professional hairstyles fall at least one inch off the shoulders. The color of your hair should enhance your natural coloring, not create a contrast. Wear your hair the way that most often brings you compliments. If you have long hair, keep it off your face. The night before an interview is not the time to get a haircut, to color your hair, or to get a permanent. You will not feel comfortable, and your discomfort will show.

Don't smoke beforehand because that smoke odor will be on your breath and clothes. Don't chew gum during the interview.

It is permissible to wear light eye shadow and mascara, some blush, and lipstick. A natural look is what you are striving for. Make sure your fingernails are manicured. If you use polish, wear clear or light-colored polish. Nails should be only 1/4 inch long. Wear light perfume. Redefine cleanliness. You are striving for perfection.

HINTS FOR MEN

Clothing

For a man applying for any kind of professional business position, a suit, shirt, and tie are essential. The most acceptable suit colors are navy blue and charcoal gray through light gray. Less popular is the brown to camel range of colors. The darker the suit, the more authority it carries. However, black is not acceptable. A 100 percent solid or muted pinstripe wool suit will look and wear better than any other material. Men should always wear white or pale blue long-sleeved cotton shirts that have been professionally laundered and starched.

Accessories

The right tie can complement the suit, bring the total outfit together, and give the best impression. A pure silk tie makes the most powerful impression. When tied, the tie should reach the trouser belt. Also, the smaller the knot, the better. If you don't have another suit for the second interview, just choose a different shirt and tie to change your overall appearance.

Ideally men should wear freshly polished black or brown laced wing tips or slip-on dress shoes. Socks should complement the suit and be long enough so that when legs are crossed bare skin will not show. Be sure to have a handkerchief in your breast pocket, but avoid the matching tie and pocket handkerchief look at all costs. Your belt should complement your shoes, and your watch should be plain and simple.

If you choose to carry a briefcase, select a black or brown leather one. Be sure to carry your Social Security card and driver's license. Inside your suitcoat pocket or briefcase, put a small calculator, a black pen, a pencil with an eraser, and your sample application form. If you are applying for a job where typing skills might be tested, be sure to include the following items in your briefcase: a typing eraser, Korrect-Type, white correction fluid, a small dictionary, and a WordPerfect/Word template and/or command sheet.

TIME OUT

What do you plan to wear on your first interview appointment? What do you plan to wear if you are called back for a second interview?

Personal Grooming

Make sure your hair is trimmed and your beard or mustache is neat. Don't put on too much aftershave lotion or cologne. Make sure your fingernails are clean and manicured. Don't smoke beforehand or chew gum during the interview.

Remember: If you look good and feel good, that will only help in the job-search process. You get just one chance to make a good personal impression!

Some people may have cultural preferences for the way they dress. Remember, however, that on an interview it is always better to be conservative; this isn't a time to express your individuality but a time to fit in with the workplace norm.

■ GETTING PSYCHED

Your main goal in the first interview is to avoid being eliminated. Generally speaking, the interviewer will try to find a reason to turn you down, thus narrowing the field of applicants to the best two or three. You have to make sure you don't provide the interviewer evidence to suggest that you could not handle the job. How you come across in that interview can be as important as your experience and job talents. Remember, you must be able to sell your abilities to the employer and to convince the interviewer that you can provide the help and assistance for which the company is looking.

Never underestimate your competition. Don't become careless during the interview and provide your competition with an opportunity to snatch the job offer away from you. Remember, companies don't hire just the best-qualified person for a particular job; but rather the person who is best at securing a job offer.

Everyone has liabilities, and you must learn how to overcome yours. First of all, recognize your liabilities as legitimate concerns for an interviewer. Whenever a liability is sighted, it implies that a particular strength is missing. Therefore, the second thing you must do is to show that you possess that missing strength. For example, you might lack related on-the-job experience. If you can show that your training has provided you with experience equivalent to an actual job situation, then you might be able to overcome the interviewer's concern. Last, you must provide evidence of that strength. To make your point, present your portfolio with examples of the work you completed during your training and show their relationship to on-the-job performance criteria.

An interview should be a two-way exchange of information, not an inquisition. Primarily you need to prove your strengths by stating what they are and providing examples to support your claims.

Much of the first interview will be spent reviewing personal information and making small talk. You will have only a short time to convince the interviewer that you are interested in the position, that you are qualified for the position, and that you are the best candidate for the position.

Most often people don't get the job they want because they don't sell themselves. Toot your own horn because no one else will.

Have a half-dozen accomplishments from life, work, or school to talk about, and show how they relate to the job. Show what you can do for the company. You know what skills the manager is looking for; so offer examples from your resumé to show that you can fill the company's needs. Show that you're a team player. Give original answers to the manager's questions—answers that will stand out and be remembered. Give complete answers and use lots of examples. A good answer should take between 30 seconds and 2 minutes to explain. Don't be a motor-mouth; know when to be quiet and listen. The interview should be a 50–50 conversation.

The skills you have to offer an employer may or may not be required for the job. The reason that you will be hired, however, is not based on skills alone. Your personality and ability to connect with the interviewer are just as important. No matter what your skills, an employer must *like you* to want to hire you. Show that you have the skills *and* personality. Show some enthusiasm. Don't be a zombie. Participate in the conversation, and look the manager in the eye. Smile and add humor and insight whenever possible and appropriate.

Do not tell an employer what your needs are. Everyone needs good pay and medical insurance. You do not want to appear to be interested in the best dollar offer. You want to promote the image of a professional searching for the career path that will provide the best opportunities for personal and professional growth.

You have to believe that you are the best applicant for the position if you want the employer to believe it! Self-confidence (not cockiness or overconfidence) is the key to a successful interview.

■ UNDERSTANDING THE INTERVIEWER

The interviewer will probably conduct the interview in his or her office or in a human resources department office. The manager will close the door, giving you his or her full attention. The interview will last about an hour.

Most managers are expert interviewers, and they know that you'll be a bit nervous. Your nervousness is natural. To help you relax and feel comfortable, most managers will conduct the interview as if it were a casual, informal, and friendly conversation.

Chances are that the first question will be "Relax and tell me a little about yourself." By far, most interviewers are pleasant and friendly. Try to enjoy yourself.

Although the interview will be informal and friendly, the manager will be looking for some serious answers. The interviewer may begin by glancing over your resumé and job application. He or she may ask questions about your work history, education, outside interests, strengths, and weaknesses. All of the questions will be designed to answer three important questions: Can you do the job? Will you do the job? Can you get along with other employees?

The process and responsibility of hiring the right person for a job can put fears into a manager's mind. The manager may fear that, if hired, you will turn out to be incompetent or you will need too much time to become productive and pull your own weight. The interviewer may fear that you won't put in an honest day's work, that you'll goof off, or that you'll need someone to constantly check your work. Perhaps you will be lazy, giving only the minimum effort, or that you will have to be told when to do everything. Another concern is that you'll frequently call in sick, arrive late, leave early, refuse overtime, or constantly ask for raises. Also, what if you're a quitter and you walk out at a time when you are most needed? Will you be a chronic complainer, a braggart, or someone who blames others for your mistakes? Will you be arrogant, conceited, rude, antagonistic, overly pushy, broody, or moody? Will you say or do

FIGURE NO. 5–2

"Do you have initiative?"

"You know, that's a word I've always meant to look up."

FIGURE NO. 5–3

"Fill out all these forms? Gee . . . that looks like a lot of work."

something to disgrace or embarrass the company, the department, the manager, or your fellow workers? Will you steal, embezzle, lie, or cheat? What if you don't show pride in your work or appearance?

So you can see that you are not the only one who is somewhat apprehensive going into the interview. The interviewer has the sole responsibility of hiring the best person for the job. You have the sole responsibility of finding the right job for you. This marriage can come about only if you relax, let your personality show, be enthusiastic and interested, and carry on a two-way conversation.

■ PRACTICING FOR THE INTERVIEW

One of the easiest ways to prepare for the interview is to practice in front of a mirror what you may say in response to questions. Watch your facial expressions and eye contact. Also, record your answers, play them back, and listen for pronunciation, voice quality and tone, and correct grammar usage. Another idea is to have a family member or friend ask you questions at random.

One of the best ways to prepare yourself is to have someone make a videotape of you being interviewed by a teacher, friend, or family member. You know the saying "A picture is worth a thousand words!" How true the saying is in this case. You need to observe your facial expressions, posture, eye contact, body movement, mannerisms, and speech patterns. You need to hear your answers and evaluate how you came across to the interviewer. Notice if your nervousness was evident and in what form it manifested itself, such as sweaty palms, quivering lip, wringing hands, stuttering, and dry mouth. Note at what point during the interview you seemed to relax and let your real personality show through.

Now that you have an idea on how to practice for the interview and have had the opportunity to see and hear yourself under simulated interview conditions, it is time to consider exactly how you will answer specific questions asked during the interview process.

CHAPTER **6** SUCCEEDING AT THE
INTERVIEW

*T*here is no formula for succeeding at the interview, but there are many things you can do to bring success closer. Review the following guidelines and refer to them often throughout the interview process.

1. Find out the exact time of the interview, the name and title of the interviewer, and the name and address of the company.

2. Learn everything you can about the job and how your previous experience, education, or training qualify you for the position.

3. Before the interview, learn as much as you can about the company, its products, services, and so on. As discussed in Chapter 3, friends, neighbors, and relatives are good sources of information. Libraries and local chambers of commerce also are helpful.

4. If you are unsure of the company's location, make a dry run the day before the interview to ensure that you will be on time. Be sure to allow for rush-hour traffic.

5. Prepare in advance any questions you may wish to ask. (See pages 125 and 126.)

FIGURE No. 6–1

U.S. HAT CO.

"No . . . I don't like to wear hats."

FIGURE No. 6–2

6. Be prepared to answer questions asked of you. (See pages 101–123.)

7. Be prepared to take tests. Have the necessary reference materials with you.

8. Make sure your grooming and dress meet the highest business standards. Be conservative. Slacks are never acceptable for women interviewing for any office position.

9. If you cannot report for an interview, always notify the interviewer as soon as possible. You should have a very good explanation. Car trouble and babysitter problems are unacceptable. If you can't make it to the interview, the employer will be afraid that you won't make it to the job. Likewise, be sure to call if you are going to be late. Remember, though, that lateness creates a negative impression before you even get your foot in the door.

10. Go to the interview by yourself.

11. Arrive approximately 10 minutes early. If possible, find a restroom to make sure your hair and clothing are still attractively arranged. Try to relax.

12. SMILE! Be friendly, and always remain polite. Be yourself, but stay on your toes. Assume that you are being observed and

FIGURE NO. 6-3

judged from the time you enter the parking lot until the time you leave.

13. Fill out forms neatly and completely.

14. Greet the interviewer, introduce yourself, and offer a firm handshake. Don't sit down until you are offered a seat. If you are not offered a seat, then start to sit down as the interviewer begins to sit.

15. Try to be relaxed and keep calm.

16. Watch your posture. While seated, sit back in the chair. Don't cross your arms or talk with your hands. Your body language is very important.

17. Be enthusiastic and act interested by asking intelligent questions that are pertinent to the job.

18. Speak clearly.

19. Watch your grammar! Speak correctly and distinctly, or you will not get the position, even if your skills are excellent.

20. During a lunch or dinner interview situation, graciously decline an alcoholic drink, even if others order them. Also, order a dish that will be easy to eat (not spaghetti, for

FIGURE NO. 6–4

FIGURE NO. 6–5

example), that will not upset a nervous stomach (something spicy), or that will cause bad breath (heavy onions or garlic).

21. Have your portfolio with you and present it at the appropriate moment during the interview as discussed in Chapter 2.

22. Have extra copies of your resumé and reference sheet to leave with the interviewer if necessary. (Keep them in the back pocket of your portfolio.)

23. At the end of the interview, ask for the interviewer's business card to have his or her correctly spelled name and title. It is very important to be sure to thank the interviewer—and even the receptionist. Then send a thank-you letter immediately to the interviewer. (See pages, 129, 131–133.)

■ ANSWERING TYPICAL QUESTIONS

Below and on the following pages are some of the most-asked questions and appropriate responses. These are just examples. There is no one right answer, and these questions could be answered in a variety of ways.

Remember, you need to personalize your responses to fit your background and experience. Practice how you would respond to these questions, but don't memorize your answers.

These questions have been grouped into nine basic areas:

Get-acquainted questions (pages 101–105).

FIGURE No. 6–6

FIGURE No. 6–7

FIGURE No. 6–8

"Ya . . ."

Previous work experience questions (pages 105–112).

Education questions (pages 112 and 113).

Interest questions (page 113).

What-can-you-do-for-me questions (pages 113 and 114).

Personality questions (page 115).

Salary questions (pages 116 and 117).

Work styles, habits, and preferences questions (pages 118–121).

Human relations questions (pages 121 and 123).

In addition to providing an appropriate response for each question, we discuss the interviewer's objective in asking the question and the goal of your response.

GET-ACQUAINTED QUESTIONS

1. *Tell Me about Yourself.*

   This is often the first question you are asked because the interviewer wants to get to know you and to give you a question that should put you at ease. Be sure to prepare a good response because this is an open-ended question with no limits on what you can say. You are trying to paint a picture of yourself—your strengths and personal qualities—without using specific adjectives. The interviewer is interested in what motivates you; how you will work with others; and your enthusiasm, drive, competitiveness, and other job-related traits.

   You might start off, for example, with some personal accomplishments and things that interest you. Then you could describe in detail your educational training. Finally, you could mention your work experience and try to relate your job skills to the available job.

   Listen to how Linda Williams, a secretarial applicant, responded:

   For the past 10 years, I have been an active volunteer at my children's elementary school. As president of the parent group, I helped organize an annual fall fund-raiser called the "Rose Kidd Spooktacular." This is a one-day event just before Halloween that consists of a great haunted house and fair. Every year 300 people volunteer to help at the event. However, our committee begins work on the project one year in advance. We grossed over $10,000 the first year for the six-hour event. This money was used to open a computer lab in the school. As my children grew older, I decided it was time to go back to school and update my office skills. So I enrolled in a comprehensive seven-month secretarial course at Modern School of Business. This course was fantastic because we learned all the

latest software packages such as WordPerfect 6.1, Lotus, dBase III Plus, and Microsoft Word. We even had an introduction to desktop publishing. I brushed up on my shorthand and can now take it at 120 wpm. In addition, my typing speed increased to 70 wpm. After graduation from Modern School of Business, I worked for two years as a secretary for Montgomery Advertising in Warren. This job gave me valuable experience. Unfortunately, because of the recession, layoffs occurred. The layoffs were based on seniority, and I was low man on the totem pole. I really like the challenge of working in an office environment, knowing that I can make a contribution. Would you care to look at my portfolio and the work I have done?

2. *What Is It about This Position that Interests You?*

When an employer asks this question, he or she is usually attempting to learn whether you will be satisfied with the job and will be likely to stay. You must prove your interest. To reassure the interviewer, you should mention many positive features about the company and the job, such as "It's the kind of work I'm good at and enjoy doing" or "Your location is convenient to my home." Mention any good things you've heard or know about the company. Ideally, this is where your research about the company pays big dividends. Discuss what you learned from your research of the company. Here is one sample answer:

I am familiar with the Atlas Corporation and know that it is a respected leader in the automotive tubing industry. Your company has been in business for a long time; it would offer me the stability I'm looking for in my career and give me the chance to contribute my expertise.

3. *What Do You See Yourself Doing Five Years from Now?* Or *What Are Your Long-Range Goals or Future Plans?*

The interviewer is trying to find out whether you are serious about staying with this company or are using this job only as a temporary income and might become dissatisfied after awhile. You need to stress that you like the company and the type of work you would be doing, that the location is ideal, and that you have no plans that would require you to leave the job. Show how you plan to make a contribution over the next couple of years.

Here is one way of answering this question:

Five years from now I hope to have established myself with a company. I would like to continue my education in the evening to improve my opportunities for promotion, and expect to prove myself to be a productive and valuable member of the office team.

4. *What Do You Expect from the Company the Hires You? How Can We Meet Your Needs?*

Your answer, of course, is personal; but most people expect fairness, respect, freedom to perform the job effectively, support, and open lines of communication. For the second part of that question, here is one possible answer:

Give me the opportunity to use my skills to benefit the company, to take responsibility for my work, to have open communications with my supervisor and co-workers, and to receive feed-back on my performance.

5. *What Are Your Plans for Self-Improvement? What Specific Improvements Have You Made This Year?*

For one thing, the fact that you are attending school is a major improvement in your life. You have established new goals and have made career decisions. Beyond that you will have to state your personal plans.

6. *Tell Me about the Two Achievements of which You Are Most Proud.*

This especially will be a personal answer. Try to think of something you did on your last job, if you had one, that earned you special recognition. Another possibility is to cite something from your educational background that sets you apart from the majority of students. Here is one student's answer:

While attending school every day from 8 AM to 3 PM for seven months, I never missed a single day. Also, I was voted "most organized" by my classmates.

7. *Describe the Leadership Positions that You Have Held in School, at Work, or in the Community.*

Again, this will be an especially personal answer. Give this request a lot of thought. Here are some examples from a school setting: student council member, class officer, yearbook staff member, or club officer. Here are some examples from a work setting: worked on the United Fund Drive; organized a company picnic, Christmas party, or retirement party; or organized the company's food and clothing drives in conjunction with the Salvation Army. In the community, you may have been elected to city office or the school board, volunteered within the school system, or volunteered at a hospital.

8. *How Did You Learn about Us?*

Obviously you read a want ad, heard about an opening from a friend, researched the company because you knew what kind of business you wanted to work for, or something similar. Here is one response given by Paul Mandziara, an applicant for an entry-level management position:

When I saw your ad in the paper, I did a little research and discovered that Metavisions is a relatively young company that is growing at a rapid pace. The job description seemed to fit my qualifications, and I am anxious to begin my career with a progressive company, where I can make a contribution and have the opportunity for professional growth.

9. *How Many Other Companies Have You Approached?*

The interviewer may be trying to determine how long you have been in the market for a job. Don't ever state a specific number. Here is one possible answer:

There are several other positions in which I have been interested. Because this is a career decision, it is important to me to explore all avenues and make a good final selection.

10. *Give an Example of Any Major Problem You Faced and How You Solved It.*

Try to give a work-related example. Stay away from personal problems. Here is what Jeanie Moore responded:

The company I worked for had an outdated filing system that made it time-consuming and cumbersome to get needed data quickly. After someone made a major error, resulting in the loss of a significant sale, I suggested we convert much of our information onto a database management system. Because I was familiar with dBase III Plus, we converted to that system. Then another employee and I entered all customer data in the database. What a savings this eventually worked out to be.

11. *What Has Been Your Greatest Accomplishment?*

Again, this can be a rather personal question. Always try to keep your answer work related. Don't exaggerate. Dan Blackwell, a designer for Dynaplast Corporation, responded this way:

Although I believe my biggest achievements lie ahead, I am proud of my involvement with the aerodynamically designed body of the Lincoln Continental for 1996. My contribution was to the front grille design. Working as part of a team was a rewarding and learning experience.

12. *What Was Your Greatest Failure?*

You never want to state a negative, so your answer will be nonspecific. Here is one response:

I can't say I've had any real failures because every time something didn't go as planned, I've learned from that experience. Each experience has made me a better person.

13. *What Was Your Biggest Disappointment?*

Again this can be a rather personal question. Here is how one interviewee handled it:

Boy that's a tough one. Right now I really can't think of anything that sticks out as a major disappointment—not that everything has always gone the way I wanted it to. However, I have a good sense of humor to see me through the rough spots and a lot of perseverance.

PREVIOUS WORK EXPERIENCE QUESTIONS

1. *Do You Have Any Experience?* Or *Have You Done This Kind of Work before?*

This question is easy to answer if you have had some kind of work experience in a field related to the job for which you are now applying. Be sure to elaborate on your job responsibilities and accomplishments. If instead you have work experience unrelated to your new career field or no experience at all, don't ever answer no. Then, stress your recent training, up-to-date skills, and the general characteristics any employer would look for in an employee—dependability, good work ethic, ability to get along well with other people, and so on. Show how your personal strengths on your last job would transfer to this new position. Here someone with unrelated job skills answers:

While I have never before worked in an office, I feel that my intensive training a Worldwide Travel School over the past seven months was the equivalent of actual on-the-job experience. We went to school daily from 8:30 AM to 2 PM, with no lunch break. We had to learn to interact with all sorts of people from different backgrounds, and we had to set priorities in order to meet our work deadlines. Sometimes we had more than one teacher for the same class, which would be like having two bosses. There was a lot of pressure, and I feel confident that I handled everything in stride with a professional attitude. Also, I learned that I can work with little supervision, adapt easily to changes, and

catch on quickly when something new is introduced. In addition, I feel that my job at Burger Heaven taught me how to deal with the public in a professional manner, to handle all situations with a smile and a sense of humor, and always to strive to do the best job possible. Would you like to see my portfolio?

Someone with related work experience answers this question differently:

Yes, as a matter of fact, my last job entailed not only direct purchasing of all supplies, evaluating source bids, and inventory control but also the daily balancing of the bookkeeping ledger. Therefore, I am confident that my experience would be easily transferable to this position and enable me to make an immediate contribution. I have always been able to learn quickly; and as a result, I have always been given added responsibilities not originally stated in my job description. I've brought my portfolio if you'd care to look at it.

2. *What Were the Circumstances Concerning Your Leaving? Or Why Are You Giving up Your Job?*

Don't ever say anything negative about a former job or employer. Try to give positive responses. Several responses follow:

FIGURE No. 6–9

"I didn't bother putting down places I worked less than a week."

There was no room for advancement.

The job wasn't challenging enough.

I wasn't given the opportunity to utilize all of my skills.

3. *Of All Your Jobs, which Did You Like Best? Why? And Least? Why?*

   It is easy to say which job you liked best. Remember, however, that the job you liked least would be because you were not kept busy enough, allowed to use all your skills, given advancement opportunities, and so on.

4. *What Will Your Last Supervisor Tell Me Are Your Three Strongest Assets? Your Three Weakest?*

   Your answer is the same as if you were asked what your strongest and weakest points are, except that you will begin your answer with "I am confident that my supervisor would say that . . ." (See Questions 1 and 3, pages 118 and 119.)

5. *How Would You Describe Your Previous Supervisor: How Did You Know if You Were Doing Well or if You Made a Mistake?*

   Again, try to keep your comments positive. Note the upbeat tone of this response:

   My supervisor and I got along really well. We had a mutual respect and open lines of communication. I always knew exactly where I stood because he was quick to pay a compliment when he was pleased and didn't hesitate to let me know when I had done something wrong. Consistently I was given an excellent rating on my yearly performance reviews. Also, I was able to gain his confidence, which ultimately led to added responsibilities not originally listed in my job description.

6. *If You Could Have Made Two Improvements in Your Last Job, What Would They Have Been? Did You Suggest These?*

   Give this question a lot of thought. Companies rely on employees to come up with new and better ideas. You will probably be able to think of many improvements you would have made. Here is how one interviewee answered the second question:

   Yes, I did make several suggestions and would never hesitate to do so if I thought my ideas had some merit or value.

7. *What Did You Do When Your Supervisor Made a Decision with Which You Strongly Disagreed?*

Most companies don't want a yes person. They also don't want a complainer or a problem employee. Here is a response given by Ralph Conan, a retail salesperson:

My former boss and I had a good line of communication so that we were able to discuss my occasional opposition to her decisions openly and honestly. However, in the end I always supported my supervisor's decisions.

8. *Last Month, How Many Days of Work or School Did You Miss?*

You have to be honest with your response. Ideally, you can say none. If, however, you were absent, you had better have a good explanation and be able to say that it was an isolated circumstance. Generally your attendance, which is very important to any company, must be excellent. Companies look for dependable employees.

9. *How Many Times Were You Late?*

Again, hopefully you can say never. Punctuality is also important.

10. *Have You Ever Been Fired from a Job?*

If you have been fired, be prepared to discuss the circumstances. If you were at fault, explain how you have learned from your mistake and offer assurances that something similar won't happen again. Here is one response that was given:

When my children were small, I had to miss a lot of work time because they were always sick. My supervisor had no choice but to fire me because I wasn't able to complete my job responsibilities on time. Simply, I was costing the company money rather than making them more profitable. I now realize the importance of being reliable, meeting deadlines, and working as part of a team doing my equal share of the work. To alleviate this problem from occurring again, I have found a wonderful neighbor who comes into my home to watch my children—even when they are ill. This has put my mind at ease, which allows me to concentrate my efforts on my work and not constantly be worried about my children.

11. *What Are the Important Traits a Supervisor Should Have? Why Are These Traits Important?*

In response to this question you will want to list attributes that a company would want any worker to have. Here is one person's answer:

I would hope that my supervisor would be fair and respect me as a person. He or she should be a leader who is not afraid to delegate work and responsibility, who has an open-door policy with regard to communication, who tells me when I have done something wrong, who praises me for my accomplishments, and who trusts that I can do the job with little supervision. I think these are important traits because honesty, trust, and respect in the workplace are essential to a healthy work environment.

12. *Describe an Experience When You Did More than What Was Ordinarily Expected.*

    Give specific examples to indicate that you are a hard worker who has the initiative to get things done without being told every step of the way what to do and how to do it.

13. *Tell Me about a Time When You Experienced Pressure on the Job.*

    Obviously, the interviewer wants a specific example with a definitive answer describing exactly how you handled the pressure. This is a response given by Sheila Dunum, a secretary with ISA Manufacturing Corporation:

    The engineering department I work in handles prototype orders of brake and fuel lines for Ford Motor Company. At 4 PM on a Friday afternoon I received a telephone call from the project engineer stating that we made a mistake on a part that was needed the next day at 9 AM out at one of Ford's plants. I was asked to locate the original blueprints for the part so that the project engineer could verify that, indeed, we had made a mistake. Then I had to obtain permission to schedule overtime for our plant to remake the necessary parts on Saturday. Next I had to arrange for delivery of the parts on Saturday afternoon to the Ford plant by special courier. Finally I typed a letter explaining how the mistake occurred and assuring Ford that this would not happen again. Because of the lateness of the day, and being on a Friday, I felt a lot of pressure because people were relying on me to get the necessary information to help save our customer's goodwill. I welcomed the challenge when this problem arose, treated it as an opportunity to help the customer, and was able to remain cool under pressure. I was very organized and methodical in my approach to this situation. In addition, I was not afraid to put in extra hours to get the job done.

    After you have given your answer, be prepared to answer several follow-up questions. Their purpose is to determine if you react defensively to a problem, try to blame others for the situation, or are able to handle the pressure and perform professionally. The interviewer then asked *"Why do you think this situation arose?"* Sheila responded:

After retrieving all the essential blueprints, from the project's concept through a number of changes, it became apparent that one of the blueprint changes had been logged in but the actual blueprint copy was missing. Therefore, when the part was checked for accuracy and quality, the checker was actually looking at an outdated blueprint compared to the part that was actually built.

Next Sheila was asked *"When exactly did it happen?"* She responded:

This happened about a year ago.

Then Sheila was asked *"Looking back, what area of your performance were you most dissatisfied with?"* This time she responded:

Actually I am quite happy that I was able to provide the needed blueprints, get confirmation for overtime in our plant, arrange for the parts delivery, and smooth some ruffled feathers with an apologetic letter. However, those blueprints are my responsibility. So I decided to implement a better sign-out system to track the blueprint trail within our company.

Next the interviewer asked *"How do you feel others could have acted more responsibly?"* Sheila answered:

I don't think anyone could have done a better job so late on a Friday afternoon under such stressful circumstances. Our company's reputation was on the line.

Finally she was asked *"Who was responsible for this situation?"* and *"How could this situation be avoided in the future?"* Sheila didn't hesitate to answer:

I think I was partly responsible because the missing blueprint was my responsibility. However, several other competent personnel also could have eliminated the problem. It was really more important to fix the problem than to fix the blame. The new plan I implemented has been working very well ever since, and I am happy to say a similar situation has not arisen.

14. *Tell Me about an Event that Really Challenged You.*

The interviewer wants to know about your problem-solving abilities. The worse you make the problem sound, the better. Answer the question, explaining how you solved the problem, and describing the benefit your company derived from your approach. Here is one such response given by Gayle Suddick, a mortgage processor:

Papers required for the closing on a customer's home mortgage were lost in the mail. An hour before the appointment time, I was notified of the situation. Fortunately, everything was computerized. So I reprinted all the documents and personally drove them to the meeting place. The customer was never aware that a problem had arisen, and I was able to gain the respect and goodwill of the real estate agent handling the closing. Our company's reputation was on the line, and I am glad I was able to alleviate a potential problem.

15. *What Have You Done that Shows Initiative and Willingness to Work?*

Here the interviewer is looking to see if you are self-motivated, able to detect a problem and deal with it before being told to do so. Give an example of how you perceived a potential problem area and by putting in the extra time and effort were able to resolve the situation promptly. Here is one such response given by a travel consultant:

My company was giving a cruise-line presentation at a hotel one evening. On my lunch break I decided to drop by the hotel to make sure the room was set up to our satisfaction. When I arrived, nothing had been done. I questioned the manager, discovered they had the right day but wrong date down on the reservation, and were not expecting us that evening. So I just stayed right there to make sure that everything was done to our satisfaction.

16. *What Is the Most Difficult Situation You Have Ever Faced?*

You need to think of a situation that was tough but that enabled you to come out on top once the situation was solved. Stay away from personal situations, and avoid any mention of a problem with a co-worker. Here is one response given:

I was asked to make travel arrangements for my supervisor's sudden trip to Japan leaving the next morning. He needed plane tickets, hotel arrangements, an interpreter, a car and driver in Japan, and a list of restaurants serving American food. By the end of the day, I had made all the necessary arrangements and had prepared a detailed itinerary for my supervisor. Plans of this magnitude are difficult to make on such short notice, and my supervisor appreciated my efforts.

17. *What Would You Do if You Had to Make a Decision, but No Procedure Existed for Making that Decision?*

This question is directed toward your analytical skills, integrity, and dedication. It tests your management ability and your adherence to company procedures. Try to give a specific, real example, if possible. This person has actually had such an experience:

While preparing the accounts payable checks, I noticed that a check written two days before had been made out for the wrong amount. Supervisory personnel were in an important meeting and could not be disturbed. So I telephoned our bank, ordered a stop payment on that check, wrote a new check for the correct amount, mailed it, and telephoned the client with an explanation. I would act without my manager's direction only if the situation were urgent and he or she were not available. I would take command of the situation with no hesitation, make a decision based on logic and facts, and implement it. At the earliest opportunity, I would update my supervisor.

EDUCATION QUESTIONS

1. *Are You Thinking of Going Back to School to Further Your Education?*

An interviewer will usually ask this question only of a younger applicant. The interviewer may be concerned that he or she will spend a lot of time and money training the new employee, only to have this person quit to return to school. Here is how one applicant for a secretarial position responded:

I realize how important it is to keep my skills up to date because software used in business today is constantly changing. If I continue my education, I am confident that I would be a more valuable employee. However, I would take classes in the evening so that they wouldn't interfere with my work.

2. *Which Courses in School Did You Like Best? Least?*

Again, try not to list anything you didn't like. Try to fit your answer to meet the needs addressed in the want ad. If the company is looking for someone with word processing experience, then WordPerfect "was my favorite subject." If the company is looking for someone good with numbers, then "Lotus, accounting principles, and computerized accounting were my favorite subjects." Offer to show your portfolio.

3. *Why Weren't Your Grades Higher than a 2.5 Average?*

The interviewer is giving you an opportunity to prove your technical competence despite your average grades. One interviewee responded:

While in school I received an award as outstanding medical assistant from my peers and was voted the top intern in my class by my teachers. Unfortunately, I have always been nervous when taking tests. This hurt my grade point average but doesn't reflect my competence.

Present your portfolio to show your competence.

INTEREST QUESTIONS

1. *What Gets You Pumped Up at Work?*

Again your answer can take a variety of forms. Be sure to pick a positive example, such as "a challenge" or "a new project where I can really show what I can do."

2. *What Do You Do to Relax after Work?*

This is a personal answer, but you might want to list some of your hobbies. Companies like to hire well-rounded individuals. Remember the saying "All work and no play makes Jack a dull boy!" Reading, travel, and sports are typical answers.

3. *Do You Have Any Hobbies?*

This is a personal answer. It would be good to try to tie one or two to the job. If you were interested in an advertising position, then one of your hobbies might be art or writing.

WHAT-CAN-YOU-DO-FOR-ME QUESTIONS

1. *Why Should You Be My First Choice for This Position?* or *Why Should I Hire You Rather than Someone Else?*

Everyone who has made it this far in the interviewing process probably has equal skills. So your skill qualifications may be irrelevant. Perhaps if you have a lot of experience you may want to mention again how this experience would benefit the company. However, what you really need to do is to sell yourself based on your personal qualities. This is a very important question because, as in Question 1 "Tell Me about Yourself," page 101, there is no limit to your answer.

Here is one sample response:

I am very confident that I could do a good job for you. The position sounds exactly like what I have been looking for. I guarantee you that I will give you 110 percent effort and that you can count on me to be here every day on time. I think I could easily fit in with your other staff because I have always been able to get along with everyone. As you described the job, it sounded like it would offer me the types of challenges and responsibilities that I am capable of handling. I work well under pressure and would welcome the opportunity to contribute to your company.

2. *When Are You Available for Work?*

   Your answer to this depends on whether you have already graduated from school and whether you are presently working. Note how two people respond to an employer who wants the applicant to start immediately:

   I won't be graduating for another two months. Could I work part-time until I graduate? I would need to finish my studies in the evening. This arrangement would be very difficult because of the stress of a new job added to the stress of trying to complete graduation requirements.

   I could start immediately, but I prefer to give two weeks' notice to my present employer. If that's not possible, I will give only one week's notice.

3. *Why Do You Want to Work for Me?*

   Again by knowing what the company does, this is your chance to pay a compliment to that organization. The important thing is always to stress what you can do for the company—not what you want from it. One person responded:

   Your company has a great reputation in the advertising industry. You handle some of the biggest accounts in the area, and I'd love the chance to be able to contribute to your efforts. I think my creativeness and organizational skills would fit right in.

4. *Give Me Two Reasons for Not Hiring You.*

   Because you want to stay positive and confident with your responses, you will never give the interviewer a reason to not hire you. This is one response:

   I can't think of a single reason why you should not hire me because I truly believe I am the best person for this job. Then go into your answer as if the question was "Why should I hire you?"

PERSONALITY QUESTIONS

1. *If You Could Change Any Single Thing about Yourself, What Would You Change?* or *What Is Your Greatest Weakness?*

   Be careful when answering this question because it is tricky. What you want to do is pick one of your strengths and make it sound like a weakness to you (but a strength for the company). Here are several responses to this question:

   I think that sometimes I am too organized. Even if I have a project deadline that is a week away, I begin preparing for it immediately. When I want something done, I want it done now, not tomorrow. I am constantly updating my "Things-to-Do" list.

   Perhaps I am too punctual. When I am invited to be somewhere at 8 PM, I'm always there 5 minutes early; and the host is not quite ready. I can't stand to be late.

   I'm a perfectionist. I always want everything done just right, and I have to learn to accept less than perfection in myself and others because I realize that no one is perfect. However, I know that I will always take great pride in the work I do.

   I get too wrapped up in my work. Before I know it, it is 5 o'clock; but I can't quit until I finish whatever I am working on. I hate to have to carry something over to the next day when I could finish it now with a little extra time.

2. *What Five Words Best Describe You?*

   It is important to put together a list of your best traits, and pick out a few that are most impressive. The interviewer is looking for your best personal characteristics. Be positive, confident, and friendly when you answer. One person answered the question like this:

   I think that I am professional, hardworking, outgoing, dependable, and enthusiastic toward my work.

3. *What Do You Consider to Be Your Greatest Strength and Your Greatest Weakness?*

   Again, you would pick your one greatest strength to elaborate on and choose another strength and make it sound like a weakness to you personally—but a definite plus for the company.

4. *What Do You Like Most about Yourself? What Do You Like Least?*

   This is just another way of asking you your strengths and weaknesses. So respond as you would to the previous question.

SALARY QUESTIONS

1. *What Is More Important to You, the Salary or the Job?*

   There is really only one way to answer this question:

   Of course, the salary is important. However, the job is more important. I know that if I am not happy in my job, then I won't do good work. There is nothing worse than having to go to a job you hate. No amount of money can make it worth your while.

   If you have previous work experience and are afraid that your last salary might scare a company off, answer this way:

   Of course, the salary is important. However, at this point in my career I realize it is more important to have a job that I enjoy going to daily. I'm looking for a position where I can really make a contribution. My training has given me an added edge to go along with my years of on-the-job experience.

2. *What Kind of Salary Are You Looking for?*

   How you answer this question will depend on when it is asked. For example, if the question is asked very early in the interview, you might want to neutralize the question by saying something similar to: *"If you wouldn't mind, I'd prefer to learn more about the position and your organization before I give you a specific answer. I'm sure we can reach mutual agreement at that time."* You could then respond with several questions that would put you on the offensive and enable you to get more information about the company's salary policies. You could ask how that organization structures its pay system, personnel policies, and promotions. You might want to ask if performance is a key factor for compensation increases and promotions or if seniority is more important. You could ask how the company reviews employees, whether individual performance is rewarded as well as group performance. If, however, you don't feel comfortable with this evasive measure, you could respond, *"How much would someone with my qualifications and experience receive in this position?"*

   If you have already discussed the position and responsibilities and then are asked your salary requirements, you could begin your answer by summarizing the responsibilities of the position. For example: *"As I understand, I would be responsible for . . . Have I covered everything, or are there other responsibilities I should be aware of?"* After the interviewer responds, you could ask, *"What is the normal range for someone with my qualifications and experience?"* Once the range has been established, you could state your salary range, making sure that it overlaps with the company's stated range. By naming a specific salary at this stage of the hiring process, you can only harm yourself. If the salary is too high, the employer may decide that he or she can't afford you. If it's lower than the company's standard pay, you may not get as much money as you could have. Again, if you are not comfortable with this negotiation tactic, one way to answer the question is *"I would be willing to consider any offer the company would care to make."* Another response is *"I expect to be paid what the company feels is fair based on my qualifications and considering the standard salary level for that position within the company."*

After you have been offered the job, you can decide if the salary is high enough. If you feel it's too low, you can suggest that you would feel more comfortable if you had some assurance that a raise or promotion would be possible in the near future if your work justified it. Always be polite, even if the offer is much too low. Always let the employer know that you're willing to negotiate and would consider any offers he or she would care to make.

Here an employer and an applicant discuss this:

I'm willing to consider any offer that you care to make. However, with my recent training from Macomb School and my previous office experience, I expect a salary offer commensurate with my background and qualifications.

Well, that's fine; but I really need you to give me a dollar amount.

I'm willing to discuss it. What is the standard salary for this type of position?

Always try to get the employer to make the first offer. If you are really pinned down and have to give a dollar amount, try to give a range.

Remember, if the benefits are good, you may be able or willing to accept a little less money. If the benefits are bad, then you need more money as compensation. In the end, however, no job decision should be based solely on salary. Remember, the job itself and whether you think you will like it are more important.

WORK STYLES, HABITS, AND PREFERENCES QUESTIONS

1. *Could You Handle Working at a Fast Pace All Day?*

   This question indicates that your job will involve working under pressure and deadlines, so reassure the interviewer by giving examples of past activities that involved deadlines or pressure. For example, (if this applies) tell how you managed to prepare for exams while holding down a job and raising a family. Mention any examples of performing under stressful conditions and describe how well you handled the crisis. You must appear self-confident for the interviewer to believe you. You might even say that you don't mind stress or pressure and that you enjoy a challenge. Here's how one applicant answered this question:

   I love working at a fast pace because I like to be kept busy and look forward to new challenges. As I mentioned before, as a volunteer in charge of this huge fund-raiser for my kid's elementary school, I worked 10- to 15-hour days the week before the event making sure that all the committees met their deadlines and pitched in wherever extra help was needed. In addition, while attending Modern School, I was able to work part time at Burger Heaven. So working at a fast pace would be no problem, and I would welcome the challenge.

   A person who really doesn't like to work at a fast pace won't answer quite as strongly:

   Working at a fast pace wouldn't be a problem. I'm sure I would have no problem handling the responsibilities.

   You need to ask questions to find out whether the pace of this job is one you would feel comfortable with. For example, you could ask "Is there a lot of overtime?" "Would I be working for more than one person?" "Could you describe my responsibilities?"

2. *How Do You Handle Stress or Pressure?*

   This question is similar to Question 1, Could You Handle Working at a Fast Pace All Day?, above. Mention any examples of performing under stressful conditions and describe how well you handled the crisis. Here is one person's answer:

   I think I can handle stress very well because when a problem occurs, I look on it as a challenge. As I said before, I welcome challenges because they bring out the best in me.

Therefore, I don't seem to feel the same stress that others do in similar circumstances. A crisis just gives me an opportunity to show what I can do. Also, I have learned not to worry about things over which I have no control. Perhaps the best example I can give is my ability to handle the daily stress of going to school and work and raising a family—all at the same time. Having a good sense of humor and a supportive family also helps.

3. *Why Did You Choose This Field?*

   Here's one possible response:

   I really enjoy doing this type of work because it offers many opportunities to use the skills I've developed, and it is something I do well. Also, I am aware of how important it is to have good support staff people in today's workplace. I wanted a career in which I knew I could make an impact.

4. *Would You Be Willing to Work Overtime if Required?*

   You should always be eager and willing to work when and where needed. If the time comes when you simply cannot work the extra hours requested, then that will be the time to discuss this with your employer. Within reason, you should make yourself available when your employer needs you.

FIGURE NO. 6–10

You didn't answer this question, "Do you work well under pressure?"'

'Hey, lighten up, will you?'

Your willingness to help is what will make you a valuable asset to the company.

If you wanted a lot of overtime and were available most of the time, you could respond with *"Yes, overtime would be no problem whatsoever."*

If you had young children to care for after work, you could say *"As long as I had some advance notice so that I could make arrangements with my babysitter, there would be no problem."*

If you really didn't want to work overtime, your best response would be *"Occasionally working overtime wouldn't be a problem."*

5. *What Are Two Things You Wish to Avoid in Your Next Job? Why?*

   Again, you are trying to keep things positive. Note how this person turns the negatives into positives:

   I really like everything about my present job; however, I want to leave to find a position in which I can make a greater contribution. You see, I work for a large company where everyone specializes in certain areas. In a smaller work environment, I should be able to contribute far more in different areas.

6. *What Hours of Work Do You Prefer? Why?*

   You should know what the company's work hours are. Those hours would then be the hours you would want to work!

7. *What Is Most Important to You about Your Job? Why?*

   Again, this will be a personal answer. Here is one individual's answer:

   That I really like my job and the people I work with are very important to me. There is diversity, challenge, and responsibility, and things are never boring. Also, we all work together as a team to accomplish a common goal. I really like that attitude.

8. *What Kind of Working Environment Do You Prefer? Why?*

   Know the size of the company you are applying to. If it is a small office, you don't want to answer that you'd like to work for a large company with several divisions and the opportunity to transfer to another city. Most people would like a friendly but professional atmosphere, where everyone works as a team to accomplish a common goal.

9. *Are You at Your Best When Working Alone or with a Group?*

If you don't want to give the wrong answer, you could say: *"I like interacting with other people on a project because you can get so many different viewpoints. However, I also enjoy taking an assignment on my own from conception through completion and need little supervision."*

10. *Would You Rather Be in Charge of a Project or Working as Part of a Team?*

Notice how this person responds, by being positive about both choices:

I feel I could capably lead a project and would be able to set priorities and delegate work responsibilities. However, whether working as a leader or as a group member, I feel one can accomplish a lot more with a cooperative team effort. I have no problem taking directions and working with my peers.

HUMAN RELATIONS QUESTIONS

1. *Describe a Personality Conflict You've Had with a Co-Worker. How Did You Deal with It?*

Try to be positive. You should probably say that you have never had a conflict with a co-worker because, while you may not always like everyone, you are able to work well and get along with others.

2. *What Would You Do if One Supervisor Told You to Do Something Now and Another Supervisor Told You to Do It Later?*

It is important never to show favoritism when working for more than one supervisor. If, in the middle of working for Supervisor A, Supervisor B asks you to do something for him or her, this is what you could say *"I'll be done with this project for Supervisor A in 30 minutes and will be glad to do it then. If you need it done immediately, however, I'll have to check with Supervisor A to see if his or her project could wait."* You don't ever want to be put in the middle of two supervisors.

3. *Discuss a Situation in Which Your Work or Idea Was Criticized.*

Never give an example of work that was criticized. Instead, pick an idea you had that sounded good at the time. What is most important in your answer is how you handle criticism. Here is one well-handled answer:

I listened carefully to my supervisor's criticism and asked for some advice. Then we tossed around some ideas on the subject, and later I brought back my same idea but in a more workable format.

4. *Tell Me about the Last Time You Were Angry on the Job.*

   It is important to show that you can remain calm and face "the heat." Pick something that would get any conscientious worker mad. Can you identify with this example?

   I feel I give 100 percent daily effort to my employer. Dealing with people who have their coats on and their desks cleaned off at 4:55 PM or who are regularly sick on Mondays and Fridays really bothers me. However, I can't say it gets me angry.

5. *What Are Some of the Things over Which You and Your Supervisor Disagreed?*

   The safest answer is that you really never disagreed. You could state that the open lines of communication you had allowed you to discuss ideas and differences openly in a professional, mutually respectful atmosphere.

6. *What Kind of People Do You Like to Work with? Describe the Kind of People Who Annoy You Most. How Have You Successfully Worked with This Type of Person?*

   You should state that you like to work with people who have pride, honesty, integrity, and dedication to their work.

   In describing someone who annoys you, again you should explain that the person annoys you because he or she lacks a strength most companies look for in an employee: *"People who always have a negative attitude annoy me;" "People who procrastinate and then complain when they don't meet a deadline annoy me;" "People who are always complaining but never offer solutions annoy me."*

   When answering how you deal with these annoying people, you might reply, *"I stick to my ideas, keep enthusiastic, and hope some of it will rub off."*

Remember, you must have a positive, can-do attitude throughout the interview. Look the interviewer in the eye while answering, display self-confidence, and show enthusiasm in your responses. This first interview will be your last chance to make an impression. If you make a good impression, you will get a second chance.

Some employer questions are in the form of negative statements. Employers may make negative statements to discourage an applicant, but these statements are opportunities for you to sell yourself.

In Exercise 6.1 (next page) are statements an employer might make to discourage an applicant. Practice responding to these statements as if you were being asked the questions during an interview. This practice will help you deal with an employer's objections in a positive manner and help you think on your feet.

Besides writing answers to objections, practice recording your responses. Play them back and see how you sound. Did your voice and answers exude confidence?

Never try to memorize any answer. However, with repetitive practice to some difficult questions, you will find that your responses come easier and your manner becomes more self-confident.

■ RESPONDING TO ILLEGAL QUESTIONS

Nine out of 10 companies will ask something they shouldn't during the preemployment interview. Some questions are just inappropriate, but others are illegal.

To ensure equal employment opportunities among all applicants, employment cannot be denied for reasons based on the person's arrest record, citizenship or national origin, disability, marital or family status, race, religion, age, or sex/gender. There are exceptions to these laws called *bona fide occupational qualifications*. For example, a movie producer might need to select an actor based on gender or physical appearance. In general, however, these areas cannot be factors in determining a person's employability.

Most interviewers are honest people legitimately trying to find the best employees for their companies. While their intentions may be good, you need to know how to deal with illegal questions. What would you do?

1. Simply answer the question. Most people take this route because they are afraid that if they don't they will risk losing the opportunity to be hired. However, what they don't realize is that if they do answer, their answer might also hurt their chances.

2. Refuse to answer or point out that this is an illegal question. This response will most certainly end your chance for the job.

3. Address the concern of the question with your answer while not divulging any information. For example, "Do you have plans to raise a family?" The interviewer's real concern is whether

EXERCISE 6.1	**OVERCOMING OBJECTIONS**

Employer: We're looking for someone with more experience.

Your Response:

_____

_____

Employer: We're really looking for someone who lives in this area.

Your Response:

_____

_____

Employer: We need someone we can depend on. There will be times when overtime is required.

Your Response:

_____

_____

Employer: You've had too many jobs in too short a time.

Your Response:

_____

_____

Employer: We need someone who can handle a fast-paced, busy office.

Your Response:

_____

_____

Employer: We're looking for someone who has good people skills—who can communicate well with our customers.

Your Response:

_____

_____

you will be a reliable, committed employee who will stay with the company. A response such as *"I appreciate your concern. I can assure you that I am a professional and would be committed to the responsibilities of the job"* would satisfy the interviewer's concern without actually answering the question.

Which strategy you adopt will depend on your own communication style, how intrusive you feel a particular question is, and how much you really want the job. If you want the job and the question is not too intrusive, answer the question. Otherwise, try to answer the concern of the illegal question whenever it is possible to do so without revealing specific information. Most employers would not like the refusal approach.

■ ASKING QUESTIONS DURING THE INTERVIEW

On the first interview, never bring up the subject of salary or benefits unless the interviewer has introduced the topic. Obviously, if you are offered the job—but the interviewer has not mentioned salary or benefits—you could say, "Before I could give you my decision I would need to know the salary and benefit package you are offering." If at the close of a second interview the salary/benefits issue has not been raised, it would be appropriate to ask in a rather off-handed manner, "Could you give me an idea of the salary range and company benefit package for this position?" If you do not inquire about this, the interviewer might think you lack assertiveness.

Basically you need to find out enough about the job and your responsibilities so that if you were offered the position you would know whether the job was something you would enjoy doing. Many of these questions will be answered throughout the interview as you exchange information. Your questions should be spontaneous as you carry on your conversation with the interviewer. Remember, your job is to find out as much about the position as possible so that you can make a good evaluation of that job.

If, as the interview draws to a close, the interviewer has not stated that he or she will be contacting you for a second interview, or if you have not been offered the job, or if you have not been told when the interviewer will be making a decision, then you should definitely ask when the interviewer will be making a decision. Then ask if it would be all right to contact him or her if you haven't heard by then. Thank the employer for the interview. If the position sounds good to you, don't be afraid to state enthusiastically that the position is what you have been looking for and that you look forward to hearing from the employer.

Some questions that you might want to have answered:

1. If hired, would I be filling a newly created job or replacing someone?

2. What happened to the person who last held this position?

3. Would you describe a typical workday and the things I'd be doing?

4. What duties are most important for this job?

5. How would I be trained or introduced to the job?

6. How is the job important to this company, or how does it contribute to the company?

7. Who would I be working with and what do they do?

8. How will I get feedback on my job performance?

9. Can someone in this job be promoted? If so, to what position?

10. If hired, would I report directly to you or to someone else?

11. Has the company had a layoff in the last three years? How long was the layoff? Was everyone recalled?

TIME OUT

List any questions you might like to ask that have not been mentioned.

_____

_____

_____

_____

_____

_____

■ HANDLING COMMITTEE INTERVIEWS

Occasionally, committees, or more than one person, interview an applicant at one time. When you are interviewed by more than one person at the same time, be enthusiastic and confident, and keep eye contact when answering questions. Don't be timid or shy. Pay attention to the names and titles of the people you are speaking with, and use their names as you answer their questions. They will be impressed by your grasp of names and will feel a more personal connection with you. Answering several persons' questions is really no different than answering one person's questions. Relax and let your personality show through.

*A*fter an interview, go home and write in your Activity Log (page 62) notes about the interview. Include information you might need to know if you were later offered a job and the date you were told to check back (if that applies). Allow three boxes per company so that you can fill in information for first, second, and third interviews, when necessary.

■ WRITING YOUR THANK-YOU LETTER

As soon as the interview is over, take time to type a brief thank-you letter to the person who interviewed you. Sending a thank-you letter is very important. Timeliness is key, so be sure to drop the letter in the mail no later than the next day. If you were interviewed by more than one person, send each person a separate thank-you note—each slightly different from the others.

In the first paragraph of the letter, you should thank the interviewer for his or her time and consideration. If you want the job, say so. In the second paragraph, restate what you can contribute if offered this position. Let the employer know that you would accept the position if it were offered to you. In the last paragraph, make it easy for the interviewer to reach you by including your telephone number.

At some point in the letter try to say something regarding a specific topic you and the interviewer discussed. Reminding the interviewer of part of your conversation may set you apart from other applicants. Try to mention something that you suspect may only have been told to you or something you discussed that may cause the interviewer to remember you. For example, "I hope your upcoming speech at the convention is a tremendous success." See the examples on pages 131–133.

■ INTERVIEWING A SECOND TIME

If the employer was impressed with you during the interview, he or she will probably invite you to a second interview. Usually the field of applicants has been narrowed down to two or three individuals at this time. You may be given a tour of the facility and may be introduced to other employees.

Expect that you may be interviewed by one or more other people. During this interview, you may be given hypothetical situations and expected to role-play how you would react to them. One example is Marilyn Richardson, who found herself in a second interview for an executive secretarial position with a large company. Here is the scenario she was asked to respond to:

> Assume the department head has three managers working underneath him. You are the secretary for all three managers. Manager A asks you to type the minutes for the monthly meeting and wants them in an hour. Manager B asks you to type the notes she will need for a meeting she will be attending tomorrow. She wants these by noon as she will be leaving the office to catch her flight. Manager C asks you to type a 30-page speech he needs to deliver at a banquet tomorrow afternoon. How would you handle this situation?

This is how Marilyn responded. *First I would explain to Manager A that Manager B is leaving town at noon and needs her notes typed before she can leave. I would then ask if the minutes for the meeting he wanted typed could wait until after lunch. Manager C's speech would be typed last because, if necessary, I would stay late to finish the job. However, I would probably suggest that in the future we have regular meetings to review the workload and determine priorities and deadline dates so that this situation doesn't occur again.*

The employer may discuss salary and the available benefits package. Once salary and benefits are brought up by the company representative, then it is fair game to ask any questions. However, as you recall, until the interviewer brings up the subject, it is off limits.

As with the first interview, you should follow up the second interview with thank-you letters to all the people with whom you interviewed. You should always send thank-you letters, even if you sent one to the same person following the first interview.

■ INQUIRING ABOUT THE JOB STATUS

If you have not received feedback from a first interview after approximately a week or 10 days, you may want to write a letter inquiring about the status of the position. On page 134 is a sample of such a letter. It is also appropriate to call the interviewer or human resources representative.

Note that a similar letter can be written to follow up a letter of application or resumé you submitted (see page 135). You may want to wait two weeks before sending such a letter or calling, however, as it generally takes more time for employers to review applicants at this stage. You should keep notes in your Activity Log so that you know when you applied and when you should call or write.

EXERCISE 7.1	**WRITING YOUR THANK-YOU LETTER**

After carefully reviewing the sample thank-you letters below and on pages 132–133, prepare a thank-you letter for a fictitious first interview situation. Address the letter to Ms. Nancy Johnson, National Dynamics Corporation, 45023 Front Street, Boston, MA 02159. Pretend that during the interview you discussed your mutual enjoyment of skiing and that the interviewer is going on a ski vacation next year to Vail, Colorado. If you are using WordPerfect or a similar software program, save this and name it **a:thankyou.ltr.** You will then be able to retrieve this letter and use it as a guide to respond to a real interviewer by changing the inside address, salutation, and specific topic discussed that will remind the interviewer of you.

THANK-YOU LETTER NO. 1

Your Street Address
Your City, State, and Zip Code
Date

Mr. Archie Montgomery
Megabucks Corporation
3456 Barlett Road
Rockville, MD 20853

Dear Mr. Montgomery:

Thank you for your consideration during my interview today for the secretarial opening with your company. I thoroughly enjoyed meeting you and your fine staff during my tour of your facility.

The job you described to me sounds exactly like the type of position for which I have been looking. My expertise in word processing and office procedures would enable me to make a contribution to your office team. I am sure that, if given the opportunity to work for you, my work ethic, my ability to get along with everyone, and my dependable nature would prove me to be an asset as your secretary.

My visit with you convinced me that Megabucks Corporation offers more challenging and exciting career opportunities than any other firm I have visited. Please feel free to call me at (301) 323–6799 if you need any further information. I look forward to hearing from you.

Sincerely,

Your Name

THANK-YOU LETTER NO. 2

Your Street Address
Your City, State, and Zip Code
Date

Mr. Vince Sajewski
Whittier Insurance Company
332 Meadowbrook Avenue
Phoenix, AZ 85012

Dear Mr. Sajewski:

Thank you, Mr. Sajewski, for giving me your undivided attention this morning during my interview. I have great expectations of becoming a successful secretary with your firm.

During my seven months of full-time training at American Business School, I have experienced almost all facets of office procedures and computer applications. If given the opportunity to work as your secretary, I am confident that my previous work experience and personal attributes would make me an asset to your firm.

After our discussion, I am certain that I would find the insurance industry to be a challenging and exciting field in which to work, especially the prospect of creating a monthly newsletter using my desktop publishing background.

Again, thank you for your consideration. I look forward to hearing from you soon with regard to this position.

Sincerely,

Your Name

THANK-YOU LETTER No. 3

Your Street Address
Your City, State, and Zip Code
Date

Mr. Gerald Grossi
Essence Manufacturing
66 Collingwood Drive
East Lansing, MI 48824-1113

Dear Mr. Grossi:

I want to thank you for interviewing me yesterday for the draftsman position in your engineering department. I was very impressed with the description you provided of your organization, and I am excited about the prospect of working for you.

My qualifications are well-matched with the position we discussed, and I have a real interest in this area of work. My CAD experience and work history will enable me to make a valuable contribution to Essence Manufacturing.

Again, thank you for the interview and your consideration. I am eager to have an opportunity of working on your staff. I look forward to hearing from you. Please feel free to call me at (616) 383-9821 if you have any further questions.

Sincerely,

Your Name

JOB STATUS LETTER NO. 1

Your Street Address
Your City, State, and Zip Code
Date

Mrs. Mary Alvin
Redkin Corporation
909 Viola Boulevard
Orlando, FL 32810

Dear Mrs. Alvin:

During my interview for the marketing position on September 16, you indicated that you hoped to make a decision within a week. As I am very interested in this position, I would like to know the status of this job. If it has not been filled, I hope that I am still in contention.

Let me restate my strong desire to join the Redkin Corporation marketing team. If given the opportunity to work for you, I am confident I will justify your decision and be able to contribute immediately.

Please feel free to contact me at (407) 555–6744 if you need any further information.

Sincerely,

Your Name

JOB STATUS LETTER NO. 2

Your Street Address
Your City, State, and Zip Code
Date

Mrs. Doris Horton
Director of Human Resources
Catskill, Inc.
1292 Independence Drive
Los Angeles, CA 89032

Dear Mrs. Horton:

On September 16 I submitted my resumé for consideration for the secretarial opening in your sales department. I am hopeful that you have had time to review it and find that my qualifications meet your requirements.

Could you possibly tell me the current status of the position and when interviews will be held. You can contact me at (318) 222–8907. I look forward to your response.

Sincerely,

Your Name

TIME OUT

What are the three most important criteria for you personally to consider when evaluating a job offer?

_____

_____

_____

_____

_____

■ EVALUATING JOB OFFERS

First, it is essential that you take notes each and every time you contact a company for a position. Based on these notes, information you have received, and your impressions, you will make your decision. Weigh the pros and the cons. Although salary is important, remember that the job is more important. If you lack work experience, you need to get your foot in the door, so to speak, and earn your promotions. Don't set unrealistic salary expectations. Company benefits are also very important. Such benefits include health and dental insurance; 401K plans, in which you are allowed to contribute to a retirement fund some of your pay before it is taxed; vacation time; life and disability insurance; employee stock purchase program matched at some percentage by the employer; education and training programs; bonuses; profit sharing; savings plans; and retirement plans. Remember, this is probably only the first job you will hold while progressing up the ladder to success. Look at future opportunities that may be presented to you through this initial position.

NEGOTIATING A HIGHER SALARY

One of your main responsibilities during the interview is to convey your value to the company. If you hesitate to accept a job because the salary offer is too low, the interview is the best time to try and negotiate a higher rate. Assume an offer has been made. You might respond by saying, "This position sounds exactly like what I have been looking for, and I really think I could make a contribution to your company. However, to be honest, I was expecting a higher starting salary. Is this negotiable?" If the answer is no, then respond "Would you consider giving me a performance review after 90 days and, if you like my work and the job I have been doing, then giving me an increase at that point? If the answer is still no, then say: "I'll need some time to think about it. When will you need my decision?"

ACCEPTING, DECLINING, OR DELAYING A DECISION

Accepting the Offer

If you are absolutely sure that the position offered is the perfect job for you, then by all means accept enthusiastically. When accepting a job with a start date that is not immediate, you should write a letter of acceptance to firm up the arrangements with your future employer. An example of such a letter is on page 138.

Declining the Offer

If, after getting answers to all of your questions, you think that this job is not right for you, then graciously decline and thank the interviewer for his or her time. One such applicant responded, "I am very impressed with Lakeside Development and your rapid rise to one of the largest land development companies in the area. However, the job you described would not give me the opportunity to use all of my secretarial skills. I would not be happy working at a computer terminal all day. Therefore, I have to decline your gracious offer. If another position should arise that might offer more diversity, I would be very interested. Thank you for your time and consideration."

Delaying Your Decision

Delaying your decision about a job offer may be necessary if you're hoping to receive another offer for a job you'd rather have. Sometimes you just need more time to think about the specific job.

If you are not sure whether to accept a job offer, say that you'd like some time to think about it. Ask when your decision is needed. Generally 48 hours is the norm.

Assume an employer makes an offer, you ask for time to make your decision, and you decide that this offer is not right for you for whatever reason. Refuse the job in writing. It is important to remain polite and professional while thanking the employer for the offer. On page 139 is an example of just such a letter.

LETTER ACCEPTING A JOB

Your Street Address
Your City, State, and Zip Code
Date

Mr. Dale Burgess
Enteck Enterprises
39209 Elliott Street
Chattanooga, TN 48054

Dear Mr. Burgess:

Thank you for giving me the opportunity to join the Enteck Enterprises team. I am pleased to accept the position as a computer operator with the accounting department. This position entails exactly the kind of work I desire.

As we discussed, I will begin working on January 3. In the meantime, I will complete all the necessary employment forms and obtain the required physical exam and drug analysis.

Again, thank you for your time and consideration. I enjoyed interviewing with you and look forward to beginning my career with Enteck.

Sincerely,

Your Name

LETTER DECLINING A JOB

Your Street Address
Your City, State, and Zip Code
Date

Mr. Merle Loch
Macabes, Inc.
1235 Ward Road
Valdosta, GA 31601

Dear Mr Loch:

Thank you for offering me a sales-consultant position with Macabes.

You can be assured that I am appreciative of your time and consideration. But foremost, I am flattered to have been selected for a position with your excellent company.

However, I must decline your offer because of other considerations. Certainly, numerous candidates will be eager to join your fine staff.

I wish you continued success.

Sincerely,

Your Name

HANDLING REJECTION

It is very important to remain objective in your job search. If you are not offered the job after being interviewed, don't take it as a personal insult or failure. Remember what was discussed earlier: To make the marriage work, the company needs to find the right person for the position it is trying to fill. If the employer doesn't believe you are right for that job, would you want it anyway? You have a lot to offer and must trust the interviewer's instincts. If you receive a favorable response in 1 out of 10 interviews, you are doing well. Persistence and self-confidence will enable you to succeed. Analyze your rejections, but don't wallow in self-pity. Our reaction to failure is what distinguishes winners from losers.

Handling rejection can be a valuable learning experience if pursued in the right vein. If you are rejected by the interviewer either in person or over the telephone, thank the interviewer for his or her consideration. Ask if he or she would share with you the reasons that you were not chosen for the position so that you will be able to improve your chances on future interviews. Stress that you really want an honest and objective opinion. Take notes and don't interrupt. Then thank the interviewer for his or her time.

Whether the interviewer's perceptions are true or not really doesn't matter. The importance lies in the fact that you need to overcome the negative perceptions you conveyed. How you say something is just as important as what you say!

To improve your interviewing technique and lessen the chance for rejection, take a close look at the interviewer's opinions to see if they have any merit. Perhaps discuss these perceptions with a friend or family member. As the job search lengthens, it is important to keep a positive outlook. If you don't, your attitude may cloud otherwise good responses.

As mentioned in the sample job acceptance letter, many companies will require you to take a physical examination after you have been offered a position and have accepted. Passing the examination cannot become a condition for employment, unless failing the examination would indicate that you were unable to perform your duties. Expect to be tested for drugs and alcohol.

Notes

CHAPTER **8** KEEPING YOUR JOB—AND YOUR SANITY

■ DO OR DIE: THE FIRST 90 DAYS ON THE JOB

During the first three months, or 90 days, on a new job, you will be watched closely by your superiors and co-workers. They will be reviewing the quality of your work, how cooperative you are, and how you get along with others on the office team. You must try to create a positive image and a can-do attitude without stepping on anyone's toes. Be perceptive and trust your instincts.

Most employees are unaware of the problems that can cost approximately 10 percent of them their new jobs. The most common reasons for losing a new job follow:

- Don't fit in.

- Lack skills.

- Don't get along with boss.

- Don't adapt to company procedures.

- Don't understand office politics.

- Downsized out of a job.

- Misjudged workload or misunderstood job requirements.

1. *You Don't Fit In.*   To begin with, many new employees never quite fit in according to management's expectations. From the employee's perspective, the key is to figure out just exactly what is expected. To do this, talk to present and past employees. Be a team player. Becoming part of the team means cooperating not only during working hours on the projects at hand but also after hours when you are asked to join in some of the social activities of your department. Remember, part of your ability to enjoy your work will depend on your ability to get to know your co-workers and establish good working relationships with them. Meeting with them outside the typical work environment will afford you an excellent opportunity to do just that. Developing a good rapport now in this way will ensure your co-workers' support later in a working environment. If you continually turn down offers to meet with the team after work, eventually you will be excluded and may feel isolated. Many new ideas are tossed around after work; and if you are not present, you will miss out on important decisions, how they were reached, and why they were necessary. This lack of information may make your work suffer, thus resulting in your dismissal.

Sometimes a new employee will be let go because he or she is unable to conform to the company's unspoken rules. For example, there may not be a dress code. Yet if everyone in the company dresses conservatively and the new employee dresses rather flamboyantly, this could result in a problem. Supervisors expect new employees to conform to the established, time-honored traditions.

During the interview process, carefully observe the company's work atmosphere and ask questions that will give you a better feel for the management style and personality. If you are fired because you don't fit in, it may be the best for you in the long run. After all, would you really want to work for a company where you don't feel comfortable? No job comes with a satisfaction or your money back guarantee.

2. *You Don't Have the Skills.*   Another problem may be that a new employee lacks the necessary skills to perform the job adequately. Good grades don't always spell success. It is necessary to have a strong foundation of skills and an understanding of the business principles involved before undertaking a new job. To avoid this pitfall, ask what training programs the company offers. Find out whether the company has a manual to explain procedures and policies. Find out if someone will assist you in your new position and for how long.

You must act confident in your ability to do the job. However, if you exaggerate your skill and overstate your experience, you may be setting yourself up for failure within the first three months on the new job. You can't just talk a good game; you must be able to produce.

3. *You Don't Get Along with the Boss.*   A new employee's inability to get along with the boss is another major concern and reason for early dismissal on a new job. You may not always like your boss; however, it is essential that the boss like you if you are going to have a chance to succeed. A mismatch may occur due to differences in personalities, ways of communicating, unclearly defined goals, and so on. However, you must be able to overcome these differences to your boss's satisfaction to have any hope for success.

4. *You Don't Adapt to Your Company.*   You may be unwilling to adapt to your new company's policies and procedures while you are getting your feet wet during the first 90 days on the job. No one wants to hear how you did something on your last job, regardless of how well it might have worked. Remember, you are the new kid on the block. As such, keep your ideas to yourself. For now, keep your eyes and ears

open, and follow the guidelines set by your company. Later on, after you've been accepted, you can make suggestions for new and perhaps better ways of doing things.

5. *You Don't Understand Office Politics.*   One of the most unfortunate reasons a new employee may lose a job is because he or she is caught in the crossfire of office politics. While you are getting your feet wet on the new job, it is important to do a lot of listening, little talking, and keep new ideas and opinions to yourself—temporarily. People who appear most friendly toward you may have ulterior motives that could be detrimental to your success during that critical 90-day period. A boss may have more tolerance for an employee whose skills are lacking than for an employee who is caught in the middle of office politics. Quite often the reason given for firing a new hire is that they just didn't work out!

6. *Downsized Out of a Job.*   Sometimes, through no fault of their own, employees are fired because the company has decided to downsize the workforce. The last hired are often the first to go. You can try to avoid becoming the victim of downsizing by doing research on the firm before you accept a position.

7. *You Misjudged the Workload or Misunderstood the Job Requirements.*   A new hire may be fired because of his or her poor judgment. Make sure you understand the task at hand, are able to put the tasks in priority and meet the imposed deadline, and know your own limitations. Don't hesitate to ask questions if you are unsure of the task at hand.

■ THE BUSINESS OF PERSONALITIES

Most often the reason an employee is fired from a position or fails to advance within a company is due to his or her inability to get along with co-workers and become part of an overall office team. A large part of this problem is the lack of understanding or misunderstanding of personalities—an individual's and his or her co-workers. Just as in life, a business is made up of many personalities, each requiring special treatment.

IDENTIFYING YOUR OWN PERSONALITY

In the next pages, you are going to take a good look at your own personality—how you see yourself, not how others see you. You might gain some insights as to what your strengths are and how to use those to your own advantage. In addition, perhaps your shortcomings will become more apparent and you might learn how to change your weaknesses into strong points.

Exercise 8.1 on page 147 is designed to assist in understanding individual tendencies and preferences found in three personality types: the organizer, the developer, and the communicator. Our personalities are composed of bits and pieces from each of these areas.

As you will see from the results of Exercise 8.1, each of you is part organizer, part developer, and part communicator. However, one of these personality types is usually dominant. Let's examine more closely each type of personality.

The Organizer

The typical organizer is someone who can get things done! He or she is normally precise, thoughtful, practical, responsible, dependable, calm, and detail-oriented. The organizer offers excellent support to any staff. An organizer has the ability to perform consistently, listen to others, find better ways to do things (although he or she must be the one to find the better way), use facts and logic, plan thoroughly, and analyze situations and people. However, if an organizer gets carried away, he or she tends to be overly cautious, takes too much time, acts reserved, delays decisions, resists change, keeps a low profile, and avoids conflict. One thing to remember about organizers, however, is that they don't get mad—they get even!

The Developer

The typical developer is someone who can make things happen; he or she has mastered the job. This personality type is good at crisis management. He or she is determined, decisive, creative, self-confident, and firm. The developer loves a challenge. The developer has the ability to make decisions, stay motivated, initiate action, sum up things concisely, and be the master of the job. Again, however, if carried to an extreme, this personality type tends to come on too strong, becomes insensitive, leaps before looking, overlooks details, generates conflict, and becomes impatient. If you have something new to do, give it to a developer. He or she likes to be constantly challenged. After the first time, however, the developer would become bored and probably would not do as good a job as an organizer would.

The Communicator

The typical communicator is someone who likes working with other people and can always work things out. He or she is enthusiastic,

EXERCISE 8.1	IDENTIFYING PERSONALITY DYNAMICS

PART ONE. Thirty pairs of words are used below. Please circle the word in each pair that best describes you. For example, are you more diplomatic or more decisive? When you have finished, count your circles to be sure that you have made one choice for each pair (30 total).

1. Diplomatic
2. Persistent
3. Poised
4. Open-minded
5. Concise
6. Tactful
7. Accurate
8. Considerate
9. Likable
10. Talkative
11. Tough-minded
12. Determined
13. Independent
14. Sociable
15. Achiever
16. Precise
17. Organized
18. Convincing
19. Sensitive
20. Change-oriented
21. Knowledgeable
22. Outgoing
23. Careful
24. Adventurous
25. Friendly
26. Factual
27. Vigorous
28. Persuasive
29. Self-assured
30. Calm

31. Decisive
32. Flexible
33. Sincere
34. Self-disciplined
35. Articulate
36. Firm
37. Creative
38. Brave
39. Loyal
40. Listener
41. Trusting
42. Spontaneous
43. Harmonious
44. Patient
45. Enthusiastic
46. Innovative
47. Assertive
48. Objective
49. Practical
50. People-oriented
51. Confident
52. Cooperative
53. Fearless
54. Optimistic
55. Logical
56. Direct
57. Affectionate
58. Consistent
59. Charming
60. Forceful

PART TWO.   Now circle every number below that matches a word you chose in Part One. When you finish, you should have 30 numbers circled. Then count the number of circles in each column and write that number in the box above each column. The three numbers should total 30.

ORGANIZER	DEVELOPER	COMMUNICATOR
□	□	□
1	2	3
6	5	4
7	11	9
8	12	10
16	13	14
17	15	18
21	20	19
23	24	22
26	27	25
30	29	28
33	31	32
34	36	35
39	37	41
40	38	42
44	46	43
48	47	45
49	51	50
52	53	54
55	56	57
58	60	59

flexible, poised, friendly, articulate, and emotional. Communicators have the ability to motivate others, generate enthusiasm, be team players, communicate verbally, solve problems, adapt to changes, and turn negatives into positives. If carried to an extreme, however, the communicator tends to lose objectivity, talks too much, becomes too trusting, compromises too often, loses track of time, and lacks self-confidence. Communicators learn from their mistakes.

MAKING SELF-IMPROVEMENTS

To manage your work and personal life better, you may need to take a good look at your daily habits and consider making some changes. Because your habits are learned and not inherited, you can make any changes you want—provided you want to change.

First, you need to decide that you want to change. Second you need to decide what you want to change. Then decide what the new habit will be. Next, write down the new habit so that it becomes more of a commitment. Finally, set a deadline. You must stick to something for 28 consecutive days before you can honestly say you have turned over a new leaf. This process may sound easy, but it is not. Habits develop over years and require real commitment to change.

For each type of personality, there are some things you can do to increase your productivity on the job and, at the same time, increase your job satisfaction. Let's look at all three major personality types to see where self-improvements might be made.

The Organizer

As an organizer, you have a commitment to accuracy and quality, which is the reason you set high standards in the workplace. To increase your productivity, however, you need to set deadlines and stick to them. Try to accept less than perfection in yourself and others. Try to be more flexible, not so set in your ways. Finally, look for any shortcuts and try using them.

To enjoy your job more, try to become more outgoing and develop warmer working relationships with co-workers. Stop worrying about things that you can't control. Try to project more confidence and show more enthusiasm in your work.

The Developer

As a developer, your initiative and can-do attitude promote progress and achievement in the workplace. However, to increase your productivity, you need to get more information and develop a plan before acting. Try to be more patient and tolerant of other workers. Most of all, avoid making snap decisions.

To increase your job satisfaction, make an effort to slow down and relax a little. Try asking other people for their ideas and input. When you want something done, ask—don't tell. Because the developer comes across as being in command of the job at all times, other workers are sometimes afraid to get to know the developer personally. Therefore, make an attempt to go out of your way to improve working relationships with co-workers.

The Communicator

The communicator's positive attitude and communication skills build teamwork and inspire others. To increase productivity, you need to prioritize your work and set deadlines, organize your work area, be more forceful and firm, ask questions, and check details.

To increase your job satisfaction, find a quiet place to think so you can put everything in perspective. There is a difference between being alone and being lonely. Use logic more, not emotion, and get the facts. Listen carefully when receiving directions and repeat them back. Finally, worry less about other people's feelings.

DEALING WITH DIFFERENT PERSONALITY TYPES

Now that you better understand yourself and how you can change to become happier and more productive in the workplace, it is time to focus on how you affect the behavior of others. Being successful in your job requires hard work, good timing, and top-notch human relations skills. Every job requires interaction with others to achieve a desired goal. Therefore, you need other people on your side to accomplish your goals. Your ability to determine what type of person you are dealing with in a business situation and to understand how to deal with that person will help you develop better working relationships, which will ease your stress and make your job a lot easier and more enjoyable.

The Organizer

If the person you are dealing with is primarily an organizer (precise, cautious, determined, practical, calm, and a perfectionist), you can get his or her attention and win favorable decisions by following these guidelines.

1. Always approach the organizer with all the facts in a logical order.

2. Don't ever criticize his or her work.

3. Don't just throw out an idea; provide options and suggest solutions. Even go so far as to offer to help. It's hard to say no to someone who has presented an idea, offered the means to carry it out, and then said he or she would do the necessary leg-work.

4. Express appreciation for agreeing to your ideas.

5. Also, give advance notice of any changes that may occur in the daily routine or procedures.

The Developer

If the person you are dealing with is a developer (bold, decisive, confident, determined, direct, and outspoken), follow these guidelines to get his or her attention and to speed a decision in your favor.

1. Approach a developer with complete information on the subject you want to discuss. Be direct, to the point, and have all

the facts. Anticipate that person's response and any questions he or she may have so that you are fully prepared with all the answers.

2. Ask the developer to think things over. You do not want him or her to give you an immediate answer. Remember that developers like to make snap decisions, which may not be in your best interest.

3. Compliment the developer who comes across as being the master of the job and rarely receives compliments. Everyone just assumes the developer must know that he or she is doing a good job. Therefore, it is most important to recognize the developer's accomplishments whenever possible.

4. Listen carefully and take notes when dealing with a developer. Typically he or she may ask you to do something a certain way—and you do it. Then the developer looks at the project and asks why you did it that way. When you state that you followed his or her instructions, the developer will deny giving those instructions and tell you to take different steps. The developer is not trying to be mean; he or she honestly believes that you misunderstood the instructions. To avoid such a situation, always take notes when directions are given. Then all you have to do when a question arises is to say, "Let me check my notes. Oh, I must have misunderstood you because that's not what my notes say. No problem, though. I'll be glad to make the change." The next time you check your notes, however, it will be the developer apologizing for the miscommunication. In the end, however, it really doesn't matter who is at fault for the miscommunication as long as the goal is achieved.

5. Show confidence in yourself. If you don't, the developer will walk all over you. If you are not self-confident, then you had better fake it until you are!

The Communicator

If the person you are dealing with is primarily a communicator (friendly, optimistic, supportive, talkative, spontaneous, and emotional), follow these guidelines to get his or her attention and quick and favorable decisions.

1. Clarify priorities and set deadlines.

2. Always use the communicator's name when talking to him or her and be friendly.

3. Ask his or her opinion on the subject you want to discuss.

4. Don't reject the communicator professionally. For example, consider the typical coffee klatch. If someone starts to make negative comments about the communicator, you have only two choices: get up and leave the discussion, or stay and defend the other person. However, to stay in silence makes you just as guilty as the person who is speaking negatively. While every personality type expects such loyalty and would be upset if it weren't present, the communicator will never be able to forgive such an act.

5. Get him or her to write down dates, information, deadlines, and so on. Don't let the communicator leave information to memory.

6. Praise the communicator's flexibility.

Communicators can appear disorganized. Generally it is because they are very busy, have more than one thing on their minds, and are constantly fueling their creative juices.

■ MANAGING YOUR TIME

In any position, time is money. Yet we all procrastinate; this can harm business relationships and lead to poor products. People procrastinate to escape the unknown, to avoid boring projects that offer no challenge, and to avoid stressful situations and people. Procrastination negatively affects a person's time management routine and can cost a person his or her job. It is easy to say "I won't procrastinate any more" but much harder to do. Perhaps these ideas will help.

Take a good look at your energy level during a typical workday. To make better use of your time and to avoid procrastination, follow these simple rules:

1. During your high-energy times, do the things you procrastinate about most. Also do the things that require more detail and thinking on your part. For example, if you have been putting off doing something and finally do it when you are low in energy, the task will take forever. So, instead, do it when you have the most energy and you'll be surprised at how quickly you can get the job done.

2. During your low-energy times, do simple tasks that require no real thinking: make telephone calls, file, photocopy, and so on. Do anything that gets you up and moving. Such activities will reenergize you.

3. Learn to set priorities and deadlines. Stick to your energy clock when planning your daily schedule. If your high-energy time is first thing in the morning, then perhaps ask your boss to give you major projects early in the day when you are freshest. You will be much more efficient that way.

It's also amazing how quickly you can accomplish a goal or meet a deadline when you reward yourself. A reward can be as simple as not taking a coffee break with others until you have completed your project. Then when you have finished, reward yourself with a coffee break.

Develop a regular work schedule to follow. Use artificial, or pretend, deadlines because of Murphy's law. You all know what that is—if something can go wrong, it will. Therefore, if the deadline is 3 PM Friday, impose an artificial deadline, such as 1 PM, to allow for things that might go wrong.

Also, include committed as well as flexible time when approaching a job. Committed time is what you actually believe it will take to complete the task. Flexible time includes extra minutes for interruptions or things over which you have no control. For example, you think a job will take an hour. As that hour draws to a close, however, you have not finished and you begin to feel stress and pressure. Instead, if you add on a little extra time and begin the project thinking it will take 1 1/2 hours, then when you finish in 70 minutes you will feel great about your accomplishment and will not feel much stress.

Get organized and use a weekly planner. Try coding your work in order of importance: either 1, 2, 3, or m, s, i (must do, should do, if I get around to it).

When handling paperwork, simplify it, don't shuffle it! Ask yourself these questions: "Can I drop it? Can I delay it? Can I delegate it? If not, I'd better do it!" Try to handle paper only once. Organize your work area; a neat and organized work area will make all of your jobs seem much more manageable. Analyze the papers that come across your desk to see if you can eliminate anything. Perhaps you get a weekly copy of new employee names. If this is something you don't really need, go to the source and ask to be taken off the list. Check your filing systems; when in doubt, throw it out. Maybe there are inactive files or accounts that could be stored elsewhere or eliminated entirely. However, before discarding anything, make sure it is no longer necessary. Over the years this must be done to facilitate better records management. Poorly managed paperwork has an adverse affect on a person's effective time management. If you keep papers and files in an orderly, neat fashion—eliminating waste and nonessential paper flow—you can perform your job in a more timely, efficient manner. This will make you a more productive, valuable employee.

TEN WAYS TO GET MORE OUT OF YOUR TIME AT WORK

1. *Take time to take breaks.* There is a misconception that the longer you work, the more productive you become. That couldn't be further from the truth. If you don't recharge your battery, you will eventually stall. When you feel the pressure rising and your level of concentration is falling, step away from your desk, take a walk, clear your mind, and refocus on your current project. Everything will be much clearer when you return to the task at hand.

2. *Set rewards for large and small accomplishments.* Determine what motivates you and use it as a way to help you accomplish your goals.

3. *Ask for temporary help.* As you become more familiar with your job, your responsibilities will grow. When you are given routine tasks that could be done by someone else, learn to delegate so that your time can be better spent on the more productive tasks.

4. *Avoid the office gossip mill.* Playing the office politics game is a waste of time and could come back to haunt you.

5. *Throughout the day, ask yourself if what you are doing is the best use of your time.* It may not be an activity you enjoy, but if it is a top priority, make the time to get it done.

6. *Don't make assumptions about your work; when in doubt, ask questions.* When you are given a job, ask questions if in doubt to ensure that you understand what needs to be done. Redoing your work is a waste of time.

7. *Get off the phone as soon as possible.* When someone keeps you on the phone for longer than necessary, gently prompt the caller to end the call. You could tell the person that you have another call or a deadline to meet. If the person has requested something, say that you want to get started on it right away.

8. *Make your environment conducive to working.* If your office is disorganized, you will easily waste time searching for files, replacing lost information, and running in place. Take time to clear your desk of any distractions. Don't locate your desk in a high-traffic area, near copy machines, or near the vending machines. Otherwise you can be guaranteed a day filled with needless interruptions.

9. *Stay focused on the activity at hand.* When you have to jump from one task to another, try to bring your progress on one project to a point where it will be easy to pick it up later before switching gears.

10. *Know when to say no.* There are often times when you want to say no but feel obligated to say yes. You must recognize that you can't be everything to all people all of the time. One strategy is to offer alternatives. When you tell someone that you can't do something, offer to help with a small task or even to switch tasks. It will be difficult at first to say no, but when you realize how much more you will be able to accomplish, saying no will become that much easier.

■ HANDLING STRESS

No one can escape stress, but you can learn to cope with it. Stress is the result of feeling a lack of control. It can come from information overload, economic pressures, overwork, perfectionism, or a crisis situation. Once you understand the causes of your stress, you need to implement a plan to handle it. Break down a job that seems large and overwhelming into small, manageable pieces. Practice positive thinking and remind yourself frequently just how well you are actually doing. Prioritize your tasks and set aside time for relaxation. Keep in mind that stress is not a one-time occurrence but an on-going circumstance. If you allow yourself to be overwhelmed, you are more likely to feel like a victim.

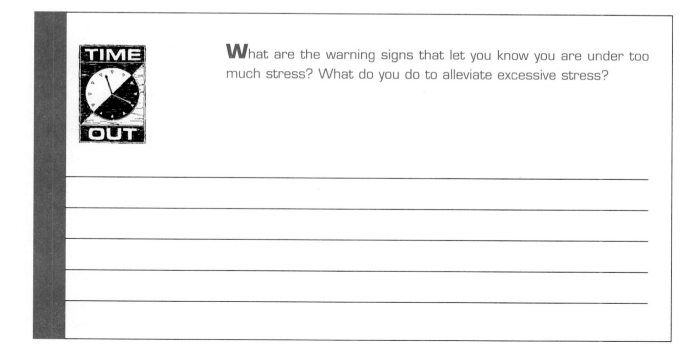

What are the warning signs that let you know you are under too much stress? What do you do to alleviate excessive stress?

While pursuing your career goal through the interviewing process, maintain a normal schedule of exercise to relieve some of the tension that might build up. In addition, get up at the same time every morning as if you had an interview scheduled for the day.

A worker's inability to effectively deal with the stress and pressures of today's business world can cost a company millions of dollars each year in sick pay, health care, and loss of productivity. Stress is exhibited in many forms, such as low morale, poor attitude, absenteeism, illness, and alcohol and drug abuse. Exercise 8.2 on page 157 may help you determine if you are at risk from stress.

TWENTY STRESS–BUSTING STRATEGIES

1. Take a warm bath.

2. Write a nasty letter to whomever is stressing you out—then tear it up.

3. Play with a pet.

4. Make decisions based as much on your heart as on your head.

5. Don't eat unless you're hungry.

6. Volunteer to do good. You'll feel better about what you've done and who you are.

7. If your company's employee assistance program offers a stress reduction program, sign up for it.

8. Cultivate a sense of humor and smile.

9. Unplug the phone, send the family to a movie, and listen to your favorite music.

10. Take control of how you react to a stressful event.

11. Don't be afraid to say no. You are in charge of your time.

12. Reduce your sugar consumption. Excess sugar can heighten your stress response.

13. Set a comfortable, steady pace at work, then focus totally on the task at hand to improve productivity.

14. Eat lots of fiber and starches; carbohydrates tend to calm you down.

15. Eat breakfast so you can start the day on a full tank. Avoid big meals late at night because they can disrupt your sleep and cause stress.

EXERCISE 8.2	STRESS INDICATORS

After each question, place a check mark under the category that most applies to your daily life.

COMMON STRESS INDICATORS	ALWAYS OR USUALLY	SELDOM OR SOMETIMES	NEVER
Do you find yourself talking fast?			
Do you hurry other people's speech by interrupting them or by completing their sentences for them?			
Do you hate to wait in line?			
Do you seem to have difficulty getting everything done?			
Do you eat too fast?			
Do you drive over the speed limit?			
Do you try to do more than one thing at a time?			
Do you become impatient if others do something too slowly?			
Do you find yourself overcommitted?			
Do you jiggle your knees or tap your fingers?			
Do you walk fast?			
Do you hate dawdling after a meal?			
Do you become irritable if kept waiting?			
Do you compete with others at work?			

If many of your check marks are in the first column, you may be under a lot of stress.

16. Don't be afraid of your tears. Sometimes a good cry is called for—it releases anxiety.

17. Schedule time for fun.

18. Leave the job at work. Leave family pressures at home.

19. Remember that some things don't have to be done perfectly.

20. Lighten up! Once you have examined a perceived failure from the past, let it go and focus on the future.

■ MAINTAINING YOUR ETHICS

Weighing a difficult decision on the job often involves a question of ethics. An employee may feel torn between his or her personal beliefs and what a company expects. To understand business ethics, you need to understand the values that form the basis of decision making: honesty, integrity, generosity, helpfulness, self-reliance, and kindness. Your values are the fundamental beliefs you were raised with and that come from home, church, school, and peers.

You should always maintain your personal integrity and ethical values in the workplace. However, situations may arise at work where the manner in which a solution is arrived at may contradict your personal standards. Then it will be up to you to decide whether the value in question is worth defending. When you decide to challenge such a decision, you should discuss the matter with your supervisor.

■ UNDERSTANDING YOUR RIGHTS

DISABILITY IN THE WORKPLACE

The Americans with Disabilities Act, which was passed by Congress in July 1992, applies to employers with 15 or more employees. The purpose of the Americans with Disabilities Act is to eliminate the obstacles that prevent qualified individuals with disabilities from enjoying the same employment opportunities available to individuals without disabilities. The act prohibits discrimination against any employee affected by a disability or chronic disease and specifically mentions the HIV virus and AIDS. The law prohibits discrimination in all employment practices, including hiring, firing, advancement, compensation, advertising, layoffs, leaves, fringe benefits, training, job application procedures, recruitment, and all other employment activities.

Employers are required to provide reasonable accommodations to the known physical or mental limitations of an otherwise qualified worker (1) to ensure equal opportunity in the application process, (2) to enable performance of essential job functions, and (3) to ensure equal benefits and privileges of employment. Some examples of accommodations that might be made include reassignment, job restructuring, equipment and devices, accessible and usable facilities, work schedule modification, and flexible leave policies. However, the key words here are *reasonable accommodations*. One must take into account the abilities and limitations of the particular disabled employee and the functional requirements of the particular job. Decisions are made on a case-by-case basis.

SEXUAL HARASSMENT

Sexual harassment is any unwelcome sexual advance or conduct on the job that creates an intimidating, hostile, or offensive working environment. No worker should have to tolerate such behavior by a co-worker or supervisor.

The following instances demonstrate the fine line between what constitutes sexual harassment and acceptable behavior. In each instance the first case is a form of sexual harassment, but the second is not. No one single instance would necessarily make a case for sexual harassment but rather a series of conditions occurring over time would be necessary to support one's claim. Remember, the worker's conduct must be intimidating, offensive, or hostile to another worker to be perceived as harassment.

- "Boy, that suit really accents your figure." Or "That is a pretty suit you have on."

- A worker puts his or her arm around you and draws you closer. Or a worker taps your arm to get your attention.

- A manager uses profane language when addressing several people in a department and then apologizes to only the female workers for the language used. Or a manager uses profane language when addressing several people in a department.

If you believe that you are being sexually harassed, there are several steps you should follow. First, verbally inform the harasser that his or her attentions are unwanted. If the harassment continues, write the harasser a memo stating your complaint and keep a copy for your records. Third, keep a written record of the harassment, noting the date, time, place, witnesses, and your response. Then look for witnesses, other victims, and further evidence to support your claim. If the harassment continues, use your in-company grievance procedures. If you need to take further action, call a legal service agency, your state discrimination agency, or the Equal Employment Opportunity Commission.

■ TACKLING THE FIRST YEAR

By now you should have taken a close look at your personality and stress level and have a better grasp of how to deal with all kinds of people. However, starting to work in an organization is a unique and important time that requires special strategies for you to be successful. You are entering a transition stage and may feel uncomfortable. While you are no longer a student, you're not yet a professional either. You have to let go of student attitudes and behavior and understand that as time passes, you will earn the rights, responsibilities, and credibility of a full-fledged professional.

As you know from your job search, first impressions are important. Those first few weeks on the job are critical because the way people perceive you at the beginning determines your opportunities to grow and contribute to the company. You need to establish a reputation as a bright, capable, and valuable employee worthy of your colleagues' respect. You want to jump on the "success spiral," where the more you demonstrate what an outstanding performer you are, the more opportunities to succeed follow.

Here are some strategies to make your first-year transition smooth:

1. *Slow Down.*   Most new hires want to impress so badly that they jump right in with new ideas, step on others' toes, and develop foot-in-mouth problems. You need to be accepted before your ideas will be. As the new kid on the block, you need to try to fit into the existing scheme of things. Realize that you have much to learn and can do so by keeping your eyes and ears open and your mouth shut.

2. *Learn the Rules.*   Understanding the personality of the office is essential. Pay attention to the way things are done, understand what people expect of you, notice the way people work together as a team, and understand the office politics. Learn your company's and department's routines and procedures.

3. *Make a Good Impression.*   At first, everything you do will be magnified because everyone will be watching. Use good judgment and build strong relationships with co-workers. Be willing to learn from the experience of older employees, yet show confidence in your own abilities without sounding cocky. Display a good work ethic and positive attitude.

4. *Accept Your New Role.* Realize that as the newcomer you need to learn the organization and be accepted. You have to pay your dues before you can earn your place in the organization.

5. *Set Realistic Expectations.* First of all, expect surprises. Things will never go as you plan. During the interview, you were told only the good things about the company. Everyone knows that there are two sides to every story. Decision making won't always seem logical because of office politics. Human relations skills and teamwork will be more important than you ever imagined. Second, be ready to handle the stress, pressure, and workload. Everyone paid a lot of attention to you while you were being recruited. Now that you're hired, however, things will go back to normal; no more special attention.

6. *Your Biggest Ally.* The most important person during your first year will be your boss. Your primary function is to support his or her efforts. Learn what your boss wants, needs, and expects—and then do it. Make your boss look good, and you will succeed. Remember, you can't become a good leader until you become a good follower. If, by chance, you get a bad boss, that is no excuse for you to give a bad performance.

Once you accept the uniqueness of this transitional first year on the job, your job can be lots of fun, very exciting, and a wonderful start to a successful new career. Once you are accepted by an organization, respected by your colleagues, and productive in your work, you will be able to assert yourself in the organization using your individual style. The first year is important because it lays the foundation for future professional growth. With this solid base, future successes will await you. If you have a difficult boss, find a support network, document problems so you cover your back, keep things in perspective, and know when to move on. Remember to ask yourself, do you work to live or do you live to work? Stick to your own standards and remain positive.

9 MOVING BEYOND YOUR
FIRST JOB

WORKPLACE TRENDS

Regardless of how great your job may be or how well you are doing in your present position, you have to be prepared to move on. To place yourself in line to obtain the best future jobs, watch trends in the marketplace, keep your skills and knowledge up to date, and keep track of your likes and dislikes about the jobs you have held.

To get a job, the job has to exist. In the not-too-distant future, the workplace as we know it will no longer exist. Certain jobs will no longer exist. It is important to look ahead and be aware of the trends in the workplace, so that you do not pursue or stay in a job that will no longer be needed. By noting workplace trends, you may learn of new fields for which few are prepared.

■ DOWNSIZING AND RESTRUCTURING

Some workplace changes have already started to occur. Companies have begun to downsize their workforces by offering early retirements and curtailing the hiring of new employees. These changes have resulted from better technology that has enabled workers in lower-level positions to make more critical decisions, thus resulting in the elimination of many management, supervisory, support staff, and lower-level positions.

To cope with downsizing, expect a wide range of feelings such as fear, anger, anxiety, distrust, confusion, and uncomfortable work relationships. Don't deny these feelings but talk about them with friends and family. Don't base your self-worth and identity on your job or on pleasing your employer. Detach yourself so your self-esteem isn't smashed if your work changes or disappears. Focus on doing quality work and providing a benefit to people instead of playing politics. Don't become overly dependent on your employer for travel benefits, savings plans, recreation, child care assistance, tuition reimbursement, or career planning. Don't rush to take a new job when you feel threatened at work. Seriously think about your options. Monitor your physical and emotional health. Set limits at work. Don't accept an unreasonable amount of work out of fear that you'll be the next one to go. Take vacations and long weekends often. Look for hidden opportunities. Is this a chance to shift career direction, learn new skills, or apply seldom-used ones? Don't wait for your employer to nudge you.

To prevent downsizing from happening to you, anticipate changes in the workplace before they happen and then position yourself to take advantage of these changes because of thorough preparation.

The company structure is being simplified. No longer can a worker expect to spend his or her entire career with one company; *job security* is a term of the past. Many of the fringe benefits that workers have enjoyed in the past are being altered. Employees today are expected to pay for more of the benefits, especially for those in the health care area.

Making a change in careers may sound scary, but in reality it can be very exciting. To prepare for the changing job environment, learn as much as possible about a company by working in different departments to improve your marketability. Take advantage of all the resources and tools available to enhance this learning process. In exchange, your value to your employer lies in your increased productivity and loyalty. The company owns the job, but you own the career path you chose to follow. Be aware of your achievements, write them down, make them part of your resumé and portfolio. If you have an idea that will benefit the company, present it to your boss. Creativity is always appreciated.

Greater emphasis is being placed on producing quality products to compete more cost efficiently in the world market. Greater effort is being given to meeting customers' demands on a more timely basis. This concept, referred to as total quality management (TQM), will be discussed in more detail later.

■ CORPORATE CULTURE

In addition, many companies are experimenting with dress down days once a week. In a study of 200 companies, nearly half reported that wearing informal attire had helped to improve employee morale. As a result, 58 percent of those surveyed have instituted these dress down days on a permanent basis.

Casual dress does not mean wear anything in your closet. You want to look relaxed, but not too relaxed. The key to dressing casual on the job is balancing comfort and appearance. Even firms with designated dress-down days expect employees to exercise discretion if they have meetings to attend or other scheduled visits with clients. People who take their work seriously have to look professional. They have to be very careful in how they present themselves, so they retain their image of command. This is especially important for women who will find their credibility or respect diminished if they look too sloppy, frivolous, or sexy. Soft-knit separates feel relaxed yet project a strong image. A fine wool jacket or blazer could be mixed with more relaxed skirts or slacks. Employees should shy away from jeans, leggings, sandals, and most shorts because they convey the message that the person is about to do something sportslike. Women often face greater difficulties than men in determining what is appropriate. For men, the most generally accepted casual outfit is a golf shirt with dress pants or not-too-worn Dockers. Some general guidelines to follow are

- Understand that neatness is extra important on casual days. Clothes should be especially clean and pressed, and shoes are recommended instead of sneakers.

- A sport coat or jacket can add just enough polish to keep an outfit from looking unprofessional.

- Know your industry. Someone in a creative field such as advertising or the media has more room for experimentation than someone in a traditionally conservative field like banking.

- When in doubt, men should wear a sport coat, slacks, and either a shirt with no tie or a neatly styled three-button polo shirt. Women can usually get away with slacks and a sweater or less formally styled shirt.

- Avoid anything too tight, too short, too attention grabbing, and too political. Leave anything imprinted with a message at home.

- Take a critical look in the mirror before walking out the door. If the clothing seems more appropriate for a sporting activity or cleaning the garage rather than going out to dinner on the weekend with friends, it's too casual.

■ TEAMWORK

To survive in the workplace of tomorrow, you need to know now what to expect of the future. People who simply process information or make routine decisions are likely to find their jobs in danger within the next 10 years. As this belt-tightening occurs, there will be fewer opportunities for advancement. Because of the lack of real job security, the average worker is predicted to work at 10 or more jobs for five or more companies before retirement.

Due to the competitive nature of business and the demands for maximum performance, workers will have to become part of the new team strategy concept. An employee's flexibility and creativity will be more important than loyalty. Being widely versed in many business areas rather than being a specialist in any one area will make a worker more valuable. Because of new information technologies, workers will receive more immediate performance feedback and will need to know either how to change their behavior or how to identify new opportunities within the organization to succeed. The ability to analyze data, draw conclusions, and make recommendations will be essential. Computer literacy and knowledge of statistics will be critical.

Company perks will be used as rewards for workers whose behavior has been valuable to the company. Disciplinary action, when required, will be handled by the worker's peers as well as by managers. Peer pressure to remain part of the team, focused on the team goals and objectives, will be enormous. Teamwork and cooperation will be the measure of an employee's worth to a company. Most workers will be offered incentive pay based on the performance of the team and company. Because a worker's income will be much more variable, everyone will need a personal financial plan for retirement.

The entire management structure will be changed. Teams will manage themselves. There will be no clearly defined jobs. Team members will move from job to job as the need arises. Employees will need to increase their speed in doing a job. Problem-solving abilities and quality control will move to the head of the list when evaluating a team's accomplishments.

In the future, a company will move away from management control and toward employee control. Supervisors will be replaced by facilitators who will help employee teams manage interpersonal relationships and technology managers who will help teams implement new technology and solve unusual problems with scheduling, organizing, directing, and controlling the work process. Companies and individuals will have to invest in more educational and skill training.

DO'S AND DON'TS FOR EXECUTIVES CLIMBING THE SUCCESS LADDER

Most executives are smart, capable, effective, and hardworking. However, sometimes peers and subordinates view those same characteristics as controlling, demeaning, and overly critical. Personal factors that can limit career advancement potential were uncovered during an eight-year study of men and women executives by Personnel Decisions, Inc. While men and women have similar flaws, the issues were particularly tough for women to deal with because the feedback they receive may be incomplete or tainted with bias, according to Ann Marsh, senior vice president at Personnel Decisions, Inc. The five most common flaws are

- Poor relationship skills.

- Failure to foster open communications.

- Inability to develop and coach subordinates.

- Failure to create win-win situations.

- Unwillingness to admit mistakes.

To prevent problems like these from putting your career advancement at risk, apply these helpful hints:

- Realize that as you move up the success ladder, interpersonal skills become more important than technical skills.

- Get feedback not only from supervisors but also from peers, direct reports, clients, and associates.

- Don't automatically write off negative feedback as a personal condemnation. Analyze it in light of other feedback you've received.

- Don't try to prove yourself by doing everything perfectly, because you might lose sight of long-term goals. Learn to delegate or drop tasks that don't contribute to your goals. Seek collaboration from other team members on projects.

- Recognize and use the hierarchy in most businesses to your advantage. You can turn your boss's wishes into a win-win situation for both of you. Go along with the plan, but then improve it with your own ideas.

- Learn to work within the team concept.

If you are a newly hired employee on the way up, these hints might prove helpful:

- Carefully observe how most people handle a variety of situations. Then try to make small changes in your handling of similar situations through your behavior and attitude.

- Don't complain.

- Be on time or early.

- Ask lots of questions to show that you are a good listener and eager to learn more.

- Volunteer for jobs no one else wants.

- Expect to make mistakes. When you do, admit to them, try to correct them, and assure your boss that you've learned from them.

■ TOTAL QUALITY MANAGEMENT

It takes training, training, and more training to become a quality company. The basic principles of quality are to focus attention on the customer and to continuously improve one's product or service. This idea sounds simple enough, and one would expect nothing less from any respectable company. However, trying to apply these principles is far from easy. Companies that want to change to a total quality management philosophy must endure a lengthy preparation process that can take a couple of years.

The critical first step is to train managers and supervisors thoroughly so that when the rest of the staff finishes their training, they won't be penalized for practicing their new skills. Building a friendly environment is hard work. The key is to change behaviors and overcome resistance to the changes. Most total quality management training covers leadership, teamwork, and technical skills. Managers must become more receptive to others' ideas, act as coaches rather than as controllers, and help their employees reach a desired outcome rather than just give orders. The technical skills training must include methods of studying a problem and displaying the results of analysis. Self-esteem boosts productivity, and it is leadership's job to enhance self-esteem.

To promote teamwork within a company, it is necessary to recognize an individual's achievements at work; encourage high ethical standards and honest, open behavior; find meaning in work tasks; and encourage collaboration on work projects. Quality and teamwork go hand in hand.

Develop a mission statement to keep team activities in focus. Find out how the team might best benefit the entire organization—not just the team members. Also, stress commitment from team members so that they will be there for the good times and when the going gets rough.

When it comes to determining a company's strategic goals, the internal company structure—particularly its reward and compensation systems—provides the answer. For a worker to get ahead under a teamwork-based total quality management system, the conventional method for employee compensation must change. For example, if a company rewards individual performance, there is no way that a teamwork philosophy will prosper. Even implemented with the best intentions, total quality management principles cannot take root in an organization until total quality values are built into the underlying structure. Progressive companies have discovered the critical link between human resource initiatives and the reward-and-compensation structure.

Currently the top four assessment factors for senior managers are (in order of importance) profitability or cash flow, individual performance, quality performance, and team performance. Soon, however, individual performance will be listed last on this list. Things will be similar for middle management and non-management. Team skills and judgment will be emphasized in the next three years when determining compensation. Quality performance will count twice as much as it does now. However, the shift to teams without recognizing the personal needs of the members who make up the teams would be a mistake. Try to be flexible because the work schedules and family responsibilities will vary by team member. Meeting times and locations might need adjusting. Stay flexible in dealing with various personalities within a group. Remember that everyone brings a different strength to the team.

Two important components of total quality management are quality results and team performance. Human resource people must be involved in this process. This all relates back to the basic principle of total quality management, which is that business, like any living thing, is a system. The interrelation of its parts is as critical to the company's mission as each part is unto itself.

■ PROFESSIONAL DEVELOPMENT

NETWORKING

As your career develops, continue to expand your networking base. Networking is building relationships with knowledgeable professionals in your field who are in a position to lead you to a new and better job opportunity. They may work for the same company you do or a competitor. Through networking, you keep abreast of potential job opportunities as you continue to grow both personally and professionally.

Begin to network by joining several trade or professional organizations within your field of work and become active in them. By attending meetings, you will come in contact with other professionals who share the same interests and goals. Getting to know these professionals in an informal setting over a lunch or dinner meeting will afford you an excellent opportunity to discover potential job leads within your area, stay abreast of rumors or trends regarding your particular industry, and develop invaluable relationships that may pay future dividends toward your career growth.

Attend conferences where you can meet other professionals in your area. Attend formal classes, seminars, and workshops, and make new friends so you can exchange career information with them. Subscribe to and study appropriate trade magazines. Create a resource contact on your local campus. Then find someone who can serve as your mentor—a person in whom you can confide your goals, ambitions, and ideas; someone knowledgeable about your area of career interest whose contacts might prove beneficial to you; someone who can give you honest advice with no strings attached.

One of the most important keys to establishing a successful network is to share what you learn with others. In that way, they will share their experiences, job leads, and contacts with you. Your network circle should be constantly expanding as you continue to grow on a professional level.

INCREASING YOUR WORTH

Because of the ever-changing workplace, downsizing, and new technology, it is imperative that you make yourself so valuable to the company that they couldn't do without your input. Continuing your education is important to your future. New technology is causing everything to change very quickly. Therefore, it is essential to stay current to meet the demands of tomorrow's workplace. Ask your supervisor what courses or direction you should follow in your educational endeavors that would benefit both you and the company the most. Remember, the more you strive to improve yourself, the more of an asset you will become to your organization. You will need to know what job areas are growing fastest and keep abreast of the skills they require.

In addition to becoming more diversified through continuing education, one of the keys to survival is to raise your output, thus increasing your individual value to the company. Competition today is fierce; productivity is the lifeline of business. As departments and companies downsize, everyone who remains on the team must pull together, each person must understand the inherent worth of his or her job, how it relates to the whole picture, and the need for meeting deadlines.

To get promoted within a company, you must gain the respect and attention of your supervisor and co-workers based on your job performance, human relations and communication skills, productivity, willingness to further your education and training, ability to perform well under pressure, and company loyalty. Your attitude, enthusiasm, and commitment to giving 110 percent effort is important. Are you willing to go the extra mile or go above and beyond what is expected for the job? These are the qualities that may move you to the top of the list when an opening occurs within your company.

MAINTAINING YOUR PORTFOLIO

Constantly update your portfolio with samples of your work. As your responsibilities grow, your work abilities will broaden as well. Your diversification should be represented in your portfolio. As you move from one job to another, ask your previous supervisor to write a letter of recommendation to add to your portfolio. Also, from time to time review your resumé to make sure that it is up to date with your current capabilities and the responsibilities of your job.

ENDING ON A GOOD NOTE

Whenever you leave a job, it is customary to give the employer two weeks' notice to find a replacement. Give this notice in writing to be sure that you are understood and clear about the final date of employment. The letter should be addressed to the head of personnel with a copy to your immediate supervisor. Below is an example of such a letter.

RESIGNATION LETTER

Your Street Address
Your City, State, and Zip Code
Date

Human Resources Director's Name
Company Name
Company Street Address
Company City, State, and Zip Code

Dear (Director's Name):

Please accept this letter as my two-week's notice of resignation from (Company Name). Accordingly, my last date of employment will be Friday, October 12, 1996.

Thank you for providing me with the opportunity to work at (Company Name). Over the past three years, I have thoroughly enjoyed working as a secretary in the sales department. Further, I appreciate Darlene Makarski's fine supervision and support. You can be assured that I have valued my association with (Company Name), both personally and professionally.

If I can be of help in training my replacement, I would be happy to do so.

Sincerely,

Your Name

C Your Supervisor

APPENDIX ***A*** **TYPING YOUR RESUMÉ USING WORDPERFECT 6.1 (WINDOWS)**

*I*nstructions for creating each of the 10 resumé styles shown on pages 34–43 are provided. If you follow these instructions, your resumé will look identical to the one you have selected.

Depending on your printer's capabilities, you may want to choose a different font than the one in the directions. If you chose a different font, then the tabs indicated in the directions may need to be altered. You will have to make the appropriate adjustments in those cases.

If you are having trouble getting your resumé to fit on one page, put the street, city, state, and zip code on the same line for each entry under "Education" and "Experience."

DIRECTIONS FOR RESUMÉ No. 1
WORDPERFECT 6.1 (WINDOWS)

GENERAL SETUP

1. From a clear screen, make sure you are in the Page Mode, with your Tool Bar, Power Bar, Ruler Bar, Status Bar, and Graphics visible—like this:

Tool Bar
Power Bar

   If they are not visible, click on **View** and then click on **Page Mode**. Then click on **View** and click on **Tool Bar**. Then click on **View** and click on **Power Bar**, click on **View** and click on **Ruler Bar**. Then click on **View** and click on **Graphics**.

2. Click on **Format**, click on **Margins**, click on the down arrow key next to top margin until it reaches .5; then click on the down arrow key next to bottom margin until it reaches .5; then click on **OK**.

3. Click on **Format**, click on **Page**, click on **Center**, click on **Current Page**, and click on **OK**.

4. Click on **Format**, click on **Line**, click on **Tab Set**, click on **Absolute**, click on **Clear**, click on the box opposite **Position** and type **2.8** and enter. Click on **Format**, click on **Line**, click on **Tab Set**, click on the box opposite **Position** and type **3.16**; then enter.

MAIN HEADING SETUP

1. Looking at your Power Bar, click on the justification button where it says **Left▾**. Click on **Center**.

2. Click on the **Font Button** in your Power Bar where it says **Courier**, scroll down the list until you get to **Times New Roman**, then click on that choice. Click on the **Point Size** button in your Power Bar where it says **12 pt.** From the pull-down list of choices, click on **16**. Then click on **b (Bold)** in your Tool Bar.

3. Now type your name in all capitals. Then click on the **Point Size** button in the Power Bar and click on **12**. Then click on **b (Bold)** in your Tool Bar to turn it off. Enter twice.

4. Type your street address; then enter. Type your city, state, and zip code; then enter. Type your area code and phone number; then enter once.

5. Click on the justification button in the Power Bar, which is now set for **Center.** Click on **Left**. Then enter once more.

6. In your menu bar click on **Graphics**. Click on **Custom Line**. Click on the arrow next to **Thickness** in lower right corner of the screen until it reaches **.047**. Click on **OK**.

7. Hit enter three times.

CAREER OBJECTIVE SETUP

1. Click on **Point Size** in your Power Bar and click on **13**. Click on **b (Bold)** and **u (Underline)** in your Tool Bar. In all capitals type **CAREER OBJECTIVE**. Then click on **Point Size** again in your Power Bar and click on **12**. Then click on **b (Bold)** and **u (Underline)** in your Tool Bar to turn them off. Now enter twice.

2. Type your career objective letting it word wrap at the end of the line. When you are through, enter twice.

EDUCATION SETUP

1. Click on **Point Size** in your Power Bar and click on **13**. Click on **b (Bold)** and **u (Underline)** in your Tool Bar. In all capitals type **EDUCATION**. Then click on **Point Size** again in your Power Bar and click on **12**. Then click on **b (Bold)** and **u (Underline)** in your Tool Bar to turn them off. Now enter twice.

2. Begin with your most recent education by typing the dates you attended, making sure that all digits align. Leave one

space before and after the hyphen. Then tab, click on **b (Bold)** in your Tool Bar, and type the name of the school. Then click on **b (Bold)** in your Tool Bar to turn it off; enter once.

3. Tab, type the street address, city, state, and zip code of your school; then enter once.

4. Tab, click on **i (Italics)** and **b (Bold)** in your Tool Bar, type your course of study or degree received, click on **i (Italics)** and **b (Bold)** in your Tool Bar to turn them off; then enter once.

5. Tab, type when you received your diploma or when it will be awarded, or the number of credits earned, if applicable; then enter twice.

6. Repeat Steps 2–5 for any other schools you want to list. Then enter twice to begin the next section.

AREAS OF SKILLS SETUP

1. Click on **Point Size** in your Power Bar and click on **13**. Click on **b (Bold)** and **u (Underline)** in your Tool Bar. In all capitals type **AREAS OF SKILLS**. Then click on **Point Size** again in your Power Bar and click on **12**. Then click on **b (Bold)** and **u (Underline)** in your Tool Bar to turn them off.

2. Tab; to create the bullet hit **CTRL+W**, type **4,0**, then enter. If none of the items in this area will take more than one line, you may tab and start to type. However, if you think the skill might wrap to a second line, then click on **Format**, click on **Paragraph**, click on **Indent**, and begin to type your skill letting it word wrap. Then enter.

3. Repeat Step 2 until all of your skills have been listed. Hit enter twice when you are through with this section.

EXPERIENCE SETUP

1. Click on **Point Size** in your Power Bar and click on **13**. Click on **b (Bold)** and **u (Underline)** in your Tool Bar. In all capitals type **EXPERIENCE**. Then click on **Point Size** again in your Power Bar and click on **12**. Then click on **b (Bold)** and **u (Underline)** in your Tool Bar to turn them off. Then enter twice.

2. Begin with your most recent experience by typing the dates you were employed, making sure that all digits align. Leave one space before and after the hyphen. Then tab, click on **b (Bold)** in your Tool Bar, and type the name of the company. Then click on **b (Bold)** in your Tool Bar to turn it off; enter once.

3. Tab, type the street address, city, state, and zip code of the company; then enter once.

4. Tab, click on *i* **(Italics)** and **b (Bold)** in your Tool Bar, and type your job title, click on *i* **(Italics)** and **b (Bold)** in your Tool Bar to turn them off; then enter once.

5. Tab; to create the bullet, hit **CTRL+W**, type **4,0** and then enter. At this point you are going to list your accomplishments and responsibilities of the job. If none of the items in this area will take more than one line, you may tab and start to type. However, if you think the item might wrap to a second line, then click on **Format**, click on **Paragraph**, click on **Indent**, and begin to type your item letting it word wrap. Then enter.

6. Repeat Step 5 until all of your accomplishments and responsibilities of the first job have been listed.

7. Hit enter twice and repeat Steps 5–6 until all of your experience has been listed. When you are through with this section, enter twice.

REFERENCE SETUP

1. Click on **Point Size** in your Power Bar and click on **13**. Click on **b (Bold)** and **u (Underline)** in your Tool Bar. In all capitals type **<u>REFERENCES</u>**. Then click on **Point Size** again in your Power Bar and click on **12**. Then click on **b (Bold)** and **u (Underline)** in your Tool Bar to turn them off. Tab and type Available upon Request.

DO NOT ENTER AFTER THE LAST LINE.

FINAL REVIEW

1. Hit your **Page Up Key** to take you to the top of your page. Click on the button in your Tool Bar that looks like a magnifying glass. While you won't actually be able to read the words, you will get an overall idea of how it looks on the page. When you are through viewing, click on the magnifying glass button to return to the regular screen.

2. To run a spell check, click on **Tools**, click on **Spell Check**, and begin the spell check process.

3. Proofread your resumé carefully. To print, click on **File** and click on **Print**. To print more than one copy, click on **Number of Copies** and type in the number you want; then enter. Click on **Print**. *As a word of caution, print just one copy the first time to make sure everything looks good. Then you can print more.*

4. To save your document to a floppy disk, click on **File**, click on **Save**, and type the path name as **a:\resume**; then enter.

5. To exit you must close your document by clicking on **File**, click on **Close**, click on **File**, and click on **Exit**.

DIRECTIONS FOR RESUMÉ NO. 2
WORDPERFECT 6.1 (WINDOWS)

GENERAL SETUP

1. From a clear screen, make sure you are in the Page Mode, with your Tool Bar, Power Bar, Ruler Bar, Status Bar, and Graphics visible—like this:

Tool Bar
Power Bar

If they are not visible, click on **View** and then click on **Page Mode**. Then click on **View** and click on **Tool Bar**. Then click on **View** and click on **Power Bar.** Then click on **View** and click on **Ruler Bar**. Then click on **View** and click on **Graphics**.

2. Click on **Format**, click on **Margins**, click on the down arrow key next to top margin until it reaches .5; then click on the down arrow key next to bottom margin until it reaches .5; then click on **OK**.

3. Click on **Format**, click on **Page**, click on **Center**, click on **Current Page**, and click on **OK**.

4. Click on **Format**, click on **Line**, click on **Tab Set**, click on **Absolute**, click on **Clear**, click on the box opposite **Position** and type **2.8** and enter. Click on **Format,** click on **Line**, click on **Tab Set**, click on the box opposite **Position** and type **5**; then enter.

MAIN HEADING SETUP

1. Looking at your Power Bar, click on the justification button where it says **Left▾**. Double click on **Center**.

2. Click on **Font** in your Power Bar where it says **Courier**, scroll down the list until you get to **Times New Roman**, then click on that choice. Click on the **Point Size** button in your Power Bar where it says **12 pt.** From the pull-down list of choices, click on **16**. Then click on **b (Bold)** in your Tool Bar.

3. Now type your name in all capitals. Then click on the **Point Size** button in the Power Bar and click on **12**. Then click on **b (Bold)** in your Tool Bar to turn it off. Enter twice.

4. Type your street address; then enter. Type your city, state, and zip code; then enter. Type your area code and phone number; then enter once.

5. Click on the justification button in the Power Bar, which is now set for **Center.** Click on **Left.** Then enter once more.

6. In your menu bar click on **Graphics.** Click on **Custom Line.** Click on **Line Style,** click on **thick/thin;** then click on **OK.** Then enter three times to continue.

CAREER OBJECTIVE SETUP

1. Click on **Point Size** in your Power Bar and click on **13.** Click on **b (Bold)** and *i* **(Italics)** in your Tool Bar. In all capitals type *CAREER OBJECTIVE.* Then click on **Point Size** again in your Power Bar and click on **12.** Then click on **b (Bold)** and *i* **(Italics)** in your Tool Bar to turn them off.

2. Click on **Format,** click on **Paragraph,** click on **Indent,** and type your career objective letting it word wrap at the end of the line. When you are through, enter twice.

EDUCATION SETUP

1. Click on **Point Size** in your Power Bar and click on **13.** Click on **b (Bold)** and *i* **(Italics)** in your Tool Bar. In all capitals type *EDUCATION.* Then click on **Point Size** in your Power Bar again and click on **12.** Then click on **b (Bold)** and *i* **(Italics)** in your Tool Bar to turn them off.

2. Tab and type the name of your most recent school; enter once.

3. Tab, type the street address, city, state, and zip code of your school; then enter once.

4. Tab, click on **b (Bold)** in your Tool Bar, type your course of study or degree received, click on **b (Bold)** in your Tool Bar to turn it off; then enter once.

5. Tab, type when you received your diploma or when it will be awarded, or the number of credits earned, if applicable; then enter twice.

6. Repeat Steps 2–5 for any other schools you want to list. Then enter twice to begin the next section.

AREAS OF SKILLS SETUP

1. Click on **Point Size** in your Power Bar and click on **13.** Click on **b (Bold)** and *i* **(Italics)** in your Tool Bar. In all capitals type

AREAS OF SKILLS. Then click on **Point Size** in your Power Bar again and click on **12**. Then click on **b (Bold)** and **i (Italics)** in your Tool Bar to turn them off.

2. Tab and type your first skill; then tab and type your second skill. Now enter and continue in the same manner until all skills have been listed. Hit enter twice when you are through with this section.

EXPERIENCE SETUP

1. Click on **Point Size** in your Power Bar and click on **13**. Click on **b (Bold)** and *i* **(Italics)** in your Tool Bar. In all capitals type *EXPERIENCE*. Then click on **Point Size** in your Power Bar again and click on **12**. Then click on **b (Bold)** and *i* **(Italics)** in your Tool Bar to turn them off.

2. Begin with your most recent experience first. Tab and type the name of the company. Then enter once.

3. Tab, type the street address, city, state, and zip code of the company; then enter once.

4. Type the dates you were employed, making sure that all digits align. Leave one space before and after the hyphen.

5. Then click on **Format**, click on **Paragraph,** and click on **Indent.** Click on **b (Bold)** in your Tool Bar, and type your job title followed by a colon; click on **b (Bold)** in your Tool Bar to turn it off. Now space twice and begin to type your job description, letting it word wrap at the end of the line. Enter twice.

6. Repeat Steps 2–5 until all your experience has been listed.

REFERENCE SETUP

1. Click on **Point Size** in your Power Bar and click on **13**. Click on **b (Bold)** and *i* **(Italics)** in your Power Bar. In all capitals type *REFERENCES*. Then click on **Point Size** again and click on **12**. Then click on **b (Bold)** and *i* **(Italics)** in your Power Bar to turn them off. Tab and type Provided upon Request.
   DO NOT ENTER AFTER THE LAST LINE.

FINAL REVIEW

1. Hit your **Page Up Key** to take you to the top of your page. Click on the button in your Tool Bar that looks like a magnifying glass. While you won't actually be able to read the

words, you will get an overall idea of how it looks on the page. When you are through viewing, click on the magnifying glass button to return to the regular screen.

2. To run a spell check, click on **Tools**, click on **Spell Check**, and begin the spell check process.

3. Proofread your resumé carefully. To print, click on **File** and click on **Print**. To print more than one copy, click on **Number of Copies** and type in the number you want; then enter. Click on **Print**. *As a word of caution, print just one copy the first time to make sure everything looks good. Then you can print more.*

4. To save your document to a floppy disk, click on **File**, click on **Save**, and type the path name as **a:\resume**; then enter.

5. To exit you must close your document by clicking on **File**, click on **Close**, click on **File**, and click on **Exit**.

DIRECTIONS FOR RESUMÉ NO. 3
WORDPERFECT 6.1 (WINDOWS)

GENERAL SETUP

1. From a clear screen, make sure you are in the Page Mode, with your Tool Bar, Power Bar, Ruler Bar, Status Bar, and Graphics visible—like this:

Tool Bar
Power Bar

If they are not visible, click on **View** and then click on **Page Mode**. Then click on **View** and click on **Tool Bar**. Then click on **View** and click on **Power Bar.** Then click on **View** and click on **Ruler Bar**. Then click on **View** and click on **Graphics**.

2. Click on **Format**, click on **Margins**, click on the down arrow key next to top margin until it reaches .5; then click on the down arrow key next to bottom margin until it reaches .5; then click on **OK**.

3. Click on **Format**, click on **Page**, click on **Center**, click on **Current Page**, and click on **OK**.

4. Click on **Format**, click on **Line**, click on **Tab Set**, click on **Absolute**, click on **Clear**, click on the box opposite **Position** and type **2.4;** and enter.

MAIN HEADING SETUP

1. Looking at your Power Bar, click on the justification button where it says **Left▾**. Double click on **Center**.

2. Click on **Font** in your Power Bar where it says **Courier**, scroll down the list until you get to **Times New Roman**, then click on that choice. Click on the **Point Size** button in your Power Bar where it says **12 pt.** From the pull-down list of choices, click on **16**. Then click on **b (Bold)** in your Tool Bar.

3. Now type your name in all capitals. Then click on the **Point Size** button in the Power Bar and click on **12**. Then click on **b (Bold)** in your Tool Bar to turn it off. Enter twice. Type your street address; then enter once. Type your city, state, and zip

code; then enter. Type your area code and phone number; then enter once.

4. Click on the justification button in the Power Bar, which is now set for **Center.** Click on **Left**. Then enter once more.

5. In your menu bar click on **Graphics**. Click on **Custom Line**. Click on **Line Style**. Click on **thin/thick**; click on **OK**. Then enter three times to continue.

CAREER OBJECTIVE SETUP

1. Click on **Point Size** in your Power Bar and click on **14**. Click on **b (Bold)** in your Tool Bar. In all capitals type **CAREER OBJECTIVE**. Then click on **Point Size** again and click on **12**. Then click on **b (Bold)** in your Tool Bar to turn it off. Enter twice and type your career objective letting it word wrap at the end of the line. When you are through, enter twice.

EXPERIENCE SETUP

1. Click on **Point Size** in your Power Bar and click on **14**. Click on **b (Bold)** in your Tool Bar. In all capitals type **EXPERIENCE**. Then click on **Point Size** again and click on **12**. Then click on **b (Bold)** in your Tool Bar to turn it off.

2. Begin with your most recent experience. Tab, click on **b (Bold)** in your Tool Bar and type the name of the company. Click on **b (Bold)** in your Tool Bar to turn it off. Then enter once.

3. Tab, type the street address, city, state, and zip code of the company; then enter once.

4. Type the beginning and ending years you were employed, making sure to leave a space before and after the hyphen.

5. Then tab, click on **b (Bold)** in your Tool Bar, and type your job title. Then click on **b (Bold)** in your Tool Bar to turn it off; then enter once.

6. Tab. To create the bullet hit **CTRL+W**, type **5,169**, then enter. If none of the items in this area will take more than one line, you may tab and start to type. However, if you think the description might wrap to a second line, then instead of tabbing, click on **Format**, click on **Paragraph**, click on **Indent**, and begin to type letting the lines word wrap. Enter once.

7. Repeat Steps 2–6 until all your experience has been listed; then enter twice to continue with next section.

EDUCATION SETUP

1. Click on **Point Size** in your Tool Bar and click on **14**. Click on **b (Bold)** in your Tool Bar. In all capitals type **EDUCATION**. Then click on **Point Size** again and click on **12**.

2. Tab and type the name of your most recent school. Then click on **b (Bold)** in your Tool Bar to turn it off; enter once.

3. Tab, type the street address, city, state, and zip code of your school; then enter once.

4. Type the beginning and ending year you attended that school leaving a space before and after the hyphen.

5. Tab, click on **b (Bold)** in your Tool Bar, type your course of study or degree received and your grade point average if it is above a 3.0; click on **b (Bold)** in your Tool Bar to turn it off and then enter once.

6. Tab, type the number of credits earned so far if you have not yet graduated or any academic honors received; then enter twice.

7. Repeat Steps 2–6 for any other schools you want to list. Then enter twice to begin the next section.

AFFILIATIONS SETUP

1. Click on **Point Size** in your Power Bar and click on **14**. Click on **b (Bold)** in your Tool Bar. In all capitals type **AFFILIA-TIONS**. Then click on **Point Size** again and click on **12**. Then click on **b (Bold)** in your Tool Bar to turn it off. Enter twice.

2. To create the bullet, hit **CTRL+W**, type **5,169**, then enter. Tab and type your first item. Then enter and repeat this step until all items have been included. Enter twice after the last item.

REFERENCE SETUP

1. Click on **Point Size** in your Power Bar and click on **11**. Hit **SHIFT+F6** (center) and type References Available upon Request.
   DO NOT ENTER AFTER THE LAST LINE.

FINAL REVIEW

1. Hit your **Page Up Key** to take you to the top of your page. Click on the button in your Tool Bar that looks like a magnifying glass. While you won't actually be able to read the

words, you will get an overall idea of how it looks on the page. When you are through viewing, click on the magnifying glass button to return to the regular screen.

2. To run a spell check, click on **Tools,** click on **Spell Check,** and begin the spell check process.

3. Proofread your resumé carefully. To print, click on **File** and click on **Print**. To print more than one copy, click on **Number of Copies** and type in the number you want; then enter. Click on **Print**. *As a word of caution, print just one copy the first time to make sure everything looks good. Then you can print more.*

4. To save your document to a floppy disk, click on **File**, click on **Save**, and type the path name as **a:\resume**; then enter.

5. To exit you must close your document by clicking on **File**, click on **Close**, click on **File**, and click on **Exit**.

DIRECTIONS FOR RESUMÉ NO. 4
WORDPERFECT 6.1 (WINDOWS)

GENERAL SETUP

1. From a clear screen, make sure you are in the Page Mode, with your Tool Bar, Power Bar, Ruler Bar, Status Bar, and Graphics visible—like this:

Tool Bar
Power Bar

If they are not visible, click on **View** and then click on **Page Mode**. Then click on **View** and click on **Tool Bar**. Then click on **View** and click on **Power Bar**. Then click on **View** and click on **Ruler Bar**. Then click on **View** and click on **Graphics.**

2. Click on **Format**, click on **Margins**, click on the down arrow key next to top margin until it reaches .5; then click on the down arrow key next to bottom margin until it reaches .5; then click on **OK**.

3. Click on **Format**, click on **Page**, click on **Center**, click on **Current Page**, and click on **OK**.

4. Click on **Format**, click on **Line**, click on **Tab Set**, click on **Absolute**, click on **Clear**, click on the box opposite **Position** and type **2.4;** and enter.

MAIN HEADING SETUP

1. Looking at your Power Bar, click on the justification button where it says **Left▾**. Click on **Center**.

2. Click on **Font** in your Power Bar and scroll down the list until you get to **Times New Roman**, then click on that choice. Click on the **Point Size** button in your Power Bar where it says **12 pt.** From the pull-down list of choices, click on **13**. Then click on **b (Bold)** in your Tool Bar.

3. Now type your name in all capitals. Then click on **Point Size** and click on **11**. Then click on **b (Bold)** in your Tool Bar to turn it off. Enter once.

4. Type your street address; then enter. Type your city, state, and zip code; then enter. Type your area code and phone number; then enter once.

5. Click on the justification button in the Power Bar, which is now set for **Center.** Click on **Left**. Then enter twice.

CAREER OBJECTIVE SETUP

1. Click on **Point Size** in your Power Bar and click on **12**. Hit **SHIFT+F6** (center) and click on **b (Bold)** and **u (Underline)** in your Tool Bar. In all capitals type **CAREER OBJECTIVE**. Then click on **b (Bold)** and **u (Underline)** in your Tool Bar to turn them off. Enter twice and type your career objective letting it word wrap at the end of the line. When you are through, enter twice.

EXPERIENCE SETUP

1. Hit **SHIFT+F6** (center). Click on **b (Bold)** and **u (Underline)** in your Tool Bar. In all capitals type **WORK EXPERIENCE**. Then click on **b (Bold)** and **u (Underline)** in your Tool Bar to turn them off. Enter twice.

2. Begin with your most recent experience by typing the dates you were employed, making sure that all the digits align. Leave one space before and after the hyphen. Then tab and in all capitals type the name of the company. Then enter once.

3. Tab, type the street address, city, state, and zip code of the company; then enter once.

4. Then tab, click on **b (Bold)** in your Tool Bar, and type your job title. Then click on **b (Bold)** in your Tool Bar to turn it off; then enter once.

5. Click on **Format**, click on **Paragraph**, click on **Indent**, and type your job description letting it word wrap; enter twice.

6. Repeat Steps 2–5 until all your experience has been listed. Hit enter twice to continue with next section.

EDUCATION SETUP

1. Hit **SHIFT+F6** (center). Click on **b (Bold)** and **u (Underline)** in your Tool Bar. In all capitals type **EDUCATION**; enter twice. Click on **b (bold)** in your Tool Bar to turn it off.

2. Begin with your most recent education by typing the dates you attended, making sure that all digits align. Leave one

space before and after the hyphen. Then tab and type the name of your school in all capitals; enter once.

3. Tab, type the street address, city, state, and zip code of your school; then enter once.

4. Tab, click on **b (Bold)** in your Tool Bar, type your course of study or degree received. Click on **b (Bold)** in your Tool Bar to turn it off and then enter once.

5. Tab and type when you received your diploma or when it will be awarded, or the number of credits earned, if applicable; then enter twice.

6. Repeat Steps 2–5 for any other schools you want to list. Then enter twice to begin the next section.

AREAS OF SKILLS SETUP

1. Click on **Format**, click on **Line**, click on **Tab Set**, click on **Absolute**, click on **Clear,** click on the box opposite **Position** and type **2.74** and enter. Click on **Format,** click on **Line**, click on **Tab Set**, click on the box opposite **Position**, and type **5.4**; then enter.

2. Hit **SHIFT+F6** (center), click on **b (Bold)** and **u (Underline)** in your Tool Bar and in all capitals type **AREAS OF SKILLS**. Click on **b (bold)** and **u (Underline)** to turn them off; then enter twice.

3. Type your first skill; tab and type your second skill; tab and type your third skill; then enter once. Repeat this step until all skills have been listed. Then enter twice to continue.

REFERENCE SETUP

1. Hit **SHIFT+F6** (center), click on **b (Bold)** and **u (Underline)** in your Tool Bar and in all capitals type **REFERENCES**. Click on **b (Bold)** and **u (Underline)** in your Tool Bar to turn them off; then enter twice.

2. Hit **SHIFT+F6** (center) and type Available upon Request.
   DO NOT ENTER AFTER THE LAST LINE.

FINAL REVIEW

1. Hit your **Page Up Key** to take you to the top of your page. Click on the button in your Tool Bar that looks like a magnifying glass. While you won't actually be able to read the words, you will get an overall idea of how it looks on the page.

When you are through viewing, click on the magnifying glass button to return to the regular screen.

2. To run a spell check, click on **Tools**, click on **Spell Check**, and begin the spell check process.

3. Proofread your resumé carefully. To print, click on **File** and click on **Print**. To print more than one copy, click on **Number of Copies** and type in the number you want; then enter. Click on **Print**. *As a word of caution, print just one copy the first time to make sure everything looks good. Then you can print more.*

4. To save your document to a floppy disk, click on **File**, click on **Save**, and type the path name as **a:\resume**; then enter.

5. To exit you must close your document by clicking on **File**, click on **Close**, click on **File**, and click on **Exit**.

DIRECTIONS FOR RESUMÉ No. 5
WORDPERFECT 6.1 (WINDOWS)

GENERAL SETUP

1. From a clear screen, make sure you are in the Page Mode, with your Tool Bar, Power Bar, Ruler Bar, Status Bar, and Graphics visible—like this:

Tool Bar
Power Bar

If they are not visible, click on **View** and then click on **Page Mode**. Then click on **View** and click on **Tool Bar**. Then click on **View** and click on **Power Bar.** Then click on **View** and click on **Ruler Bar**. Then click on **View** and click on **Graphics**.

2. Click on **Format**, click on **Margins**, click on the down arrow key next to top margin until it reaches .5; then click on the down arrow key next to bottom margin until it reaches .5; then click on **OK**.

3. Click on **Format**, click on **Page**, click on **Center**, click on **Current Page**, and click on **OK**.

4. Click on **Format**, click on **Line**, click on **Tab Set**, click on **Absolute**, click on **Clear**, click on the box opposite **Position** and type **3,** and enter. Click on **Format**, click on **Line**, click on **Tab Set**, click on the box opposite **Position** and type **3.31;** and enter. Click on **OK**.

MAIN HEADING SETUP

1. Looking at your Power Bar, click on the justification button where it says **Left▾**. Click on **Center**.

2. Click on **Font** in your Power Bar where it says **Courier**, scroll down the list until you get to **Times New Roman**, then click on that choice. Click on the **Point Size** button in your Power Bar where it says **12 pt.** From the pull-down list of choices, click on **14**. Then click on **b (Bold)** in your Tool Bar.

3. Now type your name in all capitals. Then click on the **Point Size** button in the Power Bar and click on **12**. Then click on **b (Bold)** in your Tool Bar to turn it off. Enter twice.

4. Type your street address; then enter. Type your city, state, and zip code; then enter. Type your area code and phone number; then enter once.

5. Click on the justification button in the Power Bar, which is now set for **Center.** Click on **Left**. Then enter once more.

6. In your menu bar click on **Graphics**. Click on **Custom Line**. Click on the arrow next to **Thickness** in the lower right corner of the screen until it reaches **.047**; click on **OK**; then enter three times to continue.

CAREER OBJECTIVE SETUP

1. Click on **Point Size** in your Power Bar and click on **13**. Click on **b (Bold)** and *i* **(Italics)** in your Tool Bar. In all capitals type *CAREER OBJECTIVE*. Then click on **Point Size** again and click on **12**. Then click on **b (Bold)** and *i* **(Italics)** in your Tool Bar to turn them off.

2. Click on **Format**, click on **Paragraph**, click on **Indent** and type your career objective letting it word wrap at the end of the line. When you are through, enter twice.

EDUCATION SETUP

1. Click on **Point Size** in your Power Bar and click on **13**. Click on **b (Bold)** and *i* **(Italics)** in your Tool Bar. In all capitals type *EDUCATION*. Then click on **Point Size** again and click on **12**. Then click on **b (Bold)** and *i* **(Italics)** in your Tool Bar to turn them off.

2. Tab and begin with your most recent education by typing the name of the school. Enter once.

3. Tab and type the street address. Enter once.

4. Tab and type the city, state, and zip code of your school; then enter once.

5. Tab, click on **b (Bold)** in your Tool Bar, type your course of study or degree received, click on **b (Bold)** in your Tool Bar to turn it off; then enter once.

6. Tab, type when you received your diploma or when it will be awarded, or the number of credits earned, if applicable; then enter twice.

7. Repeat Steps 2–6 for any other schools you want to list. Then enter twice to begin the next section.

EXPERIENCE SETUP

1. Click on **Point Size** in your Power Bar and click on **13**. Click on **b (Bold)** and *i* **(Italics)** in your Tool Bar. In all capitals type ***EXPERIENCE***. Then click on **Point Size** again and click on **12**. Then click on **b (Bold)** and *i* **(Italics)** in your Tool Bar to turn them off.

2. Tab and begin with your most recent experience by typing the name of the company; then enter once.

3. Tab and type the street address; then enter once.

4. Tab and type the city, state, and zip code of the company; then enter once.

5. Tab, click on **b (Bold)** in your Tool Bar, and type your job title, click on **b (Bold)** in your Tool Bar to turn it off; then enter once.

6. Tab and type your dates of employment leaving one space before and after the hyphen; then enter twice.

7. Repeat Steps 2–6 until all experience has been listed.

AFFILIATIONS SETUP

1. Click on **Point Size** in your Power Bar and click on **13**. Click on **b (Bold)** and *i* **(Italics)** in your Tool Bar. In all capitals type ***AFFILIATIONS***. Then click on **Point Size** again and click on **12**. Then click on **b (Bold)** and *i* **(Italics)** in your Tool Bar to turn them off.

2. Tab. To create the bullet hit **CTRL+W** and type **5,226**; then enter. Tab and type the name of the organization; then enter once. Repeat this step until all items have been listed. Enter twice to begin next section.

AWARDS/HONORS SETUP

1. Click on **Point Size** in your Power Bar and click on **13**. Click on **b (Bold)** and *i* **(Italics)** in your Tool Bar. In all capitals type ***AWARDS/HONORS***. Then click on **Point Size** again and click on **12**. Then click on **b (Bold)** and *i* **(Italics)** in your Tool Bar to turn them off.

2. Tab. To create the bullet hit **CTRL+W** and type **5,226**; then enter. Tab and type the name of the award or honor; then enter once. Repeat this step until all items have been listed. Enter twice to begin next section.

REFERENCE SETUP

1. Click on **Point Size** in your Power Bar and click on **13**. Click on **b (Bold)** and *i* **(Italics)** in your Tool Bar. In all capitals type ***REFERENCES***. Then click on **Point Size** again and click on **12**. Then click on **b (Bold)** and *i* **(Italics)** in your Tool Bar to turn them off. Tab and type Available upon Request.

   ### DO NOT ENTER AFTER THE LAST LINE.

FINAL REVIEW

1. Hit your **Page Up Key** to take you to the top of your page. Click on the button in your Tool Bar that looks like a magnifying glass. While you won't actually be able to read the words, you will get an overall idea of how it looks on the page. When you are through viewing, click on the magnifying glass button to return to the regular screen.

2. To run a spell check, click on **Tools**, click on **Spell Check**, and begin the spell check process.

3. Proofread your resumé carefully. To print, click on **File** and click on **Print**. To print more than one copy, click on **Number of Copies** and type in the number you want; then enter. Click on **Print**. *As a word of caution, print just one copy the first time to make sure everything looks good. Then you can print more.*

4. To save your document to a floppy disk, click on **File**, click on **Save**, and type the path name as **a:\resume**; then enter.

5. To exit you must close your document by clicking on **File**, click on **Close**, click on **File**, and click on **Exit**.

DIRECTIONS FOR RESUMÉ NO. 6
WORDPERFECT 6.1 (WINDOWS)

GENERAL SETUP

1. From a clear screen, make sure you are in the Page Mode, with your Tool Bar, Power Bar, Ruler Bar, Status Bar, and Graphics visible—like this:

Tool Bar
Power Bar

If they are not visible, click on **View** and then click on **Page Mode**. Then click on **View** and click on **Tool Bar**. Then click on **View** and click on **Power Bar.** Then click on **View** and click on **Ruler Bar**. Then click on **View** and click on **Graphics**.

2. Click on **Format**, click on **Margins**, click on the down arrow key next to top margin until it reaches .5; then click on the down arrow key next to bottom margin until it reaches .5; then click on **OK**.

3. Click on **Format**, click on **Page**, click on **Center**, click on **Current Page**, and click on **OK**.

4. Click on **Format**, click on **Line**, click on **Tab Set**, click on **Absolute**, click on **Clear**, click on the box opposite **Position** and type **3** and enter. Click on **Format**, click on **Line**, click on **Tab Set**, click on the box opposite **Position** and type **3.44** and enter. Click on **Format**, click on **Line**, click on **Tab Set**, click on the box opposite **Position** and type **6** and enter. Click on **OK**.

MAIN HEADING SETUP

1. Hit **SHIFT+F6** (center).

2. Click on the **Font Button** in your Power Bar where it says **Courier**, scroll down the list until you get to **Times New Roman**, then click on that choice. Click on the **Point Size** button in your Power Bar and click on **16**. Then click on **b (Bold)** in your Tool Bar.

3. Now type your name in all capitals. Then click on **Point Size** and click on **12**. Enter twice.

4. Type **Home Address:**, tab 3 times, and type **School Address:** and enter twice. Then click on **Point Size** click on **11**. Click on **b (Bold)** in your Tool Bar to turn it off.

5. Type your home street address; then tab three times and type your school street address; enter once.

6. Type your home city, state, and zip code; tab three times and type your school city, state, and zip code; then enter once.

7. Type your home area code and phone number; tab three times and type your school area code and phone number; then enter twice.

8. In your menu bar click on **Graphics**. Click on **Custom Line**. Click on **Line Style** and from the pull-down list of choices, click on **Double**; click on **OK**. Then enter three times to continue with next section.

CAREER OBJECTIVE SETUP

1. Click on **Point Size** in your Power Bar and click on **14**. Click on **b (Bold)** and *i (Italics)* in your Tool Bar. In all capitals type ***CAREER OBJECTIVE***. Then click on **Point Size** again and click on **12**. Then click on **b (Bold)** and *i (Italics)* in your Tool Bar to turn them off. Now enter twice and type your career objective letting it word wrap at the end of the line. When you are through, enter twice.

EDUCATION SETUP

1. Click on **Point Size** in your Power Bar and click on **14**. Click on **b (Bold)** and *i (Italics)* in your Tool Bar. In all capitals type ***EDUCATION*** and enter twice. Then click on **Point Size** again and click on **12**. Then click on **b (Bold)** and *i (Italics)* in your Tool Bar to turn them off.

2. Type the beginning and ending year you attended the school leaving one space before and after the hyphen. Tab, click on **b (Bold)** in your Tool Bar, and type the name of your most recent school in all capitals. Click on **b (Bold)** in your Tool Bar to turn it off; then enter once.

3. Tab, type the street address, city, state, and zip code of your school; then enter once.

4. Tab and type what type of diploma you will receive and when; then enter twice.

5. Repeat Steps 2–4 for any other schools you want to list. Then enter twice to begin the next section.

EXPERIENCE SETUP

1. Click on **Point Size** in your Power Bar and click on **14**. Click on **b (Bold)** and *i* **(Italics)** in your Tool Bar. In all capitals type *EXPERIENCE*. Then click on **Point Size** again and click on **12**. Then click on **b (Bold)** and *i* **(Italics)** in your Tool Bar to turn them off. Enter twice.

2. Begin with your most recent experience. Type the dates of your employment. Tab, click on **b (Bold)** in your Tool Bar and type the name of the company in all capitals. Click on **b (Bold)** in your Tool Bar to turn it off; then enter once.

3. Tab, type the street address, city, state, and zip code of the company; then enter once.

4. Then click on **Format**, click on **Paragraph**, and click on **Indent**. Click on **b (Bold)** in your Tool Bar and type your job title followed by a colon; click on **b (Bold)** in your Tool Bar to turn it off. Now space twice and begin to type your job description, letting it word wrap at the end of the line. Enter twice.

5. Repeat Steps 2–4 until all your experience has been listed. Then enter twice to begin the next section.

ACTIVITIES SETUP

1. Click on **Point Size** in your Power Bar and click on **14**. Click on **b (Bold)** and *i* **(Italics)** in your Tool Bar. In all capitals type *ACTIVITIES*. Then click on **Point Size** again and click on **12**. Then click on **b (Bold)** and *i* **(Italics)** in your Tool Bar to turn them off.

2. Tab. To create the bullet, hit **CTRL+W** and type **5,18**; then enter. Tab and type your first activity; enter once.

3. Repeat Step 2 until all activities have been listed. Then enter twice to continue with next section.

REFERENCE SETUP

1. Click on the **Point Size** button in your Power Bar and click on **14**. Click on **b (Bold)** and *i* **(Italics)** in your Tool Bar. In all capitals type *REFERENCES*. Then click on **Point Size** again and click on **12**. Then click on **b (Bold)** and *i* **(Italics)** in your Tool Bar to turn them off. Tab and type Available upon Request.

DO NOT ENTER AFTER THE LAST LINE.

FINAL REVIEW

1. Hit your **Page Up Key** to take you to the top of your page. Click on the button in your Tool Bar that looks like a magnifying glass. While you won't actually be able to read the words, you will get an overall idea of how it looks on the page. When you are through viewing, click on the magnifying glass button to return to the regular screen.

2. To run a spell check, click on **Tools**, click on **Spell Check**, and begin the spell check process.

3. Proofread your resumé carefully. To print, click on **File** and click on **Print**. To print more than one copy, click on **Number of Copies** and type in the number you want; then enter. Click on **Print**. *As a word of caution, print just one copy the first time to make sure everything looks good. Then you can print more.*

4. To save your document to a floppy disk, click on **File**, click on **Save**, and type the path name as **a:\resume**; then enter.

5. To exit you must close your document by clicking on **File**, click on **Close**, click on **File**, and click on **Exit**.

DIRECTIONS FOR RESUMÉ NO. 7
WORDPERFECT 6.1 (WINDOWS)

GENERAL SETUP

1. From a clear screen, make sure you are in the Page Mode, with your Tool Bar, Power Bar, Ruler Bar, Status Bar, and Graphics visible—like this:

Tool Bar
Power Bar

If they are not visible, click on **View** and then click on **Page Mode**. Then click on **View** and click on **Tool Bar**. Then click on **View** and click on **Power Bar.** Then click on **View** and click on **Ruler Bar**. Then click on **View** and click on **Graphics**.

2. Click on **Format**, click on **Margins**, click on the down arrow key next to top margin until it reaches .5; then click on the down arrow key next to bottom margin until it reaches .5; then click on **OK**.

3. Click on **Format**, click on **Page**, click on **Center**, click on **Current Page**, and click on **OK**.

4. Click on **Format**, click on **Line**, click on **Tab Set**, click on **Absolute**, click on **Clear**, click on the box opposite **Position** and type **2.5;** and enter. Click on **Format**, click on **Line**, click on **Tab Set**, click on the box opposite **Position** and type **5.38;** and enter. Click on **Format**, click on **Line**, click on **Tab Set**, click on the box opposite **Position** and type **6;** and enter. Click on **OK**.

MAIN HEADING SETUP

1. Hit **SHIFT+F6** (center).

2. Click on **Font** in your Power Bar, click on **1** (font), scroll down the list until you get to **Times New Roman**, then click on that choice. Click on the **Point Size** button on your Power Bar and click on **18**. Then click on **b (Bold)** in your Tool Bar.

3. Now type your name in all capitals. Then click on **Point Size** and click on **12**. Enter twice.

4. Type **School Address**, tab 3 times, and type **Home Address** and enter once. Click on **b (Bold)** in your Tool Bar to turn it off.

5. Type your school street address; then tab three times and type your home street address; enter once.

6. Type your school city, state, and zip code; tab three times and type your home city, state, and zip code; then enter once.

7. Type your school area code and phone number; tab three times and type your home area code and phone number; then enter once.

8. In your menu bar click on **Graphics**. Click on **Custom Line**. Click on the arrow next to **Thickness** in the lower right corner of the screen until it reaches **.04**; click on **OK**. Then enter twice to continue.

CAREER OBJECTIVE SETUP

1. Click on **Point Size** in your Power Bar and click on **14**. Click on **b (Bold)** and *i* **(Italics)** in your Tool Bar. In all capitals type *OBJECTIVE*. Then click on **Point Size** in your Power Bar again and click on **12**. Then click on **b (Bold)** and *i* **(Italics)** in your Tool Bar to turn them off. Click on **Format**, click on **Paragraph**, click on **Indent**, and type your career objective letting it word wrap at the end of the line. When you are through, enter twice.

EDUCATION SETUP

1. Click on **Point Size** in your Power Bar and click on **14**. Click on **b (Bold)** and *i* **(Italics)** in your Tool Bar. In all capitals type *EDUCATION.*

2. Then click on **Point Size** and click on **12**. Then click on *i* **(Italics)** in your Tool Bar to turn it off.

3. Tab and type the name of your most recent school in all capitals followed by the city, state, and zip code. Click on **b (Bold)** in your Tool Bar to turn it off; then enter once.

4. Click on **Point Size** in your Power Bar and click on **10**. Tab. To create the bullet, hit **CTRL+W** and type **5,228**; then enter once. Space once and type your college of study followed by the grade point for those courses required for graduation by that college.

5. Then tab, create a bullet by hitting **CTRL+W** and again typing **5,228**; then enter. Space once and type your overall grade point average. Enter once.

6. Tab and create a bullet by hitting **CTRL+W** and typing **5,228**; then enter. Space once and type your major area of concentration and the grade point for only those classes.

7. Tab and create a bullet by hitting **CTRL+W** and type **5,228**; then enter. Space once and type your date of graduation. Enter twice.

8. Repeat Steps 2–7 until all your education has been listed.

EXPERIENCE SETUP

1. Click on **Point Size** in your Power Bar and click on **14**. Click on **b (Bold)** and *i* **(Italics)** in your Tool Bar. In all capitals type *EXPERIENCE*.

2. Then click on **Point Size** again and click on **12**. Then click on **b (Bold)** and *i* **(Italics)** in your Tool Bar to turn them off.

3. Tab. Begin with your most recent experience. Click on **b (Bold)** in your Tool Bar and type the name of the company in all capitals followed by the city, state, and zip code. Enter once.

4. Click on **Point Size** in your Power Bar and click on **10**. Then tab and type your job title followed by your dates of employment in parentheses. Click on **b (Bold)** in your Tool Bar to turn it off. Enter once.

5. Tab and create the bullet by hitting **CTRL+W**, type **5,228**, and hit enter. Space once and begin to list your responsibilities and accomplishments on the job. Enter twice.

6. Repeat Steps 2–5 until all your experience has been listed.

AFFILIATIONS SETUP

1. Click on **Point Size** in your Power Bar and click on **14**. Click on **b (Bold)** and *i* **(Italics)** in your Tool Bar. In all capitals type *AFFILIATIONS*.

2. Then click on **Point Size** again and click on **12**. Then click on *i* **(Italics)** in your Tool Bar to turn it off.

3. Tab and type the organization's name in all capitals. Click on **b (Bold)** in your Tool Bar to turn it off. Enter once.

4. Tab. To create the bullet, hit **CTRL+W** and type **5,228**; then space once and type your first responsibility; enter once.

5. Repeat Steps 2–4 until all responsibilities for that organization have been listed. Then enter twice.

6. Repeat Steps 3–5 until all affiliations have been listed. Enter twice to continue with next section.

QUALIFICATIONS SETUP

1. Click on **Point Size** in your Power Bar and click on **14**. Click on **b (Bold)** and *i* **(Italics)** in your Tool Bar. In all capitals type *QUALIFICATIONS*.

2. Then click on **Point Size** again and click on **10**. Then click on **b (Bold)** and *i* **(Italics)** in your Tool Bar to turn them off.

3. Tab and create a bullet by hitting **CTRL+W**, then type **5,228** and enter once. Space once and begin to list your qualifications.

4. Repeat Step 3 until all qualifications have been listed. Then enter twice to continue with next section.

REFERENCES SETUP

1. Hit **SHIFT+F6** (center) and type in all capitals REFERENCES AVAILABLE UPON REQUEST.

   ### DO NOT ENTER AFTER THE LAST LINE.

FINAL REVIEW

1. Hit your **Page Up Key** to take you to the top of your page. Click on the button in your Tool Bar that looks like a magnifying glass. While you won't actually be able to read the words, you will get an overall idea of how it looks on the page. When you are through viewing, click on the magnifying glass button to return to the regular screen.

2. To run a spell check, click on **Tools**, click on **Spell Check**, and begin the spell check process.

3. Proofread your resumé carefully. To print, click on **File** and click on **Print**. To print more than one copy, click on **Number of Copies** and type in the number you want; then enter. Click on **Print**. *As a word of caution, print just one copy the first time to make sure everything looks good. Then you can print more.*

4. To save your document to a floppy disk, click on **File**, click on **Save**, and type the path name as **a:\resume**; then enter.

5. To exit you must close your document by clicking on **File**, click on **Close**, click on **File**, and click on **Exit**.

DIRECTIONS FOR RESUMÉ NO. 8
WORDPERFECT 6.1 (WINDOWS)

GENERAL SETUP

1. From a clear screen, make sure you are in the Page Mode, with your Tool Bar, Power Bar, Ruler Bar, Status Bar, and Graphics visible—like this:

 Tool Bar
Power Bar

If they are not visible, click on **View** and then click on **Page Mode**. Then click on **View** and click on **Tool Bar**. Then click on **View** and click on **Power Bar**. Then click on **View** and click on **Ruler Bar**. Then click on **View** and click on **Graphics**.

2. Click on **Format**, click on **Margins**, click on the down arrow key next to top margin until it reaches .5; then click on the down arrow key next to bottom margin until it reaches .5; then click on **OK**.

3. Click on **Format**, click on **Page**, click on **Center**, click on **Current Page**, and click on **OK**.

4. Click on **Format**, click on **Line**, click on **Tab Set**, click on **Absolute**, click on **Clear**, click on the box opposite **Position** and type **3** and enter. Click on **Format**, click on **Line**, click on **Tab Set**, click on the box opposite **Position** and type **3.25** and enter. Click on **OK**.

MAIN HEADING SETUP

1. Looking at your Power Bar, click on the justification button where it says **Left▾**. Click on **Center**.

2. Click on **Font** in your Power Bar where it says **Courier**, scroll down the list until you get to **Times New Roman**, then click on that choice. Click on the **Point Size** button in your Power Bar where it says **12 pt**. From the pull-down list of choices, click on **14**. Then click on **b (Bold)** in your Tool Bar.

3. Now type your name in all capitals. Then click on **Point Size** and click on **12**. Then click on **b (Bold)** in your Tool Bar to turn it off. Enter twice.

4. Type your street address; then enter. Type your city, state, and zip code; then enter. Type your area code and phone number; then enter twice.

5. Click on the justification button in the Power Bar, which is now set for **Center.** Click on **Left**. Then enter once more.

6. In your menu bar click on **Graphics**. Click on **Custom Line**. Click on **Line Style** and from the pull-down list of choices, click on **Double Line**; click on **OK**. Then enter three times to continue with next section.

CAREER OBJECTIVE SETUP

1. Click on **b (Bold)** and **u (Underline)** in your Tool Bar. In all capitals type **OBJECTIVE**. Then click on **b (Bold)** and **u (Underline)** in your Tool Bar to turn them off.

2. Click on **Format**, click on **Paragraph**, click on **Indent**, and type your career objective letting it word wrap at the end of the line. When you are through, enter three times.

EDUCATION SETUP

1. Click on **b (Bold)** and **u (Underline)** in your Tool Bar. In all capitals type **EDUCATION**. Then click on **b (Bold)** and **u (Underline)** in your Tool Bar to turn them off.

2. Tab and begin with your most recent education by typing the name of the school. Enter once.

3. Tab and type the street address. Enter once.

4. Tab and type the city, state, and zip code of your school; then enter once.

5. Tab and type your course of study or degree received and the date; then enter twice.

6. Repeat Steps 2–5 for any other schools you want to list. Then enter three times to begin the next section.

EXPERIENCE SETUP

1. Click on **b (Bold)** and **u (Underline)** in your Tool Bar. In all capitals type **EXPERIENCE**. Then click on **u (Underline)** in your Tool Bar to turn it off.

2. Tab and begin with your most recent experience by typing your job title. Click on **b (Bold)** to turn it off; then enter once.

3. Tab and type the company name; then enter once.

4. Tab and type the street address; then enter once.

5. Tab and type the city, state, and zip code of the company; then enter once.

6. Tab and type your dates of employment; enter twice.

7. Repeat Steps 2–6 until all experience has been listed. Enter three times to begin the next section.

ACCOMPLISHMENTS SETUP

1. Click on **b (Bold)** and **u (Underline)** in your Tool Bar. In all capitals type **ACCOMPLISHMENTS**. Then click on **b (Bold)** and **u (Underline)** in your Tool Bar to turn them off.

2. Tab. To create the bullet hit **CTRL+W** and type **4,2**; then enter. Click on **Format**, click on **Paragraph**, click on **Indent**, and type your first accomplishment letting it word wrap at the end of the line; then enter twice. Repeat this step until all items have been listed. Enter three times to begin the final section.

REFERENCE SETUP

1. Click on **b (Bold)** and **u (Underline)** in your Tool Bar. In all capitals type **REFERENCES**. Then click on **b (Bold)** and **u (Underline)** in your Power Bar to turn them off.

2. Tab and type Available upon Request.

   DO NOT ENTER AFTER THE LAST LINE.

FINAL REVIEW

1. Hit your **Page Up Key** to take you to the top of your page. Click on the button in your Tool Bar that looks like a magnifying glass. While you won't actually be able to read the words, you will get an overall idea of how it looks on the page. When you are through viewing, click on the magnifying glass button to return to the regular screen.

2. To run a spell check, click on **Tools**, click on **Spell Check**, and begin the spell check process.

3. Proofread your resumé carefully. To print, click on **File** and click on **Print**. To print more than one copy, click on **Number of Copies** and type in the number you want; then enter. Click on **Print**. *As a word of caution, print just one copy the first time to make sure everything looks good. Then you can print more.*

4. To save your document to a floppy disk, click on **File**, click on **Save**, and type the path name as **a:\resume**; then enter.

5. To exit you must close your document by clicking on **File**, click on **Close**, click on **File**, and click on **Exit**.

> ## DIRECTIONS FOR RESUMÉ NO. 9
> ## WORDPERFECT 6.1 (WINDOWS)

GENERAL SETUP

1. From a clear screen, make sure you are in the Page Mode, with your Tool Bar, Power Bar, Ruler Bar, Status Bar, and Graphics visible—like this:

Tool Bar
Power Bar

If they are not visible, click on **View** and then click on **Page Mode**. Then click on **View** and click on **Tool Bar**. Then click on **View** and click on **Power Bar**, click on **View** and click on **Ruler Bar**. Then click on **View** and click on **Graphics**.

2. Click on **Format**, click on **Margins**, click on the down arrow key next to top margin until it reaches .5; then click on the down arrow key next to bottom margin until it reaches .5; then click on **OK**.

3. Click on **Format**, click on **Page**, click on **Center**, click on **Current Page**, and click on **OK**.

4. Click on **Format**, click on **Line**, click on **Tab Set**, click on **Absolute**, click on **Clear**, click on the box opposite **Position** and type **2.8** and enter. Click on **Format**, click on **Line**, click on **Tab Set**, click on the box opposite **Position** and type **3.16**; then enter.

MAIN HEADING SETUP

1. Looking at your Power Bar, click on the justification button where it says **Left▾**. Click on **Center**.

2. Click on the **Font** button in your Power Bar where it says **Courier**, scroll down the list until you get to **Times New Roman**, then click on that choice. Click on the **Point Size** button in your Power Bar where it says **12 pt**. From the pull-down list of choices, click on **14**. Then click on **b (Bold)** in your Tool Bar.

3. Now type your name in all capitals. Then click on **Point Size** and click on **12**. Then click on **b (Bold)** in your Tool Bar to turn it off. Enter once.

4. Type your street address; then enter. Type your city, state, and zip code; then enter. Type your area code and phone number; then enter once.

5. Click on the justification button in the Power Bar, which is now set for **Center.** Click on **Left.** Then enter twice.

CAREER OBJECTIVE SETUP

1. Click on **b (Bold)** in your Tool Bar. In all capitals type **CAREER OBJECTIVE:.** Then click on **b (Bold)** in your Tool Bar to turn it off. Click on **Format**, click on **Paragraph**, click on **Indent**, and begin to type your objective letting it word wrap at the end of the line. Now enter three times.

QUALIFICATIONS SETUP

1. Click on **b (Bold)** in your Tool Bar. In all capitals type **QUALIFI-CATIONS:.** Then click on **b (Bold)** in your Tool Bar to turn it off.

2. Click on **Format**, click on **Paragraph**, and click on **Indent**. To create the bullet, hit **CTRL+W** and type **4,0**; then enter once. Tab and type your first qualification; enter once.

3. Repeat Step 2 until all qualifications have been listed. Then enter three times to begin the next section.

EDUCATION SETUP

1. Click on **b (Bold)** in your Tool Bar. In all capitals type **EDUCA-TION:.**

2. Tab. Begin with your most recent education by typing the name of the school. Then click on **b (Bold)** in your Tool Bar to turn it off; enter once.

3. Tab, type the city, state, and zip code of your school; then enter once.

4. Tab, click on *i* **(Italics)** and **b (Bold)** in your Tool Bar, type your course of study or degree received and the date; click on *i* **(Italics)** and **b (Bold)** in your Tool Bar to turn them off and then enter twice.

5. Repeat Steps 2–4 for any other schools you want to list. Then enter three times to begin the next section.

EXPERIENCE SETUP

1. Click on **b (Bold)** in your Tool Bar. In all capitals type **EXPE-**

RIENCE:. Then click on **b (Bold)** in your Tool Bar to turn it off. Enter twice.

2. Begin with your most recent experience by typing the dates you were employed, making sure that all digits align. Leave one space before and after the hyphen. Then tab, click on **b (Bold)** in your Tool Bar, and type the name of the company. Then click on **b (Bold)** in your Tool Bar to turn it off; enter once.

3. Tab, type the city, state, and zip code of the company; then enter once.

4. Tab, click on **i (Italics)** and **b (Bold)** in your Tool Bar, and type your job title, click on **i (Italics)** and **b (Bold)** in your Tool Bar to turn them off; then enter once.

5. Click on **Format**, click on **Paragraph**, click on **Indent**, and begin to type your job description letting it word wrap. Enter twice.

6. Repeat Steps 2–5 until all experience has been listed. Then enter three times to continue with the next section.

ACCOMPLISHMENTS SETUP

1. Click on **b (Bold)** in your Tool Bar and type **ACCOMPLISH-MENTS:**. Click on **b (Bold)** in your Tool Bar to turn it off.

2. Tab and create the bullet by hitting **CTRL+W** and typing **4,0**; then enter once. Tab and list your first accomplishment.

3. Repeat Step 2 until all of your accomplishments have been listed. Then enter three times to continue with the next section.

REFERENCE SETUP

1. Click on **b (Bold)** in your Tool Bar. In all capitals type **REFER-ENCES:**. Then click on **b (Bold)** in your Tool Bar to turn it off. Tab and type Available upon Request.
   DO NOT ENTER AFTER THE LAST LINE.

FINAL REVIEW

1. Hit your **Page Up Key** to take you to the top of your page. Click on the button in your Tool Bar that looks like a magnifying glass. While you won't actually be able to read the words, you will get an overall idea of how it looks on the page. When you are through viewing, click on the magnifying glass button to return to the regular screen.

2. To run a spell check, click on **Tools**, click on **Spell Check**, and begin the spell check process.

3. Proofread your resumé carefully. To print, click on **File** and click on **Print**. To print more than one copy, click on **Number of Copies** and type in the number you want; then enter. Click on **Print**. *As a word of caution, print just one copy the first time to make sure everything looks good. Then you can print more.*

4. To save your document to a floppy disk, click on **File**, click on **Save**, and type the path name as **a:\resume**; then enter.

5. To exit you must close your document by clicking on **File**, click on **Close**, click on **File**, and click on **Exit**.

**DIRECTIONS FOR RESUMÉ NO. 10
WORDPERFECT 6.1 (WINDOWS)**

GENERAL SETUP

1. From a clear screen, make sure you are in the Page Mode, with your Tool Bar, Power Bar, Ruler Bar, Status Bar, and Graphics visible—like this:

Tool Bar
Power Bar

If they are not visible, click on **View** and then click on **Page Mode**. Then click on **View** and click on **Tool Bar**. Then click on **View** and click on **Power Bar.** Then click on **View** and click on **Ruler Bar**. Then click on **View** and click on **Graphics**.

2. Click on **Format**, click on **Margins**, click on the down arrow key next to top margin until it reaches .5; then click on the down arrow key next to bottom margin until it reaches .5; then click on **OK**.

3. Click on **Format**, click on **Page**, click on **Center**, click on **Current Page**, and click on **OK**.

4. Click on **Format**, click on **Line**, click on **Tab Set**, click on **Absolute**, click on **Clear**, click on the box opposite **Position** and type **3;** and enter. Click on **Format,** click on **Line**, click on **Tab Set**, click on the box opposite **Position** and type **3.25;** then enter.

MAIN HEADING SETUP

1. Looking at your Power Bar, click on the justification button where it says **Left▾**. Click on **Center**.

2. Click on **Font** in your Power Bar where it says **Courier**, scroll down the list until you get to **Times New Roman**, then click on that choice. Click on the **Point Size** button in your Power Bar where it says **12 pt**. From the pull-down list of choices, click on **12**. Then click on **b (Bold)** in your Tool Bar.

3. Now type your name in all capitals. Then click on **b (Bold)** in your Tool Bar to turn it off. Enter twice.

4. Type your street address; then enter. Type your city, state, and zip code; then enter. Type your area code and phone number; then enter twice.

5. Click on the justification button in the Power Bar, which is now set for **Center.** Click on **Left.** Then enter once more.

6. In your menu bar click on **Graphics.** Click on **Custom Line.** Click on **Line Style,** click on **CyanMat,** and click on **OK;** then enter three times to continue with next section.

CAREER OBJECTIVE SETUP

1. Click on **b (Bold)** in your Tool Bar. In all capitals type **CAREER OBJECTIVE:.** Then click on **b (Bold)** in your Tool Bar to turn it off.

2. Click on **Format,** click on **Paragraph,** click on **Indent,** and type your career objective letting it word wrap at the end of the line. When you are through, enter three times.

QUALIFICATIONS SETUP

1. Click on **b (Bold)** in your Tool Bar. In all capitals type **QUALIFI-CATIONS:.**Then click on **b (bold)** in your Tool Bar to turn it off.

2. Tab and create the bullet by hitting **CTRL+W** and typing **4,47**; then enter. Click on **Format,** click on **Paragraph,** click on **Indent,** and type your first qualification letting it word wrap if it takes more than one line; enter once.

3. Repeat Step 2 until all qualifications have been listed. Then enter three times to continue with the next section.

SKILLS SETUP

1. Click on **b (Bold)** in your Tool Bar. In all capitals type **SKILLS:.** Then click on **b (Bold)** in your Tool Bar to turn it off.

2. Tab and create the bullet by hitting **CTRL+W** and typing **4,47**; then enter. Now tab and type your first skill; enter once.

3. Repeat Step 2 until all skills have been listed. Then enter three times to continue with the next section.

EDUCATION SETUP

1. Click on **b (Bold)** in your Tool Bar. In all capitals type **EDUCA-TION:.**

2. Tab, click on *i* **(Italics)** in your Tool Bar, and begin with your most recent education by typing the name of the school in all capitals. Click on **b (Bold)** and *i* **(Italics)** in your Tool Bar to turn them off. Enter once.

3. Tab and type the street address. Enter once.

4. Tab and type the city, state, and zip code of your school; then enter once.

5. Tab, click on **b (Bold)** in your Tool Bar, type your course of study or degree received and the date; click on **b (Bold)** in your Tool Bar to turn it off; then enter twice.

6. Repeat Steps 2–5 for any other schools you want to list. Then enter three times to begin the next section.

EXPERIENCE SETUP

1. Click on **b (Bold)** in your Tool Bar. In all capitals type **EXPE-RIENCE:**.

2. Tab, click on *i* **(Italics)** in your Tool Bar, and begin with your most recent experience by typing the name of the company in all capitals. Click on **b (Bold)** and *i* **(Italics)** in your Tool Bar to turn them off; then enter once.

3. Tab and type the street address; then enter once.

4. Tab and type the city, state, and zip code of the company; then enter once.

5. Tab, click on **b (Bold)** in your Tool Bar, and type your job title followed by the dates of your employment in parentheses. Click on **b (Bold)** in your Tool Bar to turn it off; then enter twice.

6. Repeat Steps 2–5 until all experience has been listed. Enter three times to continue with the last section.

REFERENCE SETUP

1. Click on **b (Bold)** in your Tool Bar. In all capitals type **REFER-ENCES:**. Then click on **b (Bold)** in your Tool Bar to turn it off. Tab and type Available upon Request.
   DO NOT ENTER AFTER THE LAST LINE.

FINAL REVIEW

1. Hit your **Page Up Key** to take you to the top of your page. Click on the button in your Tool Bar that looks like a magnifying

glass. While you won't actually be able to read the words, you will get an overall idea of how it looks on the page. When you are through viewing, click on the magnifying glass button to return to the regular screen.

2. To run a spell check, click on **Tools**, click on **Spell Check**, and begin the spell check process.

3. Proofread your resumé carefully. To print, click on **File** and click on **Print**. To print more than one copy, click on **Number of Copies** and type in the number you want; then enter. Click on **Print**. *As a word of caution, print just one copy the first time to make sure everything looks good. Then you can and print more.*

4. To save your document to a floppy disk, click on **File**, click on **Save**, and type the path name as **a:\resume**; then enter.

5. To exit you must close your document by clicking on **File**, click on **Close**, click on **File**, and click on **Exit**.

■ SETTING BULLETS USING WORDPERFECT

Several bullet choices are available under WordPerfect's typographic symbols. To create a bullet like the ones shown here press **Crtl+W,** type the numerical information following the symbol you want, and then enter.

•	○	■	•	○	□
4,0	4,1	4,2	4,3	4,37	4,38

●	○	■	■	□	□
4,44	4,45	4,46	4,47	4,48	4,49

TYPING YOUR RESUMÉ
USING WORDPERFECT
6.0 (DOS)

*I*nstructions for creating each of the 10 resumé styles shown on pages 34–43 are provided. If you follow these instructions, your resumé will look identical to the one you have selected.

Depending on your printer's capabilities, you may want to choose a different font than the one in the directions. If you chose a different font, then the tabs indicated in the directions may need to be altered. You will have to make the appropriate adjustments in those cases.

If you are having trouble getting your resumé to fit on one page, put the street, city, state, and zip code on the same line for each entry under "Education" and "Experience."

DIRECTIONS FOR RESUMÉ NO. 1
WORDPERFECT 6.0 (DOS)

GENERAL SETUP

1. From a clear screen, make sure you are in the **Graphics Mode**, with your **Ribbon Bar** and **Fonts Button Bar** visible—like this:

Menu Bar
Ribbon Bar
Fonts Button Bar

   If the top of your screen looks different than the example above:

   a.   Click on **View** and then click on **Graphics Mode.**

   b.   Click on **View** and click on **Ribbon.**

   c.   Click on **View** and click on **Button Bar Setup.**

   d.   Click on **Select** and highlight **FONTS**; then enter.

2. Click on **Layout,** click on **Margins,** click on the down arrow key next to top margin until it reaches .5; then click on the down arrow key next to bottom margin until it reaches .5; then click on **OK**.

3. Click on **Layout,** click on **Page,** click on **2 (Center Current Page),** and click on **OK**.

4. Click on **Layout,** click on **Line,** click on **Tab Set,** click on **Absolute,** click on **Clear All,** click on **Set Tab,** type **2.8** and enter. Click on **Set Tab** and type **3.16**; then enter. Click on **OK**.

MAIN HEADING SETUP

1. Click on the **Justification Button** in your ribbon bar where it says **Left.** Double click on **Center**.

2. Click on the **Font Button** in your ribbon bar where the default is Courier. Scroll the pull–down list until you get to **Dutch 801 Roman**; then double click on that choice.

3. Click on the **Point Size Button** in your ribbon bar. Scroll the pull–down list and double click on 16.

4. Click on **Bold** in your button bar. Type your name in all capitals.

5. Click on the **Point Size Button** in your ribbon bar. Double click on **12**. Then click on **Bold** in your button bar to turn it off. Enter twice.

6. Type your street address; then enter. Type your city, state, and zip code; then enter. Type your area code and phone number; then enter once.

7. Click on the **Justification Button** in the ribbon bar; double click on **Left**. Then enter once more.

8. In your menu bar click on **Graphics**. Click on **Graphics Lines**. Click on **Create**. Click and hold on **4** (thickness), drag mouse to **Set**, then release mouse. Type .047; then enter. Click on **OK**. Then enter three times to continue.

CAREER OBJECTIVE SETUP

1. Click on the **Point Size Button** in your ribbon bar and double click on **13**. Click on **Bold** and **Underline** in your button bar.

2. In all capitals type **CAREER OBJECTIVE**. Then click on the **Point Size Button** and double click on **12**. Then click on **Bold** and **Underline** in your button bar to turn them off. Now enter twice.

3. Type your career objective letting it word wrap at the end of the line. When you are through, enter twice.

EDUCATION SETUP

1. Click on the **Point Size Button** in your ribbon bar and double click on **13**. Click on **Bold** and **Underline** in your button bar.

2. In all capitals type **EDUCATION**. Then click on the **Point Size Button** in your ribbon bar and double click on **12**. Then click on **Bold** and **Underline** in your button bar to turn them off. Now enter twice.

3. Begin with your most recent education first by typing the dates you attended, making sure that all digits align. Leave one space before and after the hyphen. Then tab, click on **Bold** in your button bar, and type the name of the school. Then click on **Bold** in your button bar to turn it off; enter once.

4. Tab, type the street address, city, state, and zip code of your school; then enter once.

5. Tab, click on **Italics** and **Bold** in your button bar, type your course of study or degree received, click on **Italics** and **Bold** in your button bar to turn them off; then enter once.

6. Tab, type when you received your diploma or when it will be awarded, or the number of credits earned, if applicable; then enter twice.

7. Repeat Steps 2–6 for any other schools you want to list. Then enter twice to begin the next section.

AREAS OF SKILLS SETUP

1. Click on the **Point Size Button** in your ribbon bar and double click on **13**. Click on **Bold** and **Underline** in your button bar.

2. In all capitals type **AREAS OF SKILLS**. Then click on the **Point Size Button** in your ribbon bar and double click on **12**. Then click on **Bold** and **Underline** in your button bar to turn them off.

3. Tab, to create the bullet hit **CTRL+W**, type **4,0**, then enter. If none of the items in this area will take more than one line, you may tab and start to type. However, if you think the skill might wrap to a second line, then hit **F4** (indent) and begin to type your skill letting it word wrap. Then enter and repeat this step until all of your skills have been listed. Hit enter twice when you are through with this section.

EXPERIENCE SETUP

1. Click on the **Point Size Button** in your ribbon bar and double click on **13**. Click on **Bold** and **Underline** in your button bar.

2. In all capitals type **EXPERIENCE**. Then click on the **Point Size Button** in your ribbon bar and double click on **12**. Then click on **Bold** and **Underline** in your button bar to turn them off. Enter twice.

3. Begin with your most recent experience first by typing the dates you were employed, making sure that all digits align.

Leave one space before and after the hyphen. Then tab, click on **Bold** in your button bar, and type the name of the company. Then click on **Bold** in your button bar to turn it off; enter once.

4. Tab, type the street address, city, state, and zip code of the company; then enter once.

5. Tab, click on **Italics** and **Bold** in your button bar, and type your job title, click on **Italics** and **Bold** in your button bar to turn them off; then enter once.

6. Tab, hit **CTRL+W**, type **4,0** and then enter to create the bullet. At this point you are going to list your accomplishments and responsibilities of the job. If none of the items in this area will take more than one line, you may tab and start to type. However, if you think the item might wrap to a second line, then hit **F4** (indent) and begin to type your item letting it word wrap. Then enter and repeat this step until all of your accomplishments and responsibilities of the job have been listed. Hit enter twice and repeat this step until all of your experience has been listed. When you are through with this section, enter twice.

REFERENCE SETUP

1. Click on the **Point Size Button** in your ribbon bar and double click on **13**. Click on **Bold** and **Underline** in your button bar.

2. In all capitals type **REFERENCES**. Then click on the **Point Size Button** in your ribbon bar and double click on **12**. Then click on **Bold** and **Underline** in your button bar to turn them off.

3. Tab and type Available upon Request.

   DO NOT ENTER AFTER THE LAST LINE.

FINAL REVIEW

1. Hit your **Page Up Key** to take you to the top of your page. Click on **File** and click on **Print Preview**. If you don't see the entire page, click on **View** and click on **Full Page**. While you won't actually be able to read the words, you will get an overall idea of how it looks on the page. When you are through viewing, click on **Close** to return to the regular screen.

2. To run a spell check, click on **Tools**, click on **Writing Tools**, click on **Speller**, click on **Document**, and begin the spell check process.

3. Proofread your resumé carefully. To print, click on **File** and click on **Print**. To print more than one copy, click on **Number of Copies** and type in the number you want; then enter. Click on **Print**. *As a word of caution, print just one copy the first time to make sure everything looks good. Then you can print more.*

4. To save your document to a floppy disk, click on **File**, click on **Save**, and type the path name as **a:\resume**; then enter.

5. To exit you must close your document by clicking on **File**, click on **Close**, click on **File**, and click on **Exit**.

DIRECTIONS FOR RESUMÉ NO. 2
WORDPERFECT 6.0 (DOS)

GENERAL SETUP

1. From a clear screen, make sure you are in the **Graphics Mode**, with your **Ribbon Bar** and **Fonts Button Bar** visible—like this:

Menu Bar
Ribbon Bar
Fonts Button Bar

If the top of your screen looks different from the example above:

   a.   Click on **View** and then click on **Graphics Mode.**

   b.   Click on **View** and click on **Ribbon.**

   c.   Click on **View** and click on **Button Bar Setup.**

   d.   Click on **Select** and highlight **FONTS**; then enter.

2. Click on **Layout**, click on **Margins**, click on the down arrow key next to top margin until it reaches .5; then click on the down arrow key next to bottom margin until it reaches .5; then click on **OK**.

3. Click on **Layout**, click on **Page**, click on **2 (Center Current Page)**, and click on **OK**.

4. Click on **Layout**, click on **Line**, click on **Tab Set**, click on **Absolute**, click on **Clear All**, click on **Set Tab**, type **2.8** and enter. Click on **Set Tab** and type **5**; then enter. Click on **OK**.

MAIN HEADING SETUP

1. Click on the **Justification Button** in your ribbon bar where it says **Left**. Double click on **center**.

2. Click on the **Font Button** in your ribbon bar and scroll down the list until you get to **Dutch 801 Roman**; then double click on that choice.

3. Click on the **Point Size Button** in your ribbon bar. Scroll down the pull–down list and double click on **16**.

4. Click on **Bold** in your button bar. Type your name in all capitals.

5. Click on the **Point Size Button** in your ribbon bar. Double click on **12**. Then click on **Bold** in your button bar to turn it off. Enter twice.

6. Type your street address; then enter. Type your city, state, and zip code; then enter. Type your area code and phone number; then enter once.

7. Click on the **Justification Button** in the ribbon bar and double click on **Left**. Then enter once more.

8. In your menu bar click on **Graphics**. Click on **Graphics Lines**. Click on **Create**. Click on **6** (line style), click on **thick/thin**; then click on **OK**. Then enter three times to continue.

CAREER OBJECTIVE SETUP

1. Click on the **Point Size Button** in your ribbon bar and double click on **13**. Click on **Bold** and **Italics** in your button bar.

2. In all capitals type *CAREER OBJECTIVE*. Then click on the **Point Size Button** and double click on **12**. Then click on **Bold** and **Italics** in your button bar to turn them off.

3. Now hit **F4** (indent) and type your career objective letting it word wrap at the end of the line. When you are through, enter twice.

EDUCATION SETUP

1. Click on the **Point Size Button** in your ribbon bar and double click on **13**. Click on **Bold** and **Italics** in your button bar.

2. In all capitals type *EDUCATION*. Then click on the **Point Size Button** in your ribbon bar and double click on **12**. Then click on **Bold** and **Italics** in your button bar to turn them off.

3. Tab and type the name of your most recent school; enter once.

4. Tab, type the street address, city, state, and zip code of your school; then enter once.

5. Tab, click on **Bold** in your button bar, type your course of study or degree received, click on **Bold** in your button bar to turn it off; then enter once.

6. Tab, type when you received your diploma or when it will be awarded, or the number of credits earned, if applicable; then enter twice.

7. Repeat Steps 2–6 for any other schools you want to list. Then enter twice to begin the next section.

AREAS OF SKILLS SETUP

1. Click on the **Point Size Button** in your ribbon bar and double click on **13**. Click on **Bold** and **Italics** in your button bar.

2. In all capitals type *AREAS OF SKILLS*. Then click on **Point Size** again and double click on **12**. Then click on **Bold** and **Italics** in your button bar to turn them off.

3. Tab and type your first skill; then tab and type your second skill. Now enter and continue in the same manner until all skills have been listed. Hit enter twice when you are through with this section.

EXPERIENCE SETUP

1. Click on the **Point Size Button** in your ribbon bar and double click on **13**. Click on **Bold** and **Italics** in your button bar.

2. In all capitals type *EXPERIENCE*. Then click on **Point Size** again and double click on **12**. Then click on **Bold** and **Italics** in your button bar to turn them off.

3. Begin with your most recent experience first. Tab and type the name of the company. Then enter once.

4. Tab, type the street address, city, state, and zip code of the company; then enter once.

5. Type the dates you were employed, making sure that all digits align. Leave one space before and after the hyphen.

6. Then hit **F4** (indent), click on **Bold** in your button bar, and type your job title followed by a colon; click on **Bold** in your button bar to turn it off. Now space twice and begin to type your job description, letting it word wrap at the end of the line. Enter twice.

7. Repeat Steps 2–6 until all your experience has been listed.

REFERENCE SETUP

1. Click on the **Point Size Button** in your ribbon bar and double click on **13**. Click on **Bold** and **Italics** in your button bar.

2. In all capitals type *REFERENCES*. Then click on **Point Size** again and double click on **12**. Then click on **Bold** and **Italics** in your button bar to turn them off.

3. Tab and type Provided upon Request.

DO NOT ENTER AFTER THE LAST LINE.

FINAL REVIEW

1. Hit your **Page Up Key** to take you to the top of your page. Click on **File** and click on **Print Preview**. If you don't see the entire page, click on **View** and click on **Full Page**. While you won't actually be able to read the words, you will get an overall idea of how it looks on the page. When you are through viewing, click on **Close** to return to the regular screen.

2. To run a spell check, click on **Tools**, click on **Writing Tools**, click on **Speller**, click on **Document**, and begin the spell check process.

3. Proofread your resumé carefully. To print, click on **File** and click on **Print**. To print more than one copy, click on **Number of Copies** and type in the number you want; then enter. Click on **Print**. *As a word of caution, print just one copy the first time to make sure everything looks good. Then you can print more.*

4. To save your document to a floppy disk, click on **File**, click on **Save**, and type the path name as **a:\resume**; then enter.

5. To exit you must close your document by clicking on **File**, click on **Close**, click on **File**, and click on **Exit**.

DIRECTIONS FOR RESUMÉ No. 3
WORDPERFECT 6.0 (DOS)

GENERAL SETUP

1. From a clear screen, make sure you are in the **Graphics Mode**, with your **Ribbon Bar** and **Fonts Button Bar** visible—like this:

Menu Bar
Ribbon Bar
Fonts Button Bar

If the top of your screen looks different from the example above:

a. Click on **View** and then click on **Graphics Mode.**

b. Click on **View** and click on **Ribbon.**

c. Click on **View** and click on **Button Bar Setup.**

d. Click on **Select** and highlight **FONTS**; then enter.

2. Click on **Layout**, click on **Margins**, click on the down arrow key next to top margin until it reaches .5; then click on the down arrow key next to bottom margin until it reaches .5; then click on **OK**.

3. Click on **Layout**, click on **Page**, click on **2 (Center Current Page)**, and click on **OK**.

4. Click on **Layout**, click on **Line**, click on **Tab Set**, click on **Absolute**, click on **Clear All**, click on **Set Tab**, type **2.88** and enter. Click on **Set Tab** and type **3.13**; then enter. Click on **OK**.

MAIN HEADING SETUP

1. Click on the **Justification Button** in your ribbon bar where it says **Left.** Double click on **center**.

2. Click on the **Font Button** in your ribbon bar and scroll down the list until you get to **Dutch 801 Roman**; then double click on that choice.

3. Click on the **Point Size Button** in your ribbon bar. Scroll down the pull–down list and double click on **16**.

4. Click on **Bold** in your button bar. Type your name in all capitals.

5. Click on the **Point Size Button** in your ribbon bar. Double click on **12**. Then click on **Bold** in your button bar to turn it off. Enter twice.

6. Type your street address; then enter. Type your city, state, and zip code; then enter. Type your area code and phone number; then enter once.

7. Click on the **Justification Button** in the ribbon bar and double click on **Left**. Then enter once more.

8. In your menu bar click on **Graphics**. Click on **Graphics Lines**. Click on **Create**. Click on **6** (line style), click on **thin/thick**; click on **OK**. Then enter three times.

CAREER OBJECTIVE SETUP

1. Click on the **Point Size Button** in your ribbon bar and double click on **14**. Click on **Bold** in your button bar.

2. In all capitals type **CAREER OBJECTIVE**. Then click on the **Point Size Button** and double click on **12**. Then click on **Bold** in your button bar to turn it off.

3. Enter twice and type your career objective letting it word wrap at the end of the line. When you are through, enter twice.

EXPERIENCE SETUP

1. Click on the **Point Size Button** in your ribbon bar and double click on **14**. Click on **Bold** in your button bar.

2. In all capitals type **EXPERIENCE**. Then click on **Point Size** again and double click on **12**. Then click on **Bold** in your button bar to turn it off.

3. Begin with your most recent experience. Tab, click on **Bold** in your button bar and type the name of the company. Click on **Bold** in your button bar to turn it off. Then enter once.

4. Tab, type the street address, city, state, and zip code of the company; then enter once.

5. Type the beginning and ending years you were employed, making sure to leave a space before and after the hyphen.

6. Then tab, click on **Bold** in your button bar, and type your job title. Then click on **Bold** in your button bar to turn it off; then enter once.

7. Tab. To create the bullet hit **CTRL+W**, type **5,169**, then enter. If none of the items in this area will take more than one line, you may tab and start to type. However, if you think the description might wrap to a second line, then instead of tabbing, hit **F4** (indent) and begin to type letting the lines word wrap. Enter once.

8. Repeat Steps 2–7 until all your experience has been listed.

EDUCATION SETUP

1. Click on the **Point Size Button** in your ribbon bar and double click on **14**. Click on **Bold** in your button bar.

2. In all capitals type **EDUCATION**. Then click on **Point Size** again and double click on **12**.

3. Tab and type the name of your most recent school. Then click on **Bold** in your button bar to turn if off; enter once.

4. Tab, type the street address, city, state, and zip code of your school; then enter once.

5. Type the beginning and ending year you attended that school leaving a space before and after the hyphen.

6. Tab, click on **Bold** in your button bar, type your course of study or degree received and your grade point average if it is above a 3.0; click on **Bold** in your button bar to turn it off and then enter once.

7. Tab, type the number of credits earned so far if you have not yet graduated or any academic honors received; then enter twice.

8. Repeat Steps 2–7 for any other schools you want to list. Then enter twice to begin the next section.

AFFILIATIONS SETUP

1. Click on the **Point Size Button** in your ribbon bar and double click on **14**. Click on **Bold** in your button bar.

2. In all capitals type **AFFILIATIONS**. Then click on **Point Size** again and double click on **12**. Then click on **Bold** in your button bar to turn it off. Enter twice.

3. To create the bullet, hit **CTRL+W**, type **5,169**, then enter. Tab and type your first item. Then enter and repeat this step until all items have been included. Enter twice after the last item.

REFERENCE SETUP

1. Click on the **Point Size Button** in your ribbon bar and double click on **11**.

2. Hit **SHIFT+F6** (center) and type References Available upon Request.

    DO NOT ENTER AFTER THE LAST LINE.

FINAL REVIEW

1. Hit your **Page Up Key** to take you to the top of your page. Click on **File** and click on **Print Preview**. If you don't see the entire page, click on **View** and click on **Full Page**. While you won't actually be able to read the words, you will get an overall idea of how it looks on the page. When you are through viewing, click on **Close** to return to the regular screen.

2. To run a spell check, click on **Tools**, click on **Writing Tools**, click on **Speller**, click on **Document**, and begin the spell check process.

3. Proofread your resumé carefully. To print, click on **File** and click on **Print**. To print more than one copy, click on **Number of Copies** and type in the number you want; then enter. Click on **Print**. *As a word of caution, print just one copy the first time to make sure everything looks good. Then you can print more.*

4. To save your document to a floppy disk, click on **File**, click on **Save**, and type the path name as **a:\resume**; then enter.

5. To exit you must close your document by clicking on **File**, click on **Close**, click on **File**, and click on **Exit**.

DIRECTIONS FOR RESUMÉ No. 4
WORDPERFECT 6.0 (DOS)

GENERAL SETUP

1. From a clear screen, make sure you are in the **Graphics Mode**, with your **Ribbon Bar** and **Fonts Button Bar** visible—like this:

Menu Bar
Ribbon Bar
Fonts Button Bar

If the top of your screen looks different from the example above:

a. Click on **View** and then click on **Graphics Mode.**

b. Click on **View** and click on **Ribbon.**

c. Click on **View** and click on **Button Bar Setup.**

d. Click on **Select** and highlight **FONTS**; then enter.

2. Click on **Layout**, click on **Margins**, click on the down arrow key next to top margin until it reaches .5; then click on the down arrow key next to bottom margin until it reaches .5; then click on **OK.**

3. Click on **Layout**, click on **Page**, click on **2 (Center Current Page)**, and click on **OK.**

4. Click on **Layout**, click on **Line**, click on **Tab Set**, click on **Absolute**, click on **Clear All**, click on **Set Tab**, type **2.4** and enter. Click on **OK.**

MAIN HEADING SETUP

1. Click on the **Justification Button** in your ribbon bar where it says **Left.** Double click on **Center.**

2. Click on the **Font Button** in your ribbon bar where the default is Courier. Scroll the pull–down list until you get to **Dutch 801 Roman**; then double click on that choice.

3. Click on the **Point Size Button** in your ribbon bar. Scroll the pull–down list and double click on **13.**

4. Click on **Bold** in your button bar. Type your name in all capitals.

5. Click on the **Point Size Button** in your ribbon bar and double click on **11**. Then click on **Bold** in your button bar to turn it off. Enter once.

6. Type your street address; then enter. Type your city, state, and zip code; then enter. Type your area code and phone number; then enter once.

7. Click on the **Justification Button** in the ribbon bar; double click on **Left**. Then enter three times.

CAREER OBJECTIVE SETUP

1. Click on the **Point Size Button** in your ribbon bar and double click on **12**.

2. Hit **SHIFT+F6** (center) and click on **Bold** and **Underline** in your button bar.

3. In all capitals type **CAREER OBJECTIVE**. Then click on **Bold** and **Underline** in your button bar to turn them off.

4. Enter twice and type your career objective letting it word wrap at the end of the line. When you are through, enter twice.

EXPERIENCE SETUP

1. Hit **SHIFT+F6** (center). Click on **Bold** and **Underline** in your button bar.

2. In all capitals type **WORK EXPERIENCE**. Then click on **Bold** and **Underline** in your button bar to turn them off. Enter twice.

3. Begin with your most recent experience by typing the dates you were employed, making sure that all digits align. Leave one space before and after the hyphen. Then tab and in all capitals type the name of the company. Then enter once.

4. Tab, type the street address, city, state, and zip code of the company; then enter once.

5. Then tab, click on **Bold** in your button bar, and type your job title. Then click on **Bold** in your button bar to turn it off; then enter once.

6. Hit **F4** (indent) and type your job description letting it word wrap; enter twice.

7. Repeat Steps 2–6 until all your experience has been listed. Hit enter twice to continue with next section.

EDUCATION SETUP

1. Hit **SHIFT+F6** (center). Click on **Bold** and **Underline** in your button bar.

2. In all capitals type **EDUCATION**; enter twice.

3. Begin with your most recent education by typing the dates you attended, making sure that all digits align. Leave one space before and after the hyphen. Then tab and type the name of your school in all capitals; enter once.

4. Tab, type the street address, city, state, and zip code of your school; then enter once.

5. Tab, click on **Bold** in your button bar, type your course of study or degree received. Click on **Bold** in your button bar to turn it off and then enter once.

6. Tab and type when you received your diploma or when it will be awarded, or the number of credits earned, if applicable; then enter twice.

7. Repeat Steps 2–6 for any other schools you want to list. Then enter twice to begin the next section.

AREAS OF SKILLS SETUP

1. Click on **Layout**, click on **Line**, click on **Tab Set**, click on **Absolute**, click on **Clear All**, click on **Set Tab**, type **2.74** and enter. Click on **Tab Set**, type **5.4**; then enter. Click on **OK**.

2. Hit **SHIFT+F6** (center), click on **Bold** and **Underline** in your button bar and in all capitals type **AREAS OF SKILLS**; then enter twice.

3. Type your first skill; tab and type your second skill; tab and type your third skill; then enter once. Repeat this step until all skills have been listed. Then enter twice to continue.

REFERENCE SETUP

1. Hit **SHIFT+F6** (center), click on **Bold** and **Underline** in your button bar and in all capitals type **REFERENCES**. Click on **Bold** and **Underline** in your button bar to turn them off; then enter twice.

2. Hit **SHIFT+F6** (center) and type Available upon Request.

DO NOT ENTER AFTER THE LAST LINE.

FINAL REVIEW

1. Hit your **Page Up Key** to take you to the top of your page. Click on **File** and click on **Print Preview**. If you don't see the entire page, click on **View** and click on **Full Page**. While you won't actually be able to read the words, you will get an over-all idea of how it looks on the page. When you are through viewing, click on **Close** to return to the regular screen.

2. To run a spell check, click on **Tools**, click on **Writing Tools**, click on **Speller**, click on **Document**, and begin the spell check process.

3. Proofread your resumé carefully. To print, click on **File** and click on **Print**. To print more than one copy, click on **Number of Copies** and type in the number you want; then enter. Click on **Print**. *As a word of caution, print just one copy the first time to make sure everything looks good. Then you can print more.*

4. To save your document to a floppy disk, click on **File**, click on **Save**, and type the path name as **a:\resume**; then enter.

5. To exit you must close your document by clicking on **File**, click on **Close**, click on **File**, and click on **Exit**.

DIRECTIONS FOR RESUMÉ No. 5
WORDPERFECT 6.0 (DOS)

GENERAL SETUP

1. From a clear screen, make sure you are in the **Graphics Mode**, with your **Ribbon Bar** and **Fonts Button Bar** visible—like this:

Menu Bar
Ribbon Bar
Fonts Button Bar

If the top of your screen looks different from the example above:

a. Click on **View** and then click on **Graphics Mode**.

b. Click on **View** and click on **Ribbon**.

c. Click on **View** and click on **Button Bar Setup**.

d. Click on **Select** and highlight **FONTS**; then enter.

2. Click on **Layout**, click on **Margins**, click on the down arrow key next to top margin until it reaches .5; then click on the down arrow key next to bottom margin until it reaches .5; then click on **OK**.

3. Click on **Layout**, click on **Page**, click on **2 (Center Current Page)**, and click on **OK**.

4. Click on **Layout**, click on **Line**, click on **Tab Set**, click on **Absolute**, click on **Clear All**, click on **Set Tab** and type **3** and enter. Click on **Set Tab** and type **3.31;** and enter. Click on **OK**.

MAIN HEADING SETUP

1. Click on the **Justification Button** in your ribbon bar where it says **Left**. Double click on **Center**.

2. Click on the **Font Button** in your ribbon bar where the default is Courier. Scroll the pull-down list until you get to **Dutch 801 Roman**; then double click on that choice.

3. Click on the **Point Size Button** in your ribbon bar. Scroll the pull-down list and double click on **14**.

4. Click on **Bold** in your button bar. Type your name in all capitals.

5. Click on the **Point Size Button** in your ribbon bar. Double click on **12**. Then click on **Bold** in your button bar to turn it off. Enter twice.

6. Type your street address; then enter. Type your city, state, and zip code; then enter. Type your area code and phone number; then enter once.

7. Click on the **Justification Button** in the ribbon bar and double click on **Left**. Then enter once more.

8. In your menu bar click on **Graphics**. Click on **Graphics Lines**. Click on **Create**. Click and hold on **4** (thickness), drag mouse to **Set**, then release mouse. Type **.047**; then enter. Click on **OK**; then enter three times to continue.

CAREER OBJECTIVE SETUP

1. Click on the **Point Size Button** in your ribbon bar and double click on **13**. Click on **Bold** and **Italics** in your button bar.

2. In all capitals type *CAREER OBJECTIVE*. Then click on **Point Size** again and double click on **12**. Then click on **Bold** and **Italics** in your button bar to turn them off.

3. Hit **F4** (indent) and type your career objective letting it word wrap at the end of the line. When you are through, enter twice.

EDUCATION SETUP

1. Click on the **Point Size Button** in your ribbon bar and double click on **13**. Click on **Bold** and **Italics** in your button bar.

2. In all capitals type *EDUCATION*. Then click on **Point Size** again and double click on **12**. Then click on **Bold** and **Italics** in your button bar to turn them off.

3. Tab and begin with your most recent education by typing the name of the school. Enter once.

4. Tab and type the street address. Enter once.

5. Tab and type the city, state, and zip code of your school; then enter once.

6. Tab, click on **Bold** in your button bar, type your course of study or degree received, click on **Bold** in your button bar to turn it off; then enter once.

7. Tab, type when you received your diploma or when it will be awarded, or the number of credits earned, if applicable; then enter twice.

8. Repeat Steps 2–7 for any other schools you want to list. Then enter twice to begin the next section.

EXPERIENCE SETUP

1. Click on the **Point Size Button** in your ribbon bar and double click on **13**. Click on **Bold** and **Italics** in your button bar.

2. In all capitals type ***EXPERIENCE***. Then click on **Point Size** again and double click on **12**. Then click on **Bold** and **Italics** in your button bar to turn them off.

3. Tab and begin with your most recent experience by typing the name of the company; then enter once.

4. Tab and type the street address; then enter once.

5. Tab and type the city, state, and zip code of the company; then enter once.

6. Tab, click on **Bold** in your button bar, and type your job title, click on **Bold** in your button bar to turn it off; then enter once.

7. Tab and type your dates of employment leaving one space before and after the hyphen; then enter twice.

8. Repeat Steps 2–7 until all experience has been listed.

AFFILIATIONS SETUP

1. Click on the Point Size Button in your ribbon bar and double click on 13. Click on Bold and Italics in your button bar.

2. In all capitals type *AFFILIATIONS*. Then click on **Point Size** again and double click on 12. Then click on **Bold** and **Italics** in your button bar to turn them off.

3. Tab. To create the bullet hit **CTRL+W** and type **5,226**; then enter. Tab and type the name of the organization; then enter once. Repeat this step until all items have been listed. Enter twice to begin next section.

AWARDS/HONORS SETUP

1. Click on the **Point Size Button** in your ribbon bar and double click on **13**. Click on **Bold** and **Italics** in your button bar.

2. In all capitals type ***AWARDS/HONORS***. Then click on **Point Size** again and double click on **12**. Then click on **Bold** and **Italics** in your button bar to turn them off.

3. Tab. To create the bullet hit **CTRL+W** and type **5,226**; then enter. Tab and type the name of the award or honor; then enter once. Repeat this step until all items have been listed. Enter twice to begin next section.

REFERENCE SETUP

1. Click on the **Point Size Button** in your ribbon bar and double click on **13**. Click on **Bold** and **Italics** in your button bar.

2. In all capitals type *REFERENCES*. Then click on **Point Size** again and double click on **12**. Then click on **Bold** and **Italics** in your button bar to turn them off.

3. Tab and type Available upon Request.
   DO NOT ENTER AFTER THE LAST LINE.

FINAL REVIEW

1. Hit your **Page Up Key** to take you to the top of your page. Click on **File** and click on **Print Preview**. If you don't see the entire page, click on **View** and click on **Full Page**. While you won't actually be able to read the words, you will get an overall idea of how it looks on the page. When you are through viewing, click on **Close** to return to the regular screen.

2. To run a spell check, click on **Tools**, click on **Writing Tools**, click on **Speller**, click on **Document**, and begin the spell check process.

3. Proofread your resumé carefully. To print, click on **File** and click on **Print**. To print more than one copy, click on **Number of Copies** and type in the number you want; then enter. Click on **Print**. *As a word of caution, print just one copy the first time to make sure everything looks good. Then you can print more.*

4. To save your document to a floppy disk, click on **File**, click on **Save**, and type the path name as **a:\resume**; then enter.

5. To exit you must close your document by clicking on **File**, click on **Close**, click on **File**, and click on **Exit**.

DIRECTIONS FOR RESUMÉ NO. 6
WORDPERFECT 6.0 (DOS)

GENERAL SETUP

1. From a clear screen, make sure you are in the **Graphics Mode**, with your **Ribbon Bar** and **Fonts Button Bar** visible—like this:

Menu Bar
Ribbon Bar
Fonts Button Bar

If the top of your screen looks different from the example above:

   a. Click on **View** and then click on **Graphics Mode.**

   b. Click on **View** and click on **Ribbon.**

   c. Click on **View** and click on **Button Bar Setup.**

   d. Click on **Select** and highlight **FONTS**; then enter.

2. Click on **Layout**, click on **Margins**, click on the down arrow key next to top margin until it reaches .5; then click on the down arrow key next to bottom margin until it reaches .5; then click on **OK.**

3. Click on **Layout**, click on **Page**, click on **2 (Center Current Page)**, and click on **OK.**

4. Click on **Layout**, click on **Line**, click on **Tab Set**, click on **Absolute**, click on **Clear All**, click on **Set Tab**, type **3** and enter. Click on **Set Tab** and type **3.44**; then enter. Click on **Tab Set** and type **6**; then enter. Click on **OK.**

MAIN HEADING SETUP

1. Hit **SHIFT+F6** (center).

2. Click on the **Font Button** in your ribbon bar where the default is Courier. Scroll the pull–down list until you get to **Dutch 801 Roman**; then double click on that choice.

3. Click on the **Point Size Button** in your ribbon bar. Scroll the pull–down list and double click on **16.**

4. Click on **Bold** in your button bar. Type your name in all capitals.

5. Click on the **Point Size Button** in your ribbon bar and double click on **12**. Enter twice.

6. Type **Home Address:**, tab 3 times, and type **School Address:** and enter twice. Then click on **Point Size** and double click on **11**. Click on **Bold** in your button bar to turn it off.

7. Type your home street address; then tab three times and type your school street address; enter once.

8. Type your home city, state, and zip code; tab three times and type your school city, state, and zip code; then enter once.

9. Type your home area code and phone number; tab three times and type your school area code and phone number; then enter twice.

10. In your menu bar click on **Graphics**. Click on **Graphics Lines**. Click on **Create**. Click on **6** (line style), click on **Double**; click on **OK**. Then enter three times to continue with next section.

CAREER OBJECTIVE SETUP

1. Click on the **Point Size Button** in your ribbon bar and double click on **14**. Click on **Bold** and **Italics** in your button bar.

2. In all capitals type *CAREER OBJECTIVE*. Then click on **Point Size** again and double click on **12**. Then click on **Bold** and **Italics** in your button bar to turn them off.

3. Now enter twice and type your career objective letting it word wrap at the end of the line. When you are through, enter twice.

EDUCATION SETUP

1. Click on the **Point Size Button** in your ribbon bar and double click on **14**. Click on **Bold** and **Italics** in your button bar.

2. In all capitals type *EDUCATION* and enter twice. Click on **Point Size** again and double click on **12**. Then click on **Bold** and **Italics** in your button bar to turn them off.

3. Type the beginning and ending year you attended the school leaving one space before and after the hyphen. Tab, click on **Bold** in your button bar, and type the name of your most recent school in all capitals. Click on **Bold** in your button bar to turn it off; then enter once.

4. Tab, type the street address, city, state, and zip code of your school; then enter once.

5. Tab and type what type of diploma you will receive and when; then enter twice.

6. Repeat Steps 2–5 for any other schools you want to list. Then enter twice to begin the next section.

EXPERIENCE SETUP

1. Click on the **Point Size Button** in your ribbon bar and double click on **14**. Click on **Bold** and **Italics** in your button bar.

2. In all capitals type ***EXPERIENCE***. Then click on **Point Size** again and double click on **12**. Then click on **Bold** and **Italics** in your button bar to turn them off. Enter twice.

3. Begin with your most recent experience. Type the dates of your employment. Tab, click on **Bold** in your button bar and type the name of the company in all capitals. Click on **Bold** in your button bar to turn it off; then enter once.

4. Tab, type the street address, city, state, and zip code of the company; then enter once.

5. Then hit **F4** (indent), click on **Bold** in your button bar, and type your job title followed by a colon; click on **Bold** in your button bar to turn it off. Now space twice and begin to type your job description, letting it word wrap at the end of the line. Enter twice.

6. Repeat Steps 2–4 until all your experience has been listed. Hit enter twice to continue with the next section.

ACTIVITIES SETUP

1. Click on the **Point Size Button** in your ribbon bar and double click on **14**. Click on **Bold** and **Italics** in your button bar.

2. In all capitals type ***ACTIVITIES***. Then click on **Point Size** again and double click on **12**. Then click on **Bold** and **Italics** in your button bar to turn them off.

3. Tab. To create the bullet, hit **CTRL+W** and type **5,18**; then enter. Tab and type your first activity; enter once.

4. Repeat Step 3 until all activities have been listed. Then enter twice to continue with next section.

REFERENCE SETUP

1. Click on the **Point Size Button** in your ribbon bar and double click on **14**. Click on **Bold** and **Italics** in your button bar.

2. In all capitals type ***REFERENCES***. Then click on **Point Size** again and double click on **12**. Then click on **Bold** and **Italics** in your button bar to turn them off.

3. Tab and type Available upon Request.
   DO NOT ENTER AFTER THE LAST LINE.

FINAL REVIEW

1. Hit your **Page Up Key** to take you to the top of your page. Click on **File** and click on **Print Preview**. If you don't see the entire page, click on **View** and click on **Full Page**. While you won't actually be able to read the words, you will get an overall idea of how it looks on the page. When you are through viewing, click on **Close** to return to the regular screen.

2. To run a spell check, click on **Tools**, click on **Writing Tools**, click on **Speller**, click on **Document**, and begin the spell check process.

3. Proofread your resumé carefully. To print, click on **File** and click on **Print**. To print more than one copy, click on **Number of Copies** and type in the number you want; then enter. Click on **Print**. *As a word of caution, print just one copy the first time to make sure everything looks good. Then you can print more.*

4. To save your document to a floppy disk, click on **File**, click on **Save**, and type the path name as **a:\resume**; then enter.

5. To exit you must close your document by clicking on **File**, click on **Close**, click on **File**, and click on **Exit**.

DIRECTIONS FOR RESUMÉ NO. 7
WORDPERFECT 6.0 (DOS)

GENERAL SETUP

1. From a clear screen, make sure you are in the **Graphics Mode**, with your **Ribbon Bar** and **Fonts Button Bar** visible—like this:

Menu Bar
Ribbon Bar
Fonts Button Bar

| File | Edit | View | Layout | Tools | Font | Graphics | Window | Help |

| Marg | ▼ | None | ▼ | 1 Col | ▼ | Left | ▼ | Courier | ▼ | 12pt ▼ |

| FFF Font | a Normal | a Bold | a UnderIn | a DblUndIn | *a* Italics | Fine | Small | Large | VryLarge | X Large | NormSize | a² Suprscpt |

If the top of your screen looks different from the example above:

a. Click on **View** and then click on **Graphics Mode.**

b. Click on **View** and click on **Ribbon.**

c. Click on **View** and click on **Button Bar Setup.**

d. Click on **Select** and highlight **FONTS**; then enter.

2. Click on **Layout**, click on **Margins**, click on the down arrow key next to top margin until it reaches .5; then click on the down arrow key next to bottom margin until it reaches .5; then click on **OK**.

3. Click on **Layout**, click on **Page**, click on **2 (Center Current Page)**, and click on **OK**.

4. Click on **Layout**, click on **Line**, click on **Tab Set**, click on **Absolute**, click on **Clear All**, click on **Set Tab**, type **2.5** and enter. Click on **Set Tab** and type **5.38**; then enter. Click on **Tab Set** and type **6**; then enter. Click on **OK**.

MAIN HEADING SETUP

1. Hit **SHIFT+F6** (center).

2. Click on the **Font Button** in your ribbon bar and scroll the pull–down list until you get to **Dutch 801 Roman**; then double click on that choice.

3. Click on the **Point Size Button** in your ribbon bar. Scroll the pull–down list and double click on **18**.

4. Click on **Bold** in your button bar. Type your name in all capitals.

5. Click on the **Point Size Button** in your ribbon bar. Double click on **12**. Enter twice.

6. Type **School Address**, tab 3 times, and type **Home Address** and enter once.

7. Type your school street address; then tab three times and type your home street address; enter once.

8. Type your school city, state, and zip code; tab three times and type your home city, state, and zip code; then enter once.

9. Type your school area code and phone number; tab three times and type your home area code and phone number; then enter once.

10. In your menu bar click on **Graphics**. Click on **Graphics Lines**. Click on **Create**. Click and hold on **4** (thickness), drag mouse to **set**, then release mouse. Type **.04**; then enter. Then click on **OK**. Then enter twice to continue.

CAREER OBJECTIVE SETUP

1. Click on the **Point Size Button** in your ribbon bar and double click on **14**. Click on **Bold** and **Italics** in your button bar.

2. In all capitals type *OBJECTIVE*. Then click on **Point Size** and double click on **12**. Then click on **Bold** and **Italics** in your button bar to turn them off.

3. Hit **F4** (indent) and type your career objective letting it word wrap at the end of the line. When you are through, enter twice.

EDUCATION SETUP

1. Click on the **Point Size Button** in your ribbon bar and double click on **14**. Click on **Bold** and **Italics** in your button bar.

2. In all capitals type *EDUCATION.*

3. Click on the **Point Size Button** in your ribbon bar and double click on **12**. Then click on **Italics** in your button bar to turn it off.

4. Tab and type the name of your most recent school in all capitals followed by the city, state, and zip code.

5. Click on **Bold** in your button bar to turn it off; then enter once.

6. Click on the **Point Size Button** in your ribbon bar and double click on **10**.

7. Tab. To create the bullet, hit **CTRL+W** and type **5,228**; then enter once. Space once and type your college of study followed by the grade point for those courses required for graduation by that college.

8. Tab and create a bullet by hitting **CTRL+W** and again typing **5,228**; then enter. Space once and type your overall grade point average. Enter once.

9. Tab and create a bullet by hitting **CTRL+W** and typing **5,228**; then enter. Space once and type your major area of concentration and the grade point for only those classes.

10. Tab and create a bullet by hitting **CTRL+W** and type **5,228**; then enter. Space once and type your date of graduation. Enter twice.

11. Repeat Steps 2–10 until all your education has been listed.

EXPERIENCE SETUP

1. Click on the **Point Size Button** in your ribbon bar and double click on **14**. Click on **Bold** and **Italics** in your button bar.

2. In all capitals type *EXPERIENCE*.

3. Click on **Point Size** and double click on **12**. Click on **Bold** and **Italics** in your button bar to turn them off.

4. Tab. Begin with your most recent experience. Click on **Bold** in your button bar and type the name of the company in all capitals followed by the city, state, and zip code. Enter once.

5. Click on the **Point Size Button** in your ribbon bar and double click on **10**.

6. Tab and type your job title followed by your dates of employment in parentheses. Click on **Bold** in your button bar to turn it off. Enter once.

7. Tab and create the bullet by hitting **CTRL+W**, type **5,228**, and hit enter. Space once and begin to list your responsibilities and accomplishments on the job. Enter twice.

8. Repeat Steps 2–7 until all your experience has been listed.

AFFILIATIONS SETUP

1. Click on the **Point Size Button** in your ribbon bar and double click on **14**. Click on **Bold** and **Italics** in your button bar.

2. In all capitals type *AFFILIATIONS*.

3. Then click on **Point Size** and double click on **12**. Then click on **Italics** in your button bar to turn it off.

4. Tab and type the organization's name in all capitals. Click on **bold** in your button bar to turn it off. Enter once.

5. Tab. To create the bullet, hit **CTRL+W** and type **5,228**; then space once and type your first responsibility; enter once.

6. Repeat Step 5 until all responsibilities for that organization have been listed. Then enter twice.

7. Repeat Steps 4–6 until all affiliations have been listed. Enter twice to continue with next section.

QUALIFICATIONS SETUP

1. Click on the **Point Size Button** in your ribbon bar and double click on **14**. Click on **Bold** and **Italics** in your button bar.

2. In all capitals type *QUALIFICATIONS*.

3. Then click on **Point Size** again and double click on **10**. Then click on **Bold** and **Italics** in your button bar to turn them off.

4. Tab and create a bullet by hitting **CTRL+W**, then type **5,228** and enter once. Space once and begin to list your qualifications.

5. Repeat Step 4 until all qualifications have been listed. Then enter twice to continue with next section.

REFERENCES SETUP

1. Hit **SHIFT+F6** (center).

2. Type in all capitals REFERENCES AVAILABLE UPON REQUEST. **DO NOT ENTER AFTER THE LAST LINE.**

FINAL REVIEW

1. Hit your **Page Up Key** to take you to the top of your page. Click on **File** and click on **Print Preview**. If you don't see the entire page, click on **View** and click on **Full Page**. While you won't actually be able to read the words, you will get an overall idea of how it looks on the page. When you are through viewing, click on **Close** to return to the regular screen.

2. To run a spell check, click on **Tools,** click on **Writing Tools**, click on **Speller,** click on **Document,** and begin the spell check process.

3. Proofread your resumé carefully. To print, click on **File** and click on **Print**. To print more than one copy, click on **Number of Copies** and type in the number you want; then enter. Click on **Print**. *As a word of caution, print just one copy the first time to make sure everything looks good. Then you can print more.*

4. To save your document to a floppy disk, click on **File**, click on **Save**, and type the path name as **a:\resume**; then enter.

5. To exit you must close your document by clicking on **File**, click on **Close**, click on **File**, and click on **Exit**.

DIRECTIONS FOR RESUMÉ NO. 8
WORDPERFECT 6.0 (DOS)

GENERAL SETUP

1. From a clear screen, make sure you are in the **Graphics Mode**, with your **Ribbon Bar** and **Fonts Button Bar** visible—like this:

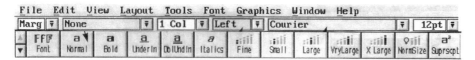

Menu Bar
Ribbon Bar
Fonts Button Bar

    If the top of your screen looks different from the example above:

    a. Click on **View** and then click on **Graphics Mode.**

    b. Click on **View** and click on **Ribbon.**

    c. Click on **View** and click on **Button Bar Setup.**

    d. Click on **Select** and highlight **FONTS**; then enter.

2. Click on **Layout**, click on **Margins**, click on the down arrow key next to top margin until it reaches .5; then click on the down arrow key next to bottom margin until it reaches .5; then click on **OK**.

3. Click on **Layout**, click on **Page**, click on **2 (Center Current Page)**, and click on **OK**.

4. Click on **Layout**, click on **Line**, click on **Tab Set**, click on **Absolute**, click on **Clear All**, click on **Set Tab** and type **3** and enter. Click on **Set Tab** and type **3.25** and enter. Click on **OK**.

MAIN HEADING SETUP

1. Click on the **Justification Button** in your ribbon bar. Double click on **Center**.

2. Click on the **Font Button** in your ribbon bar and scroll the pull–down list until you get to **Dutch 801 Roman**; then double click on that choice.

3. Click on the **Point Size Button** in your ribbon bar. Scroll the pull–down list and double click on **14**.

4. Click on **Bold** in your button bar. Now type your name in all capitals.

5. Click on **Point Size** and double click on **12**. Then click on **Bold** to turn it off. Enter twice.

6. Type your street address; then enter. Type your city, state, and zip code; then enter. Type your area code and phone number; then enter twice.

7. Click on the **Justification Button** in the ribbon bar and double click on **Left**. Then enter once more.

8. In your menu bar click on **Graphics**. Click on **Graphics Lines**. Click on **Create**. Click on **6** (line style), click on **Double Line**, click on **OK**; then enter three times to continue with next section.

CAREER OBJECTIVE SETUP

1. Click on **Bold** and **Underline** in your button bar. In all capitals type **OBJECTIVE**. Then click on **Bold** and **Underline** in your button bar to turn them off.

2. Hit **F4** (indent) and type your career objective letting it word wrap at the end of the line. When you are through, enter three times.

EDUCATION SETUP

1. Click on **Bold** and **Underline** in your button bar. In all capitals type **EDUCATION**. Then click on **Bold** and **Underline** in your button bar to turn them off.

2. Tab and begin with your most recent education by typing the name of the school. Enter once.

3. Tab and type the street address. Enter once.

4. Tab and type the city, state, and zip code of your school; then enter once.

5. Tab and type your course of study or degree received and the date; then enter twice.

6. Repeat Steps 2–5 for any other schools you want to list. Then enter three times to begin the next section.

EXPERIENCE SETUP

1. Click on **Bold** and **Underline** in your button bar. In all capitals type **EXPERIENCE**. Then click on **Bold** and **Underline** in your button bar to turn them off.

2. Tab, click on **Bold** in your button bar, and begin with your most recent experience by typing your job title. Click on **Bold** to turn it off; then enter once.

3. Tab and type the company name; then enter once.

4. Tab and type the street address; then enter once.

5. Tab and type the city, state, and zip code of the company; then enter once.

6. Tab and type your dates of employment; enter twice.

7. Repeat Steps 2–6 until all experience has been listed. Enter three times to begin the next section.

ACCOMPLISHMENTS SETUP

1. Click on **Bold** and **Underline** in your button bar. In all capitals type **ACCOMPLISHMENTS**. Then click on **Bold** and **Underline** in your button bar to turn them off.

2. Tab. To create the bullet hit **CTRL+W** and type **4,2**; then enter. Hit **F4** (indent) and type your first accomplishment letting it word wrap at the end of the line; then enter twice Repeat this step until all items have been listed. Enter three times to begin the final section.

REFERENCE SETUP

1. Click on **Bold** and **Underline** in your button bar. In all capitals type **REFERENCES**. Then click on **Bold** and **Underline** in your button bar to turn them off.

2. Tab and type Available upon Request.
   DO NOT ENTER AFTER THE LAST LINE.

FINAL REVIEW

1. Hit your **Page Up Key** to take you to the top of your page. Click on **File** and click on **Print Preview**. If you don't see the entire page, click on **View** and click on **Full Page**. While you won't actually be able to read the words, you will get an overall idea of how it looks on the page. When you are through viewing, click on **Close** to return to the regular screen.

2. To run a spell check, click on **Tools**, click on **Writing Tools**, click on **Speller**, click on **Document**, and begin the spell check process.

3. Proofread your resumé carefully. To print, click on **File** and click on **Print**. To print more than one copy, click on **Number of Copies** and type in the number you want; then enter. Click on **Print**. *As a word of caution, print just one copy the first time to make sure everything looks good. Then you can print more.*

4. To save your document to a floppy disk, click on **File**, click on **Save**, and type the path name as **a:\resume**; then enter.

5. To exit you must close your document by clicking on **File**, click on **Close**, click on **File**, and click on **Exit**.

DIRECTIONS FOR RESUMÉ NO. 9
WORDPERFECT 6.0 (DOS)

GENERAL SETUP

1. From a clear screen, make sure you are in the **Graphics Mode**, with your **Ribbon Bar** and **Fonts Button Bar** visible—like this:

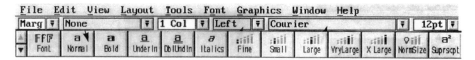

Menu Bar
Ribbon Bar
Fonts Button Bar

If the top of your screen looks different from the example above:

   a. Click on **View** and then click on **Graphics Mode.**

   b. Click on **View** and click on **Ribbon.**

   c. Click on **View** and click on **Button Bar Setup.**

   d. Click on **Select** and highlight **FONTS**; then enter.

2. Click on **Layout**, click on **Margins**, click on the down arrow key next to top margin until it reaches .5; then click on the down arrow key next to bottom margin until it reaches .5; then click on **OK**.

3. Click on **Layout**, click on **Page**, click on **2 (Center Current Page)**, and click on **OK**.

4. Click on **Layout**, click on **Line**, click on **Tab Set**, click on **Absolute**, click on **Clear All**, click on **Set Tab**, type **2.8** and enter. Click on **Set Tab** and type **3.16**; then enter. Click on **OK**.

MAIN HEADING SETUP

1. Click on the **Justification Button** in your ribbon bar. Double click on **center**.

2. Click on the **Font Button** in your ribbon bar and scroll the pull–down list until you get to **Dutch 801 Roman**; then double click on that choice.

3. Click on the **Point Size Button** in your ribbon bar. Scroll the pull–down list and double click on **14**.

4. Click on **Bold** in your button bar. Now type your name in all capitals.

5. Click on **Point Size** and double click on **12**. Then click on **Bold** to turn it off. Enter once.

6. Type your street address; then enter. Type your city, state, and zip code; then enter. Type your area code and phone number; then enter once.

7. Click on the **Justification Button** in the ribbon bar and double click on **Left**. Then enter twice.

CAREER OBJECTIVE SETUP

1. Click on **Bold** in your button bar. In all capitals type **CAREER OBJECTIVE:**. Then click on **Bold** in your button bar to turn it off.

2. Hit **F4** (indent) and begin to type your objective letting it word wrap at the end of the line. Now enter three times.

QUALIFICATIONS SETUP

1. Click on **Bold** in your button bar. In all capitals type **QUALIFI-CATIONS:**. Then click on **Bold** in your button bar to turn it off.

2. Hit **F4** (indent). To create the bullet, hit **CTRL+W** and type **4,0**; then enter once. Space once and type your first qualification; enter once.

3. Repeat Step 2 until all qualifications have been listed. Then enter three times to begin the next section.

EDUCATION SETUP

1. Click on **Bold** in your button bar. In all capitals type **EDUCA-TION:**.

2. Tab. Begin with your most recent education by typing the name of the school. Then click on **Bold** in your button bar to turn it off; enter once.

3. Tab, type the city, state, and zip code of your school; then enter once.

4. Tab, click on **Italics** and **Bold** in your button bar, type your course of study or degree received and the date; click on **Italics** and **Bold** in your button bar to turn them off and then enter twice.

5. Repeat Steps 2–4 for any other schools you want to list. Then enter three times to begin the next section.

EXPERIENCE SETUP

1. Click on **Bold** in your button bar. In all capitals type **EXPERI-ENCE:**. Then click on **Bold** in your button bar to turn it off. Enter twice.

2. Begin with your most recent experience by typing the dates you were employed, making sure that all digits align. Leave one space before and after the hyphen. Then tab, click on **Bold** in your button bar, and type the name of the company. Then click on **Bold** in your button bar to turn it off; enter once.

3. Tab, type the city, state, and zip code of the company; then enter once.

4. Tab, click on **Italics** and **Bold** in your button bar, and type your job title, click on **Italics** and **Bold** in your button bar to turn them off; then enter once.

5. Hit **F4** (indent) and begin to type your job description letting it word wrap. Enter twice.

6. Repeat Steps 2–5 until all experience has been listed. Then enter three times to continue with the next section.

ACCOMPLISHMENTS SETUP

1. Click on **Bold** in your button bar and type **ACCOMPLISH-MENTS:**. Click on **Bold** in your button bar to turn it off.

2. Tab and create the bullet by hitting **CTRL+W** and typing **4,0**; then enter once. Space once and list your first accomplishment.

3. Repeat Step 2 until all of your accomplishments have been listed. Then enter three times to continue with the next section.

REFERENCE SETUP

1. Click on **Bold** in your button bar. In all capitals type **REFER-ENCES:**. Then click on **Bold** in your button bar to turn it off. Tab and type Available upon Request.
   ### DO NOT ENTER AFTER THE LAST LINE.

FINAL REVIEW

1. Hit your **Page Up Key** to take you to the top of your page. Click on **File** and click on **Print Preview**. If you don't see the

entire page, click on **View** and click on **Full Page**. While you won't actually be able to read the words, you will get an overall idea of how it looks on the page. When you are through viewing, click on **Close** to return to the regular screen.

2. To run a spell check, click on **Tools**, click on **Writing Tools**, click on **Speller**, click on **Document**, and begin the spell check process.

3. Proofread your resumé carefully. To print, click on **File** and click on **Print**. To print more than one copy, click on **Number of Copies** and type in the number you want; then enter. Click on **Print**. *As a word of caution, print just one copy the first time to make sure everything looks good. Then you can print more.*

4. To save your document to a floppy disk, click on **File**, click on **Save**, and type the path name as **a:\resume**; then enter.

5. To exit you must close your document by clicking on **File**, click on **Close**, click on **File**, and click on **Exit**.

**DIRECTIONS FOR RESUMÉ NO. 10
WORDPERFECT 6.0 (DOS)**

GENERAL SETUP

1. From a clear screen, make sure you are in the **Graphics Mode**, with your **Ribbon Bar** and **Fonts Button Bar** visible—like this:

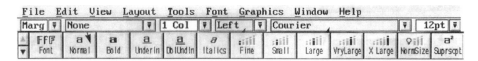

Menu Bar
Ribbon Bar
Fonts Button Bar

If the top of your screen looks different from the example above:

   a. Click on **View** and then click on **Graphics Mode.**

   b. Click on **View** and click on **Ribbon.**

   c. Click on **View** and click on **Button Bar Setup.**

   d. Click on **Select** and highlight **FONTS**; then enter.

2. Click on **Layout**, click on **Margins**, click on the down arrow key next to top margin until it reaches .5; then click on the down arrow key next to bottom margin until it reaches .5; then click on **OK**.

3. Click on **Layout**, click on **Page**, click on **2 (Center Current Page)**, and click on **OK**.

4. Click on **Layout**, click on **Line**, click on **Tab Set**, click on **Absolute**, click on **Clear All**, click on **Set Tab** and type **3** and enter. Click on **Set Tab** and type **3.25** and enter. Click on **OK**.

MAIN HEADING SETUP

1. Click on the **Justification Button** in your ribbon bar. Double click on **center**.

2. Click on the **Font Button** in your ribbon bar and scroll the pull–down list until you get to **Dutch 801 Roman**; then double click on that choice.

3. Click on the **Point Size Button** in your ribbon bar and double click on **12**. Then click on **Bold** in your button bar.

4. Now type your name in all capitals. Then click on **Bold** to turn it off. Enter twice.

5. Type your street address; then enter. Type your city, state, and zip code; then enter. Type your area code and phone number; then enter twice.

6. Click on the **Justification Button** in the ribbon bar and double click on **Left**. Then enter once more.

7. In your menu bar click on **Graphics**. Click on **Graphics Lines**. Click on **Create**. Click on **6** (line style), click on **CyanMat**, and click on **OK**; then enter three times to continue with next section.

CAREER OBJECTIVE SETUP

1. Click on **Bold** in your button bar. In all capitals type **CAREER OBJECTIVE:**. Then click on **Bold** in your button bar to turn it off.

2. Hit **F4** (indent) and type your career objective letting it word wrap at the end of the line. When you are through, enter three times.

QUALIFICATIONS SETUP

1. Click on **Bold** in your button bar. In all capitals type **QUALIFI-CATIONS:**. Click on **Bold** in your button bar to turn it off.

2. Tab and create the bullet by hitting **CTRL+W** and typing **4,47**; then enter. Now hit **F4** (indent) and type your first qualification letting it word wrap if it takes more than one line; enter once.

3. Repeat Step 2 until all qualifications have been listed. Then enter three times to continue with the next section.

SKILLS SETUP

1. Click on **Bold** in your button bar. In all capitals type **SKILLS:**. Click on **Bold** in your button bar to turn it off.

2. Tab and create the bullet by hitting **CTRL+W** and typing **4,47**; then enter. Now tab and type your first skill; enter once.

3. Repeat Step 2 until all skills have been listed. Then enter three times to continue with the next section.

EDUCATION SETUP

1. Click on **Bold** in your button bar. In all capitals type **EDUCA-TION:**.

2. Tab, click on **Italics** in your button bar, and begin with your most recent education by typing the name of the school in all capitals. Click on **Bold** and **Italics** in your button bar to turn them off. Enter once.

3. Tab and type the street address. Enter once.

4. Tab and type the city, state, and zip code of your school; then enter once.

5. Tab, click on **Bold** in your button bar, type your course of study or degree received and the date; click on **Bold** in your button bar to turn it off; then enter twice.

6. Repeat Steps 2–5 for any other schools you want to list. Then enter three times to begin the next section.

EXPERIENCE SETUP

1. Click on **Bold** in your button bar. In all capitals type **EXPERI-ENCE:**.

2. Tab, click on **Italics** in your button bar, and begin with your most recent experience by typing the name of the company in all capitals. Click on **Bold** and **Italics** in your button bar to turn them off; then enter once.

3. Tab and type the street address; then enter once.

4. Tab and type the city, state, and zip code of the company; then enter once.

5. Tab, click on **Bold** in your button bar, and type your job title followed by the dates of your employment in parentheses. Click on **Bold** in your button bar to turn it off; then enter twice.

6. Repeat Steps 2–5 until all experience has been listed. Enter three times to continue with the last section.

REFERENCE SETUP

1. Click on **Bold** in your button bar. In all capitals type **REFER-ENCES:**. Then click on **Bold** in your button bar to turn it off. Tab and type Available upon Request.
   DO NOT ENTER AFTER THE LAST LINE.

FINAL REVIEW

1. Hit your **Page Up Key** to take you to the top of your page. Click on **File** and click on **Print Preview**. If you don't see the

entire page, click on **View** and click on **Full Page**. While you won't actually be able to read the words, you will get an overall idea of how it looks on the page. When you are through viewing, click on **Close** to return to the regular screen.

2. To run a spell check, click on **Tools**, click on **Writing Tools**, click on **Speller**, click on **Document**, and begin the spell check process.

3. Proofread your resumé carefully. To print, click on **File** and click on **Print**. To print more than one copy, click on **Number of Copies** and type in the number you want; then enter. Click on **Print**. *As a word of caution, print just one copy the first time to make sure everything looks good. Then you can print more.*

4. To save your document to a floppy disk, click on **File**, click on **Save**, and type the path name as **a:\resume**; then enter.

5. To exit you must close your document by clicking on **File**, click on **Close**, click on **File**, and click on **Exit**.

Notes

APPENDIX **C** TYPING YOUR RESUMÉ
USING MICORSOFT
WORD 6.0 (WINDOWS)

*I*nstructions for creating each of the 10 resumé styles shown on pages 34–43 are provided. If you follow these instructions, your resumé will look identical to the one you have selected.

Depending on your printer's capabilities, you may want to choose a different font than the one in the directions. If you chose a different font, then the tabs indicated in the directions may need to be altered. You will have to make the appropriate adjustments in those cases.

If you are having trouble getting your resumé to fit on one page, put the street, city, state, and zip code on the same line for each entry under "Education" and "Experience."

DIRECTIONS FOR RESUMÉ NO. 1
MICROSOFT WORD 6.0 (WINDOWS)

GENERAL SETUP

1. From a clear screen, make sure you are in the Page Layout mode with your Standard Bar, Format Bar, and Ruler Bar visible—like this:

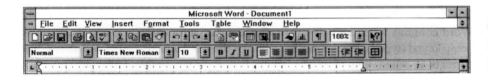

Standard Bar
Format Bar
Ruler Bar

   If they are not visible, click on **View** and then click on **Page Layout**. Then click on **View** and click on **Ruler**.

2. Click on **File**, click on **Page Setup**, click on **Margins**, click on the down arrow key next to top margin until it reaches .5; then click on the down arrow key next to bottom margin until it reaches .5; then click on **OK**.

3. Click on **File**, click on **Page Setup**, click on **Layout**, click on the down arrow under **Vertical Alignment**, click on **Center**, and click on **OK**.

4. Click on **Format**, click on **Tabs**, and click on **Clear All**. With your cursor in the **Tab Stop Position Box**, type **2.8**; then enter.

MAIN HEADING SETUP

1. Click on the **Center Justification Button** in your Format Tool Bar.

2. Click on the **Font Button** in your Format Bar, scroll down the list until you get to **Times New Roman**, then click on that choice. Click on the **Point Size** button in your Format Bar. From the pull-down list of choices, click on **16**. Then click on **b (Bold)** in your Format Bar.

3. Now type your name in all capitals. Then click on the **Point Size** button in the Format Bar and click on **12**. Then click on **b (Bold)** in your Format Bar to turn it off. Enter twice.

4. Type your street address; then enter. Type your city, state, and zip code; then enter. Type your area code and phone number; then enter once.

5. Click on the **Left Justification Button** in the Format Bar. Then enter once more.

6. To create the horizontal line, click on **View**, click on **Toolbars**, click on **Borders**, and click on **OK**. The first box in the Borders Toolbar is the Line Style Option Box. Click on the **down arrow in the Line Style Option Box** and from the pull-down list, click on **4½ pt**. To make the line appear, click on the **second box in the Borders Toolbar (Top Border)** and your line will be inserted.

7. Hit enter three times.

CAREER OBJECTIVE SETUP

1. Click on **Point Size** in your Format Bar and click on **14**. Click on **b (Bold)** and **u (Underline)** in your Format Bar. In all capitals type **CAREER OBJECTIVE**. Then click on **Point Size** again in your Format Bar and click on **12**. Then click on **b (Bold)** and **u (Underline)** in your Format Bar to turn them off. Now enter twice.

2. Type your career objective letting it word wrap at the end of the line. When you are through, enter twice.

EDUCATION SETUP

1. Click on **Point Size** in your Format Bar and click on **14**. Click on **b (Bold)** and **u (Underline)** in your Format Bar. In all capitals type **EDUCATION**. Then click on **Point Size** again in your Format Bar and click on **12**. Then click on **b (Bold)** and **u (Underline)** in your Format Bar to turn them off. Now enter twice.

2. Begin with your most recent education by typing the dates you attended, making sure that all digits align. Leave one

space before and after the hyphen. Then tab, click on **b (Bold)** in your Format Bar, and type the name of the school. Then click on **b (Bold)** in your Format Bar to turn it off; enter once.

3. Tab, type the street address, city, state, and zip code of your school; then enter once.

4. Tab, click on *i* **(Italics)** and **b (Bold)** in your Format Bar, type your course of study or degree received, click on *i* **(Italics)** and **b (Bold)** in your Format Bar to turn them off; then enter once.

5. Tab, type when you received your diploma or when it will be awarded, or the number of credits earned, if applicable; then enter twice.

6. Repeat Steps 2–5 for any other schools you want to list. Then enter twice to begin the next section.

AREAS OF SKILLS SETUP

1. Click on **Point Size** in your Format Bar and click on **14**. Click on **b (Bold)** and **u (Underline)** in your Format Bar. In all capitals type **AREAS OF SKILLS**. Then click on **Point Size** again in your Format Bar and click on **12**. Then click on **b (Bold)** and **u (Underline)** in your Format Bar to turn them off.

2. Tab. Click on **Insert**, click on **Symbol**, click on the down arrow next to the **Font Dialog Box**, and click on **Wingdings**. Click on the symbol you'd like to use as a bullet. Then click on **Insert** and click on **Close.** Type your first skill; then enter.

3. Repeat Step 2 until all of your skills have been listed.

4. Hit enter twice when you are through with this section.

EXPERIENCE SETUP

1. Click on **Point Size** in your Format Bar and click on **13**. Click on **b (Bold)** and **u (Underline)** in your Format Bar. In all capitals type **EXPERIENCE**. Then click on **Point Size** again in your Format Tool Bar and click on **12**. Then click on **b (Bold)** and **u (Underline)** in your Format Bar to turn them off. Then enter twice.

2. Begin with your most recent experience by typing the dates you were employed, making sure that all digits align. Leave one

space before and after the hyphen. Then tab, click on **b (Bold)** in your Format Bar, and type the name of the company. Then click on **b (Bold)** in your Format Bar to turn it off; enter once.

3. Tab, type the street address, city, state, and zip code of the company; then enter once.

4. Tab, click on *i* **(Italics)** and **b (Bold)** in your Format Bar, and type your job title, click on *i* **(Italics)** and **b (Bold)** in your Format Bar to turn them off; then enter once.

5. Tab. Click on **Insert**, click on **Symbol**, click on the down arrow next to the **Font Dialog Box**, and click on **Wingdings.** Click on the symbol you'd like to use as a bullet. Then click on **Insert** and click on **Close.** Type your first accomplishment or responsibility of your job; then enter.

6. Repeat Step 5 until all of your skills have been listed.

7. Hit enter twice and repeat Steps 2–6 until all of your experience has been listed. When you are through with this section, enter twice.

REFERENCE SETUP

1. Click on **Point Size** in your Format Bar and click on **13**. Click on **b (Bold)** and **u (Underline)** in your Format Bar. In all capitals type **<u>REFERENCES</u>**. Then click on **Point Size** again in your Format Bar and click on **12**. Then click on **b (Bold)** and **u (Underline)** in your Format Bar to turn them off. Tab and type Available upon Request.

   DO NOT ENTER AFTER THE LAST LINE.

FINAL REVIEW

1. Hit your **Page Up Key** to take you to the top of your page. Click on the button in your Format Bar that looks like a magnifying glass. While you won't actually be able to read the words, you will get an overall idea of how it looks on the page. When you are through viewing, click on the **Close** button to return to the regular screen.

2. To run a spell check, click on **Tools**, click on **Spelling**, and begin the spell check process.

3. Proofread your resumé carefully. To print, click on **File** and click on **Print**. To print more than one copy, click on **Copies** and type in the number you want; then enter. Click on **OK**. *As a word of caution, print just one copy the first time to make sure everything looks good. Then you can print more.*

4. To save your document to a floppy disk, click on **File**, click on **Save**, and type the path name as **a:\resume**; then enter.

5. To exit you must close your document by clicking on **File**, click on **Close**, click on **File**, and click on **Exit**.

DIRECTIONS FOR RESUMÉ NO. 2
MICROSOFT WORD 6.0 (WINDOWS)

GENERAL SETUP

1. From a clear screen, make sure you are in the Page Layout Mode with your Standard Bar, Format Bar, and Ruler Bar visible—like this:

Standard Bar
Format Bar
Ruler Bar

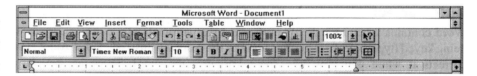

If they are not visible, click on **View** and then click on **Page Layout**. Then click on **View** and click on **Ruler**.

2. Click on **File**, click on **Page Setup**, click on **Margins**, click on the down arrow key next to top margin until it reaches .5; then click on the down arrow key next to bottom margin until it reaches .5; then click on **OK**.

3. Click on **File**, click on **Page Setup**, click on **Layout**, click on **Vertical Alignment**, click on **Center**, and click on **OK**.

4. Click on **Format**, click on **Tabs**, and click on **Clear All**. With your cursor in the **Tab Stop Position Box**, type **2.8**; then enter. With your cursor again in the **Tab Stop Position Box**, type **5**; then enter.

MAIN HEADING SETUP

1. Click on the **Center Justification Button** in your Format Bar.

2. Click on the **Font Button** in your Format Bar and scroll down the list until you get to **Times New Roman**, then click on that choice. Click on the **Point Size** button in your Format Bar where it says **12 pt.** From the pull-down list of choices, click on **16**. Then click on **b (Bold)** in your Format Bar.

3. Now type your name in all capitals. Then click on the **Point Size** button in the Format Bar and click on **12**. Then click on **b (Bold)** in your Format Bar to turn it off. Enter twice.

4. Type your street address; then enter. Type your city, state, and zip code; then enter. Type your area code and phone number; then enter once.

5. Click on the **Left Justification Button** in the Format Bar; then enter once more.

6. To create the horizontal line, click on **View**, click on **Toolbars**, click on **Borders**, and click on **OK**. The first box in the Borders Toolbar is the Line Style Option Box. Click on the **down arrow in the Line Style Option Box** and from the pull–down list, click on the line of your choice. To make the line appear, click on the **second box in the Borders Toolbar (Top Border)** and your line will be inserted.

7. Then enter three times to continue.

CAREER OBJECTIVE SETUP

1. Click on **Point Size** in your Format Bar and click on **13**. Click on **b (Bold)** and *i* **(Italics)** in your Format Bar. In all capitals type *CAREER OBJECTIVE*. Then click on **Point Size** again in your Format Bar and click on **12**. Then click on **b (Bold)** and *i* **(Italics)** in your Format Bar to turn them off.

2. Click on **Format**, click on **Paragraph**, click on **Indent**, and type your career objective letting it word wrap at the end of the line. When you are through, enter twice.

EDUCATION SETUP

1. Click on **Point Size** in your Format Bar and click on **13**. Click on **b (Bold)** and *i* **(Italics)** in your Format Bar. In all capitals type *EDUCATION*. Then click on **Point Size** in your Format Bar again and click on **12**. Then click on **b (Bold)** and *i* **(Italics)** in your Format Bar to turn them off.

2. Tab and type the name of your most recent school; enter once.

3. Tab, type the street address, city, state, and zip code of your school; then enter once.

4. Tab, click on **b (Bold)** in your Format Bar, type your course of study or degree received, click on **b (Bold)** in your Format Bar to turn it off; then enter once.

5. Tab, type when you received your diploma or when it will be awarded, or the number of credits earned, if applicable; then enter twice.

6. Repeat Steps 2–5 for any other schools you want to list. Then enter twice to begin the next section.

AREAS OF SKILLS SETUP

1. Click on **Point Size** in your Format Bar and click on **13**. Click on **b (Bold)** and *i (Italics)* in your Format Bar. In all capitals type ***AREAS OF SKILLS***. Then click on **Point Size** in your Format Bar again and click on **12**. Then click on **b (Bold)** and *i (Italics)* in your Format Bar to turn them off.

2. Tab and type your first skill; then tab and type your second skill. Now enter and continue in the same manner until all skills have been listed. Hit enter twice when you are through with this section.

EXPERIENCE SETUP

1. Click on **Point Size** in your Format Bar and click on **13**. Click on **b (Bold)** and *i (Italics)* in your Format Bar. In all capitals type ***EXPERIENCE***. Then click on **Point Size** in your Format Bar again and click on **12**. Then click on **b (Bold)** and *i (Italics)* in your Format Bar to turn them off.

2. Begin with your most recent experience first. Tab and type the name of the company. Then enter once.

3. Tab, type the street address, city, state, and zip code of the company; then enter once.

4. Type the dates you were employed, making sure that all digits align. Leave one space before and after the hyphen.

5. Then tab. Click on **b (Bold)** in your Format Bar, and type your job title followed by a colon; click on **b (Bold)** in your Format Bar to turn it off. Now space twice and begin to type your job description, letting it word wrap at the end of the line.

6. To properly align Step 5, use your mouse to highlight the section you just typed. Then click on **Format**, click on **Paragraph**, click on the up arrow next to Indentation until it reaches 2.8. Then click on **OK**. This should make this section properly aligned.

7. Enter twice.

8. Repeat Steps 2–7 until all your experience has been listed.

REFERENCE SETUP

1. Click on **Point Size** in your Format Bar and click on **13**. Click on **b (Bold)** and *i (Italics)* in your Format Bar. In all capitals

type ***REFERENCES***. Then click on **Point Size** again and click on **12**. Then click on **b (Bold)** and *i* **(Italics)** in your Format Bar to turn them off. Tab and type Provided upon Request.

DO NOT ENTER AFTER THE LAST LINE.

FINAL REVIEW

1. Hit your **Page Up Key** to take you to the top of your page. Click on the button in your Format Bar that looks like a magnifying glass. While you won't actually be able to read the words, you will get an overall idea of how it looks on the page. When you are through viewing, click on the **Close** button to return to the regular screen.

2. To run a spell check, click on **Tools**, click on **Spelling**, and begin the spell check process.

3. Proofread your resumé carefully. To print, click on **File** and click on **Print**. To print more than one copy, click on **Copies** and type in the number you want; then enter. Click on **OK**. *As a word of caution, print just one copy the first time to make sure everything looks good. Then you can print more.*

4. To save your document to a floppy disk, click on **File**, click on **Save**, and type the path name as **a:\resume**; then enter.

5. To exit you must close your document by clicking on **File**, click on **Close**, click on **File**, and click on **Exit**.

DIRECTIONS FOR RESUMÉ NO. 3
MICROSOFT WORD 6.0 (WINDOWS)

GENERAL SETUP

1. From a clear screen, make sure you are in the Page Layout Mode with your Standard Bar, Format Bar, and Ruler Bar visible—like this:

Standard Bar
Format Bar
Ruler Bar

   If they are not visible, click on **View** and then click on **Page Layout**. Then click on **View** and click on **Ruler**.

2. Click on **File**, click on **Page Setup**, click on **Margins**, click on the down arrow key next to top margin until it reaches .5; then click on the down arrow key next to bottom margin until it reaches .5; then click on **OK**.

3. Click on **File**, click on **Page Setup**, click on **Layout**, click on **Vertical Alignment**, click on **Center**, and click on **OK**.

4. Click on **Format**, click on **Tabs**, and click on **Clear All**. With your cursor in the **Tab Stop Position Box**, type **2.4**; then enter.

MAIN HEADING SETUP

1. Click on the **Center Justification Button** in your Format Bar.

2. Click on the **Font Button** in your Format Bar and scroll down the list until you get to **Times New Roman**, then click on that choice. Click on the **Point Size** button in your Format Bar where it says **12 pt.** From the pull-down list of choices, click on **16**. Then click on **b (Bold)** in your Format Bar.

3. Now type your name in all capitals. Then click on the **Point Size** button in the Format Bar and click on **12**. Then click on **b (Bold)** in your Format Bar to turn it off. Enter twice.

4. Type your street address; then enter. Type your city, state, and zip code; then enter. Type your area code and phone number; then enter once.

5. Click on the **Left Justification Button** in the Format Bar; then enter once more.

6. To create the horizontal line, click on **View**, click on **Toolbars**, click on **Borders**, and click on **OK**. The first box in the Borders Toolbar is the Line Style Option Box. Click on the **down arrow in the Line Style Option Box** and from the pull–down list, select the line style you desire. To make the line appear, click on the **second box in the Borders Toolbar (Top Border)** and your line will be inserted.

7. Hit enter three times.

CAREER OBJECTIVE SETUP

1. Click on **Point Size** in your Format Bar and click on **14**. Click on **b (Bold)** in your Format Bar. In all capitals type **CAREER OBJECTIVE**. Then click on **Point Size** again and click on **12**. Then click on **b (Bold)** in your Format Bar to turn it off. Enter twice and type your career objective letting it word wrap at the end of the line. When you are through, enter twice.

EXPERIENCE SETUP

1. Click on **Point Size** in your Format Bar and click on **14**. Click on **b (Bold)** in your Format Bar. In all capitals type **EXPERI-ENCE**. Then click on **Point Size** again and click on **12**. Then click on **b (Bold)** in your Format Bar to turn it off.

2. Begin with your most recent experience. Tab, click on **b (Bold)** in your Format Bar and type the name of the company. Click on **b (Bold)** in your Format Bar to turn it off. Then enter once.

3. Tab, type the street address, city, state, and zip code of the company; then enter once.

4. Type the beginning and ending years you were employed, making sure to leave a space before and after the hyphen.

5. Then tab, click on **b (Bold)** in your Format Bar, and type your job title. Then click on **b (Bold)** in your Format Bar to turn it off; then enter once.

6. Tab. Click on **Insert**, click on **Symbol**, click on the down arrow next to the **Font Dialog Box**, and click on **Wingdings**. Click on the symbol you'd like to use as a bullet. Then click on **Insert** and click on **Close**. At this point you are going to type your first accomplishment or responsibility of the job.

7. If any item will take more than one line, let it word wrap back to the margin. Then to make that item properly aligned you will have to highlight the lines, click on **Format**, click on

Paragraph, click on the up arrow in the **Indentation Box** until it reaches 2.4; then enter. Click on **OK**. This should make any item that is more than one line long properly indented and aligned.

8. Repeat Step 6 until all of your items have been listed.

9. Repeat Steps 2–7 until all your experience has been listed; then enter twice to continue with next section.

EDUCATION SETUP

1. Click on **Point Size** in your Format Bar and click on **14**. Click on **b (Bold)** in your Format Bar. In all capitals type **EDUCATION**. Then click on **Point Size** again and click on **12**.

2. Tab and type the name of your most recent school. Then click on **b (Bold)** in your Format Bar to turn it off; enter once.

3. Tab, type the street address, city, state, and zip code of your school; then enter once.

4. Type the beginning and ending year you attended that school leaving a space before and after the hyphen.

5. Tab, click on **b (Bold)** in your Format Bar, type your course of study or degree received and your grade point average if it is above a 3.0; click on **b (Bold)** in your Format Bar to turn it off and then enter once.

6. Tab, type the number of credits earned so far if you have not yet graduated or any academic honors received; then enter twice.

7. Repeat Steps 2–6 for any other schools you want to list. Then enter twice to begin the next section.

AFFILIATIONS SETUP

1. Click on **Point Size** in your Format Bar and click on **14**. Click on **b (Bold)** in your Format Bar. In all capitals type **AFFILIATIONS**. Then click on **Point Size** again and click on **12**. Then click on **b (Bold)** in your Format Bar to turn it off. Enter twice.

2. Tab; click on **Insert**, click on **Symbol**, click on the down arrow next to the **Font Dialog Box**, and click on **Wingdings**. Click on the symbol you'd like to use as a bullet. Then click on **Insert** and click on **Close**. Type your first item.

3. If any item will take more than one line, let it word wrap back to the margin. Then to make that item properly aligned you

will have to highlight the lines, click on **Format**, click on **Paragraph**, click on the up arrow in the Indentation Box until it reaches 2.4; then enter. Click on **OK**. This should make any item that is more than one line long properly indented and aligned.

4. Repeat Step 2 until all of your items have been listed.

5. Enter twice after the last item.

REFERENCE SETUP

1. Click on **Point Size** in your Format Bar and click on **11**. Click on the center justification button in your format bar and type References Available upon Request.

    DO NOT ENTER AFTER THE LAST LINE.

FINAL REVIEW

1. Hit your **Page Up Key** to take you to the top of your page. Click on the button in your Format Bar that looks like a magnifying glass. While you won't actually be able to read the words, you will get an overall idea of how it looks on the page. When you are through viewing, click on the **Close** button to return to the regular screen.

2. To run a spell check, click on **Tools**, click on **Spelling** and begin the spell check process.

3. Proofread your resumé carefully. To print, click on **File** and click on **Print**. To print more than one copy, click on **Copies** and type in the number you want; then enter. Click on **OK**. *As a word of caution, print just one copy the first time to make sure everything looks good. Then you can print more.*

4. To save your document to a floppy disk, click on **File**, click on **Save**, and type the path name as **a:\resume**; then enter.

5. To exit you must close your document by clicking on **File**, click on **Close**, click on **File**, and click on **Exit**.

DIRECTIONS FOR RESUMÉ No. 4
MICROSOFT WORD 6.0 (WINDOWS)

GENERAL SETUP

1. From a clear screen, make sure you are in the Page Layout Mode with your Standard Bar, Format Bar, and Ruler Bar visible—like this:

Standard Bar
Format Bar
Ruler Bar

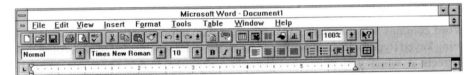

If they are not visible, click on **View** and then click on **Page Layout**. Then click on **View** and click on **Ruler**.

2. Click on **File**, click on **Page Setup**, click on **Margins**, click on the down arrow key next to top margin until it reaches .5; then click on the down arrow key next to bottom margin until it reaches .5; then click on **OK**.

3. Click on **File**, click on **Page Setup**, click on **Layout**, click on **Vertical Alignment**, click on **Center**, and click on **OK**.

4. Click on **Format**, click on **Tabs**, and click on **Clear All**. With your cursor in the **Tab Stop Position Box**, type **2.4**; then enter.

MAIN HEADING SETUP

1. Click on the **Center Justification Button** in your Format Tool Bar.

2. Click on **Font** in your Format Bar and scroll down the list until you get to **Times New Roman**, then click on that choice. Click on the **Point Size** button in your Format Bar where it says **12 pt.** From the pull-down list of choices, click on **13**. Then click on **b (Bold)** in your Format Bar.

3. Now type your name in all capitals. Then click on **Point Size** and click on **11**. Then click on **b (Bold)** in your Format Bar to turn it off. Enter once.

4. Type your street address; then enter. Type your city, state, and zip code; then enter. Type your area code and phone number; then enter once.

CAREER OBJECTIVE SETUP

1. Click on **Point Size** in your Format Bar and click on **12**. Click on **b (Bold)** and **u (Underline)** in your Format Bar. In all capitals type **CAREER OBJECTIVE**. Then click on **b (Bold)** and **u (Underline)** in your Format Bar to turn them off.

2. Click on the **Left Justification Button** in your Format Bar. Enter twice and type your career objective letting it word wrap at the end of the line. When you are through, enter twice.

EXPERIENCE SETUP

1. Click on the **Center Justification Button** in your Format Bar. Click on **b (Bold)** and **u (Underline)** in your Format Bar. In all capitals type **WORK EXPERIENCE**. Then click on **b (Bold)** and **u (Underline)** in your Format Bar to turn them off. Click on the **Left Justification Button** in your Format Bar. Enter twice.

2. Begin with your most recent experience by typing the dates you were employed, making sure that all digits align. Leave one space before and after the hyphen. Then tab and in all capitals type the name of the company. Then enter once.

3. Tab, type the street address, city, state, and zip code of the company; then enter once.

4. Then tab, click on **b (Bold)** in your Format Bar, and type your job title. Then click on **b (Bold)** in your Format Bar to turn it off; then enter once.

5. Type the information stressing your job accomplishments and responsibilities. To properly align this paragraph with the rest of your text, select (highlight) this text, click on **Format**, click on **Paragraph**, click on the up arrow next to Indentation until it reaches **2.4**, then enter and click on **OK**. This text should now be aligned with your job title.

6. Repeat Steps 2–5 until all your experience has been listed. Hit enter twice to continue with next section.

EDUCATION SETUP

1. Click on the **Center Justification Button** in your Format Bar. Click on **b (Bold)** and **u (Underline)** in your Format Bar. In all capitals type **EDUCATION**; enter twice. Click on **b (bold)** and **u (Underline)** in your Format Bar to turn them off. Click on the **Left Justification Button** in your Format Bar.

2. Begin with your most recent education by typing the dates you attended, making sure that all digits align. Leave one space before and after the hyphen. Then tab and type the name of your school in all capitals; enter once.

3. Tab, type the street address, city, state, and zip code of your school; then enter once.

4. Tab, click on **b (Bold)** in your Format Bar, type your course of study or degree received. Click on **b (Bold)** in your Format Bar to turn it off and then enter once.

5. Tab and type when you received your diploma or when it will be awarded, or the number of credits earned, if applicable; then enter twice.

6. Repeat Steps 2–5 for any other schools you want to list. Then enter twice to begin the next section.

AREAS OF SKILLS SETUP

1. Click on **Format** and click on **Tabs**. With your cursor in the **Tab Stop Position Box**, type **2.74**; then enter. Click on **Format,** click on **Tabs**, and with your cursor again in the **Tab Stop Position Box**, type **5**; then enter.

2. Click on the **Center Justification Button** in your Format Bar. Click on **b (Bold)** and **u (Underline)** in your Format Bar and in all capitals type **<u>AREAS OF SKILLS</u>**. Click on **b (bold)** and **u (Underline)** to turn them off. Click on the **Left Justification Button** in your Format Bar; then enter twice.

3. Type your first skill; tab and type your second skill; tab and type your third skill; then enter once. Repeat this step until all skills have been listed. Then enter twice to continue.

REFERENCE SETUP

1. Click on the **Center Justification Button** in your Format Bar. Click on **b (Bold)** and **u (Underline)** in your Format Bar and in all capitals type **<u>REFERENCES</u>**. Click on **b (Bold)** and **u (Underline)** in your Format Bar to turn them off; then enter twice.

2. Type Available upon Request.
   DO NOT ENTER AFTER THE LAST LINE.

FINAL REVIEW

1. Hit your **Page Up Key** to take you to the top of your page. Click on the button in your Format Bar that looks like a magnifying

glass. While you won't actually be able to read the words, you will get an overall idea of how it looks on the page. When you are through viewing, click on the **Close** button to return to the regular screen.

2. To run a spell check, click on **Tools**, click on **Spelling** and begin the spell check process.

3. Proofread your resumé carefully. To print, click on **File** and click on **Print**. To print more than one copy, click on **Copies** and type in the number you want; then enter. Click on **OK**. *As a word of caution, print just one copy the first time to make sure everything looks good. Then you can print more.*

4. To save your document to a floppy disk, click on **File**, click on **Save**, and type the path name as **a:\resume**; then enter.

5. To exit you must close your document by clicking on **File**, click on **Close**, click on **File**, and click on **Exit**.

DIRECTIONS FOR RESUMÉ NO. 5
MICROSOFT WORD 6.0 (WINDOWS)

GENERAL SETUP

1. From a clear screen, make sure you are in the Page Layout Mode with your Standard Bar, Format Bar, and Ruler Bar visible—like this:

Standard Bar
Format Bar
Ruler Bar

If they are not visible, click on **View** and then click on **Page Layout**. Then click on **View** and click on **Ruler**.

2. Click on **File**, click on **Page Setup**, click on **Margins**, click on the down arrow key next to top margin until it reaches .5; then click on the down arrow key next to bottom margin until it reaches .5; then click on **OK**.

3. Click on **File**, click on **Page Setup**, click on **Layout**, click on **Vertical Alignment**, click on **Center**, and click on **OK**.

4. Click on **Format**, click on **Tabs**, and click on **Clear All**. With your cursor in the **Tab Stop Position Box**, type **3**; then enter. With your cursor again in the **Tab Stop Position Box**, type **3.31**; then enter.

MAIN HEADING SETUP

1. Click on the **Center Justification Button** in your Format Bar.

2. Click on **Font** in your Format Bar and scroll down the list until you get to **Times New Roman**, then click on that choice. Click on the **Point Size** button in your Format Bar where it says **12 pt.** From the pull-down list of choices, click on **14**. Then click on **b (Bold)** in your Format Bar.

3. Now type your name in all capitals. Then click on the **Point Size** button in the Format Bar and click on **12**. Then click on **b (Bold)** in your Format Bar to turn it off. Enter twice.

4. Type your street address; then enter. Type your city, state, and zip code; then enter. Type your area code and phone number; then enter once.

5. Click on the **Left Justification Button** in the Format Bar; then enter once more.

6. To create the horizontal line, click on **View**, click on **Toolbars**, click on **Borders**, and click on **OK**. The first box in the Borders Toolbar is the Line Style Option Box. Click on the down **arrow in the Line Style Option Box** and from the pull–down list, select **4¹/₂ pt**. To make the line appear, click on the **second box in the Borders Toolbar (Top Border)** and your line will be inserted.

7. Then enter three times to continue.

CAREER OBJECTIVE SETUP

1. Click on **Point Size** in your Format Bar and click on **13**. Click on **b (Bold)** and *i* **(Italics)** in your Format Bar. In all capitals type ***CAREER OBJECTIVE***. Then click on **Point Size** again and click on **12**. Then click on **b (Bold)** and *i* **(Italics)** in your Format Bar to turn them off.

2. Tab. Type your career objective letting it word wrap at the end of the line.

3. To properly align Step 2, click on **Format**, click on **Paragraph**, click on the up arrow next to Indentation until it reaches **3**; then enter and click on **OK**.

4. Enter twice.

EDUCATION SETUP

1. Click on **Point Size** in your Format Bar and click on **13**. Click on **b (Bold)** and *i* **(Italics)** in your Format Bar. In all capitals type ***EDUCATION***. Then click on **Point Size** again and click on **12**. Then click on **b (Bold)** and *i* **(Italics)** in your Format Bar to turn them off.

2. Tab and begin with your most recent education by typing the name of the school. Enter once.

3. Tab and type the street address. Enter once.

4. Tab and type the city, state, and zip code of your school; then enter once.

5. Tab, click on **b (Bold)** in your Format Bar, type your course of study or degree received, click on **b (Bold)** in your Format Bar to turn it off; then enter once.

6. Tab, type when you received your diploma or when it will be awarded, or the number of credits earned, if applicable; then enter twice.

7. Repeat Steps 2–6 for any other schools you want to list. Then enter twice to begin the next section.

EXPERIENCE SETUP

1. Click on **Point Size** in your Format Bar and click on **13**. Click on **b (Bold)** and *i* **(Italics)** in your Format Bar. In all capitals type ***EXPERIENCE***. Then click on **Point Size** again and click on **12**. Then click on **b (Bold)** and *i* **(Italics)** in your Format Bar to turn them off.

2. Tab and begin with your most recent experience by typing the name of the company; then enter once.

3. Tab and type the street address; then enter once.

4. Tab and type the city, state, and zip code of the company; then enter once.

5. Tab, click on **b (Bold)** in your Format Bar, and type your job title, click on **b (Bold)** in your Format Bar to turn it off; then enter once.

6. Tab and type your dates of employment leaving one space before and after the hyphen; then enter twice.

7. Repeat Steps 2–6 until all experience has been listed.

AFFILIATIONS SETUP

1. Click on **Point Size** in your Format Bar and click on **13**. Click on **b (Bold)** and *i* **(Italics)** in your Format Bar. In all capitals type ***AFFILIATIONS***. Then click on **Point Size** again and click on **12**. Then click on **b (Bold)** and *i* **(Italics)** in your Format Bar to turn them off.

2. Tab; click on **Insert**, click on **Symbol**, click on the down arrow next to the **Font Dialog Box**, and click on **Wingdings**. Click on the symbol you'd like to use as a bullet. Then click on **Insert** and click on **Close**. Type the name of the first organization; then enter once.

3. Repeat this Step 2 until all items have been listed.

4. Enter twice to begin next section.

AWARDS/HONORS SETUP

1. Click on **Point Size** in your Format Bar and click on **13**. Click on **b (Bold)** and *i* **(Italics)** in your Format Bar. In all capitals type *AWARDS/HONORS*. Then click on **Point Size** again and click on **12**. Then click on **b (Bold)** and *i* **(Italics)** in your Format Bar to turn them off.

2. Tab; click on **Insert**, click on **Symbol**, click on the down arrow next to the **Font Dialog Box**, and click on **Wingdings**. Click on the symbol you'd like to use as a bullet. Then click on **Insert** and click on **Close**. Type the name of the award or honor; then enter once.

3. Repeat Step 2 until all items have been listed.

4. Enter twice to begin next section.

REFERENCE SETUP

1. Click on **Point Size** in your Format Bar and click on **13**. Click on **b (Bold)** and *i* **(Italics)** in your Format Bar. In all capitals type *REFERENCES*. Then click on **Point Size** again and click on **12**. Then click on **b (Bold)** and *i* **(Italics)** in your Format Bar to turn them off. Tab and type Available upon Request.

   DO NOT ENTER AFTER THE LAST LINE.

FINAL REVIEW

1. Hit your **Page Up Key** to take you to the top of your page. Click on the button in your Format Bar that looks like a magnifying glass. While you won't actually be able to read the words, you will get an overall idea of how it looks on the page. When you are through viewing, click on the **Close** button to return to the regular screen.

2. To run a spell check, click on **Tools**, click on **Spelling**, and begin the spell check process.

3. Proofread your resumé carefully. To print, click on **File** and click on **Print**. To print more than one copy, click on **Copies** and type in the number you want; then enter. Click on **OK**. *As a word of caution, print just one copy the first time to make sure everything looks good. Then you can print more.*

4. To save your document to a floppy disk, click on **File**, click on **Save**, and type the path name as **a:\resume**; then enter.

5. To exit you must close your document by clicking on **File**, click on **Close**, click on **File**, and click on **Exit**.

**DIRECTIONS FOR RESUMÉ NO. 6
MICROSOFT WORD 6.0 (WINDOWS)**

GENERAL SETUP

1. From a clear screen, make sure you are in the Page Layout Mode with your Standard Bar, Format Bar, and Ruler Bar visible—like this:

Standard Bar
Format Bar
Ruler Bar

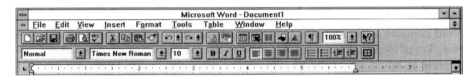

If they are not visible, click on **View** and then click on **Page Layout**. Then click on **View** and click on **Ruler**.

2. Click on **File**, click on **Page Setup**, click on **Margins**, click on the down arrow key next to top margin until it reaches .5; then click on the down arrow key next to bottom margin until it reaches .5; then click on **OK**.

3. Click on **File**, click on **Page Setup**, click on **Layout**, click on **Vertical Alignment**, click on **Center**, and click on **OK**.

4. Click on **Format**, click on **Tabs**, and click on **Clear All**. With your cursor in the **Tab Stop Position Box**, type **3**; then enter. With your cursor again in the **Tab Stop Position Box**, type **3.44**; then enter. With your cursor again in the **Tab Stop Position Box,** type 6; then enter.

MAIN HEADING SETUP

1. Click on the **Center Justification Button** in your Format Bar.

2. Click on the **Font Button** in your Format Bar and scroll down the list until you get to **Times New Roman**, then click on that choice. Click on the **Point Size** button in your Format Bar and click on **16**. Then click on **b (Bold)** in your Format Bar.

3. Now type your name in all capitals. Then click on **Point Size** and click on **12**. Click on the **Left Justification Button** in your Format Bar. Enter twice.

4. Type **Home Address:**, tab 3 times, and type **School Address:** and enter twice. Then click on **Point Size** and click on **11**. Click on **b (Bold)** in your Format Bar to turn it off.

5. Type your home street address; then tab three times and type your school street address; enter once.

6. Type your home city, state, and zip code; tab three times and type your school city, state, and zip code; then enter once.

7. Type your home area code and phone number; tab three times and type your school area code and phone number; then enter twice.

8. To create the horizontal line, click on **View**, click on **Toolbars**, click on **Borders**, and click on **OK**. The first box in the Borders Toolbar is the Line Style Option Box. Click on the **down arrow in the Line Style Option Box** and from the pull–down list, select the line style you desire. To make the line appear, click on the **second box in the Borders Toolbar (Top Border)** and your line will be inserted.

9. Then enter three times to continue with next section.

CAREER OBJECTIVE SETUP

1. Click on **Point Size** in your Format Bar and click on **14**. Click on **b (Bold)** and *i* **(Italics)** in your Format Bar. In all capitals type *CAREER OBJECTIVE*. Then click on **Point Size** again and click on **12**. Then click on **b (Bold)** and *i* **(Italics)** in your Format Bar to turn them off. Now enter twice and type your career objective letting it word wrap at the end of the line. When you are through, enter twice.

EDUCATION SETUP

1. Click on **Point Size** in your Format Bar and click on **14**. Click on **b (Bold)** and *i* **(Italics)** in your Format Bar. In all capitals type *EDUCATION* and enter twice. Then click on **Point Size** again and click on **12**. Then click on **b (Bold)** and *i* **(Italics)** in your Format Bar to turn them off.

2. Type the beginning and ending year you attended the school leaving one space before and after the hyphen. Tab, click on **b (Bold)** in your Format Bar, and type the name of your most recent school in all capitals. Click on **b (Bold)** in your Format Bar to turn it off; then enter once.

3. Tab, type the street address, city, state, and zip code of your school; then enter once.

4. Tab and type what type of diploma you will receive and when; then enter twice.

5. Repeat Steps 2–4 for any other schools you want to list. Then enter twice to begin the next section.

EXPERIENCE SETUP

1. Click on **Point Size** in your Format Bar and click on **14**. Click on **b (Bold)** and *i (Italics)* in your Format Bar. In all capitals type ***EXPERIENCE***. Then click on **Point Size** again and click on **12**. Then click on **b (Bold)** and *i (Italics)* in your Format Bar to turn them off. Enter twice.

2. Begin with your most recent experience. Type the dates of your employment. Tab, click on **b (Bold)** in your Format Bar and type the name of the company in all capitals. Click on **b (Bold)** in your Format Bar to turn it off; then enter once.

3. Tab, type the street address, city, state, and zip code of the company; then enter once.

4. Tab. Click on **b (Bold)** in your Format Bar and type your job title followed by a colon; click on **b (Bold)** in your Format Bar to turn it off. Now space twice and begin to type your job description, letting it word wrap at the end of the line.

5. To make Step 4 properly aligned, select (highlight) that text. Click on **Format**, click on **Paragraph**, click on the up arrow key next to Indentation until it reaches **3**, enter and click on **OK**.

6. Enter twice.

7. Repeat Steps 2–6 until all your experience has been listed. Then enter twice to begin the next section.

ACTIVITIES SETUP

1. Click on **Point Size** in your Format Bar and click on **14**. Click on **b (Bold)** and *i (Italics)* in your Format Bar. In all capitals type ***ACTIVITIES***. Then click on **Point Size** again and click on **12**. Then click on **b (Bold)** and *i (Italics)* in your Format Bar to turn them off.

2. Tab. Click on **Insert**, click on **Symbol**, click on the down arrow next to the **Font Dialog Box**, and click on **Wingdings**. Click on the symbol you'd like to use as a bullet. Then click on **Insert** and click on **Close**. Type your first activity; enter once.

3. Repeat Step 2 until all activities have been listed. Then enter twice to continue with next section.

REFERENCE SETUP

1. Click on the **Point Size** button in your Format Bar and click on **14**. Click on **b (Bold)** and *i (Italics)* in your Format Bar. In all capitals type ***REFERENCES***. Then click on **Point Size** again and click on **12**. Then click on **b (Bold)** and *i (Italics)* in your Format Bar to turn them off. Tab and type Available upon Request.

   DO NOT ENTER AFTER THE LAST LINE.

FINAL REVIEW

1. Hit your **Page Up Key** to take you to the top of your page. Click on the button in your Format Bar that looks like a magnifying glass. While you won't actually be able to read the words, you will get an overall idea of how it looks on the page. When you are through viewing, click on the **Close** button to return to the regular screen.

2. To run a spell check, click on **Tools**, click on **Spelling** and begin the spell check process.

3. Proofread your resumé carefully. To print, click on **File** and click on **Print**. To print more than one copy, click on **Copies** and type in the number you want; then enter. Click on **OK**. *As a word of caution, print just one copy the first time to make sure everything looks good. Then you can print more.*

4. To save your document to a floppy disk, click on **File**, click on **Save**, and type the path name as **a:\resume**; then enter.

5. To exit you must close your document by clicking on **File**, click on **Close**, click on **File**, and click on **Exit**.

**DIRECTIONS FOR RESUMÉ NO. 7
MICROSOFT WORD 6.0 (WINDOWS)**

GENERAL SETUP

1. From a clear screen, make sure you are in the Page Layout Mode with your Standard Bar, Format Bar, and Ruler Bar visible—like this:

Standard Bar
Format Bar
Ruler Bar

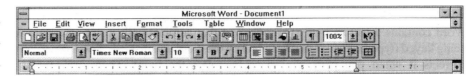

If they are not visible, click on **View** and then click on **Page Layout**. Then click on **View** and click on **Ruler**.

2. Click on **File**, click on **Page Setup**, click on **Margins**, click on the down arrow key next to top margin until it reaches .5; then click on the down arrow key next to bottom margin until it reaches .5; then click on **OK**.

3. Click on **File**, click on **Page Setup**, click on **Layout**, click on **Vertical Alignment**, click on **Center**, and click on **OK**.

4. Click on **Format**, click on **Tabs**, and click on **Clear All**. With your cursor in the **Tab Stop Position Box**, type **2.5**; then enter. With your cursor again in the **Tab Stop Position Box**, type **5.38**; then enter. With your cursor again in the **Tab Stop Position Box**, type **6**; then enter.

MAIN HEADING SETUP

1. Click on the **Center Justification Button** in your Format Bar.

2. Click on **Font** in your Format Bar and scroll down the list until you get to **Times New Roman**, then click on that choice. Click on the **Point Size** button on your Format Bar and click on **18**. Then click on **b (Bold)** in your Format Bar.

3. Now type your name in all capitals. Then click on **Point Size** and click on **12**. Click on the **Left Justification Button** in your Format Bar. Enter twice.

4. Type **School Address**, tab 3 times, and type **Home Address** and enter once. Click on **b (Bold)** in your Format Bar to turn it off.

5. Type your school street address; then tab three times and type your home street address; enter once.

6. Type your school city, state, and zip code; tab three times and type your home city, state, and zip code; then enter once.

7. Type your school area code and phone number; tab three times and type your home area code and phone number; then enter once.

8. To create the horizontal line, click on **View**, click on **Toolbars**, click on **Borders**, and click on **OK**. The first box in the Borders Toolbar is the Line Style Option Box. Click on the **down arrow in the Line Style Option Box** and from the pull–down list, select the line style you desire. To make the line appear, click on the **second box in the Borders Toolbar (Top Border)** and your line will be inserted.

9. Then enter twice to continue.

CAREER OBJECTIVE SETUP

1. Click on **Point Size** in your Format Bar and click on **14**. Click on **b (Bold)** and *i* **(Italics)** in your Format Bar. In all capitals type *OBJECTIVE*. Then click on **Point Size** in your Format Bar again and click on **12**. Then click on **b (Bold)** and *i* **(Italics)** in your Format Bar to turn them off.

2. Tab and type your career objective letting it word wrap at the end of the line. When you are through, enter twice.

3. To make Step 2 properly aligned, select (highlight) your objective statement, click on **Format**, click on **Paragraph**, click on the up arrow next to Indentation until it reaches **2.5**, then enter and click on **OK**.

EDUCATION SETUP

1. Click on **Point Size** in your Format Bar and click on **14**. Click on **b (Bold)** and *i* **(Italics)** in your Format Bar. In all capitals type *EDUCATION.*

2. Then click on **Point Size** and click on **12**. Then click on *i* **(Italics)** in your Format Bar to turn it off.

3. Tab and type the name of your most recent school in all capitals followed by the city, state, and zip code. Click on **b (Bold)** in your Format Bar to turn it off; then enter once.

4. Click on **Point Size** in your Format Bar and click on **10**. Tab. Click on **Insert**, click on **Symbol**, click on the down arrow next

to the **Font Dialog Box**, and click on **Wingdings**. Click on the symbol you'd like to use as a bullet. Then click on **Insert** and click on **Close**. Type your college of study followed by the grade point for those courses required for graduation by that college.

5. Then tab, click on **Insert**, click on **Symbol**, click on the down arrow next to the **Font Dialog Box**, and click on **Wingdings**. Click on the symbol you'd like to use as a bullet. Then click on **Insert** and click on **Close**. Type your overall grade point average. Enter once.

6. Tab. Click on **Insert**, click on **Symbol**, click on the down arrow next to the **Font Dialog Box**, and click on **Wingdings**. Click on the symbol you'd like to use as a bullet. Then click on **Insert** and click on **Close**. Type your major area of concentration and the grade point for only those classes.

7. Tab. Click on **Insert**, click on **Symbol**, click on the down arrow next to the **Font Dialog Box**, and click on **Wingdings**. Click on the symbol you'd like to use as a bullet. Then click on **Insert** and click on **Close**. Type your date of graduation. Enter twice.

8. Repeat Steps 3–7 until all your education has been listed.

EXPERIENCE SETUP

1. Click on **Point Size** in your Format Bar and click on **14**. Click on **b (Bold)** and *i* **(Italics)** in your Format Bar. In all capitals type ***EXPERIENCE***.

2. Then click on **Point Size** again and click on **12**. Then click on **b (Bold)** and *i* **(Italics)** in your Format Bar to turn them off.

3. Tab. Begin with your most recent experience. Click on **b (Bold)** in your Format Bar and type the name of the company in all capitals followed by the city, state, and zip code. Enter once.

4. Click on **Point Size** in your Format Bar and click on **10**. Then tab and type your job title followed by your dates of employment in parentheses. Click on **b (Bold)** in your Format Bar to turn it off. Enter once.

5. Tab. Click on **Insert**, click on **Symbol**, click on the down arrow next to the **Font Dialog Box**, and click on **Wingdings**. Click on the symbol you'd like to use as a bullet. Then click on **Insert** and click on **Close**. Type your first responsibility or accomplishment on the job. Then enter.

6. Repeat Step 5 until your list is completed for that entry. Enter twice.

7. Repeat Steps 3–6 until all your experience has been listed.

AFFILIATIONS SETUP

1. Click on **Point Size** in your Format Bar and click on **14**. Click on **b (Bold)** and *i* **(Italics)** in your Format Bar. In all capitals type *AFFILIATIONS*.

2. Then click on **Point Size** again and click on **12**. Then click on *i* **(Italics)** in your Format Bar to turn it off.

3. Tab and type the organization's name in all capitals. Click on **b (Bold)** in your Format Bar to turn it off. Enter once.

4. Tab. Click on **Insert**, click on **Symbol**, click on the down arrow next to the **Font Dialog Box**, and click on **Wingdings**. Click on the symbol you'd like to use as a bullet. Then click on **Insert** and click on **Close**. Type your first responsibility; enter once.

5. Repeat Step 4 until all responsibilities for that organization have been listed. Then enter twice.

6. Repeat Steps 3–5 until all affiliations have been listed. Enter twice to continue with next section.

QUALIFICATIONS SETUP

1. Click on **Point Size** in your Format Bar and click on **14**. Click on **b (Bold)** and *i* **(Italics)** in your Format Bar. In all capitals type *QUALIFICATIONS*.

2. Then click on **Point Size** again and click on **10**. Then click on **b (Bold)** and *i* **(Italics)** in your Format Bar to turn them off.

3. Tab. Click on **Insert**, click on **Symbol**, click on the down arrow next to the **Font Dialog Box**, and click on **Wingdings**. Click on the symbol you'd like to use as a bullet. Then click on **Insert** and click on **Close**. List your first qualification.

4. Repeat Step 3 until all qualifications have been listed. Then enter twice to continue with next section.

REFERENCES SETUP

1. Click on the **Center Justification Button** in your Format Bar and type in all capitals REFERENCES AVAILABLE UPON REQUEST.

DO NOT ENTER AFTER THE LAST LINE.

FINAL REVIEW

1. Hit your **Page Up Key** to take you to the top of your page. Click on the button in your Format Bar that looks like a magnifying glass. While you won't actually be able to read the words, you will get an overall idea of how it looks on the page. When you are through viewing, click on the **Close** button to return to the regular screen.

2. To run a spell check, click on **Tools**, click on **Spelling** and begin the spell check process.

3. Proofread your resumé carefully. To print, click on **File** and click on **Print**. To print more than one copy, click on **Copies** and type in the number you want; then enter. Click on **OK**. *As a word of caution, print just one copy the first time to make sure everything looks good. Then you can print more.*

4. To save your document to a floppy disk, click on **File**, click on **Save**, and type the path name as **a:\resume**; then enter.

5. To exit you must close your document by clicking on **File**, click on **Close**, click on **File**, and click on **Exit**.

> ## DIRECTIONS FOR RESUMÉ 8
> ## MICROSOFT WORD 6.0 (WINDOWS)

GENERAL SETUP

1. From a clear screen, make sure you are in the Page Layout Mode with your Standard Bar, Format Bar, and Ruler Bar visible—like this:

Standard Bar
Format Bar
Ruler Bar

   If they are not visible, click on **View** and then click on **Page Layout**. Then click on **View** and click on **Ruler**.

2. Click on **File**, click on **Page Setup**, click on **Margins**, click on the down arrow key next to top margin until it reaches .5; then click on the down arrow key next to bottom margin until it reaches .5; then click on **OK**.

3. Click on **File**, click on **Page Setup**, click on **Layout**, click on **Vertical Alignment**, click on **Center**, and click on **OK**.

4. Click on **Format**, click on **Tabs**, and click on **Clear All**. With your cursor in the **Tab Stop Position Box**, type **3**; then enter. With your cursor again in the **Tab Stop Position Box**, type **3.25**; then enter.

MAIN HEADING SETUP

1. Click on the **Center Justification Button** in your Format Bar.

2. Click on **Font** in your Format Bar and scroll down the list until you get to **Times New Roman**, then click on that choice. Click on the **Point Size** button in your Format Bar where it says **12 pt.** From the pull-down list of choices, click on **14**. Then click on **b (Bold)** in your Format Bar.

3. Now type your name in all capitals. Then click on **Point Size** and click on **12**. Then click on **b (Bold)** in your Format Bar to turn it off. Enter twice.

4. Type your street address; then enter. Type your city, state, and zip code; then enter. Type your area code and phone number; then enter twice.

5. Click on the **Left Justification Button** in your Button Bar.

6. To create the horizontal line, click on **View**, click on **Toolbars**, click on **Borders**, and click on **OK**. The first box in the Borders Toolbar is the Line Style Option Box. Click on the **down arrow in the Line Style Option Box** and from the pull–down list, select the line style you desire. To make the line appear, click on the **second box in the Borders Toolbar (Top Border)** and your line will be inserted.

7. Then enter three times to continue with next section.

CAREER OBJECTIVE SETUP

1. Click on **b (Bold)** and **u (Underline)** in your Format Bar. In all capitals type **OBJECTIVE**. Then click on **b (Bold)** and **u (Underline)** in your Format Bar to turn them off.

2. Tab. Type your objective letting it word wrap at the end of the line. When you are through, enter three times.

3. To make Step 2 properly aligned, select (highlight) your objective statement, click on **Format**, click on **Paragraph**, click on the up arrow next to Indentation until it reaches **3,** then enter and click on **OK**.

EDUCATION SETUP

1. Click on **b (Bold)** and **u (Underline)** in your Format Bar. In all capitals type **EDUCATION**. Then click on **b (Bold)** and **u (Underline)** in your Format Bar to turn them off.

2. Tab and begin with your most recent education by typing the name of the school. Enter once.

3. Tab and type the street address. Enter once.

4. Tab and type the city, state, and zip code of your school; then enter once.

5. Tab and type your course of study or degree received and the date; then enter twice.

6. Repeat Steps 2–5 for any other schools you want to list. Then enter three times to begin the next section.

EXPERIENCE SETUP

1. Click on **b (Bold)** and **u (Underline)** in your Format Bar. In all capitals type **EXPERIENCE**. Then click on **u (Underline)** in your Format Bar to turn it off.

2. Tab and begin with your most recent experience by typing your job title. Click on **b (Bold)** to turn it off; then enter once.

3. Tab and type the company name; then enter once.

4. Tab and type the street address; then enter once.

5. Tab and type the city, state, and zip code of the company; then enter once.

6. Tab and type your dates of employment; enter twice.

7. Repeat Steps 2–6 until all experience has been listed. Enter three times to begin the next section.

ACCOMPLISHMENTS SETUP

1. Click on **b (Bold)** and **u (Underline)** in your Format Bar. In all capitals type **ACCOMPLISHMENTS**. Then click on **b (Bold)** and **u (Underline)** in your Format Bar to turn them off.

2. Tab. Click on **Insert**, click on **Symbol**, click on the down arrow next to the **Font Dialog Box**, and click on **Wingdings**. Click on the symbol you'd like to use as a bullet. Then click on **Insert** and click on **Close**. Type your first accomplishment letting it word wrap at the end of the line; then enter twice.

3. Repeat Step 2 for all other items you want to list.

4. For those items that occupy more than one line, you will need to do the following to make that section properly aligned: select (highlight) the text, click on **Format**, click on **Paragraph**, click on the up arrow next to Indentation until it reaches **3**, then enter and click on **OK**.

5. After the last item in your list, enter three times to begin the final section.

REFERENCE SETUP

1. Click on **b (Bold)** and **u (Underline)** in your Format Bar. In all capitals type **REFERENCES**. Then click on **b (Bold)** and **u (Underline)** in your Format Bar to turn them off.

2. Tab and type Available upon Request.
   ### DO NOT ENTER AFTER THE LAST LINE.

FINAL REVIEW

1. Hit your **Page Up Key** to take you to the top of your page. Click on the button in your Format Bar that looks like a magnifying

glass. While you won't actually be able to read the words, you will get an overall idea of how it looks on the page. When you are through viewing, click on the **Close** button to return to the regular screen.

2. To run a spell check, click on **Tools**, click on **Spelling**, and begin the spell check process.

3. Proofread your resumé carefully. To print, click on **File** and click on **Print**. To print more than one copy, click on **Copies** and type in the number you want; then enter. Click on **OK**. *As a word of caution, print just one copy the first time to make sure everything looks good. Then you can print more.*

4. To save your document to a floppy disk, click on **File**, click on **Save**, and type the path name as **a:\resume**; then enter.

5. To exit you must close your document by clicking on **File**, click on **Close**, click on **File**, and click on **Exit**.

> **DIRECTIONS FOR RESUMÉ NO. 9**
> **MICROSOFT WORD 6.0 (WINDOWS)**

GENERAL SETUP

1. From a clear screen, make sure you are in the Page Layout Mode with your Standard Bar, Format Bar, and Ruler Bar visible—like this:

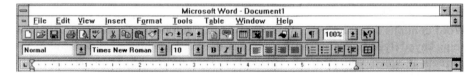

Standard Bar
Format Bar
Ruler Bar

If they are not visible, click on **View** and then click on **Page Layout**. Then click on **View** and click on **Ruler**.

2. Click on **File**, click on **Page Setup**, click on **Margins**, click on the down arrow key next to top margin until it reaches .5; then click on the down arrow key next to bottom margin until it reaches .5; then click on **OK**.

3. Click on **File**, click on **Page Setup**, click on **Layout**, click on **Vertical Alignment**, click on **Center**, and click on **OK**.

4. Click on **Format**, click on **Tabs**, and click on **Clear All**. With your cursor in the **Tab Stop Position Box**, type **2.8**; then enter. With your cursor again in the **Tab Stop Position Box**, type **3.16**; then enter.

MAIN HEADING SETUP

1. Click on the **Center Justification Button** in your Format Bar.

2. Click on the **Font** button in your Format Bar and scroll down the list until you get to **Times New Roman**, then click on that choice. Click on the **Point Size** button in your Format Bar where it says **12 pt**. From the pull-down list of choices, click on **14**. Then click on **b (Bold)** in your Format Bar.

3. Now type your name in all capitals. Then click on **Point Size** and click on **12**. Then click on **b (Bold)** in your Format Bar to turn it off. Enter once.

4. Type your street address; then enter. Type your city, state, and zip code; then enter. Type your area code and phone number; then enter once.

5. Click on the **Left Justification Button** in your Format Bar.

CAREER OBJECTIVE SETUP

1. Click on **b (Bold)** in your Format Bar. In all capitals type **CAREER OBJECTIVE:**. Then click on **b (Bold)** in your Format Bar to turn it off. Tab and begin to type your objective letting it word wrap at the end of the line. Now enter three times.

2. To make your objective statement properly aligned, select it (highlight), click on **Format**, click on **Paragraph**, click on the up arrow next to Indentation until it reaches **2.8**, enter and click on **OK**.

QUALIFICATIONS SETUP

1. Click on **b (Bold)** in your Format Bar. In all capitals type **QUALIFICATIONS:**. Then click on **b (Bold)** in your Format Bar to turn it off.

2. Tab. Click on **Insert**, click on **Symbol**, click on the down arrow next to the **Font Dialog Box**, and click on **Wingdings**. Click on the symbol you'd like to use as a bullet. Then click on **Insert** and click on **Close**. Type your first qualification; enter once.

3. Repeat Step 2 until all qualifications have been listed. Then enter three times to begin the next section.

EDUCATION SETUP

1. Click on **b (Bold)** in your Format Bar. In all capitals type **EDUCATION:**.

2. Tab. Begin with your most recent education by typing the name of the school. Then click on **b (Bold)** in your Format Bar to turn it off; enter once.

3. Tab, type the city, state, and zip code of your school; then enter once.

4. Tab, click on *i* **(Italics)** and **b (Bold)** in your Format Bar, type your course of study or degree received and the date; click on *i* **(Italics)** and **b (Bold)** in your Format Bar to turn them off and then enter twice.

5. Repeat Steps 2–4 for any other schools you want to list. Then enter three times to begin the next section.

EXPERIENCE SETUP

1. Click on **b (Bold)** in your Format Bar. In all capitals type **EXPERIENCE:**. Then click on **b (Bold)** in your Format Bar to turn it off. Enter twice.

2. Begin with your most recent experience by typing the dates you were employed, making sure that all digits align. Leave one space before and after the hyphen. Then tab, click on **b (Bold)** in your Format Bar, and type the name of the company. Then click on **b (Bold)** in your Format Bar to turn it off; enter once.

3. Tab, type the city, state, and zip code of the company; then enter once.

4. Tab, click on *i* **(Italics)** and **b (Bold)** in your Format Bar, and type your job title, click on *i* **(Italics)** and **b (Bold)** in your Format Bar to turn them off; then enter once.

5. Tab and begin to type your job description letting it word wrap. Enter twice.

6. To make Step 5 properly aligned, select (highlight) the text, click on **Format**, click on **Paragraph**, click on the up arrow next to Indentation until it reaches **2.8**, then enter and click on **OK.**

7. Repeat Steps 2–6 until all experience has been listed. Then enter three times to continue with the next section.

ACCOMPLISHMENTS SETUP

1. Click on **b (Bold)** in your Format Bar and type **ACCOM-PLISHMENTS:.** Click on **b (Bold)** in your Format Bar to turn it off.

2. Tab. Click on **Insert**, click on **Symbol**, click on the down arrow next to the **Font Dialog Box**, and click on **Wingdings**. Click on the symbol you'd like to use as a bullet. Then click on **Insert** and click on **Close**. List your first accomplishment; then enter.

3. Repeat Step 2 until all of your accomplishments have been listed. Then enter three times to continue with the next section.

REFERENCE SETUP

1. Click on **b (Bold)** in your Format Bar. In all capitals type **REF-ERENCES:.** Then click on **b (Bold)** in your Format Bar to turn it off. Tab and type Available upon Request.
   DO NOT ENTER AFTER THE LAST LINE.

FINAL REVIEW

1. Hit your **Page Up Key** to take you to the top of your page. Click on the button in your Format Bar that looks like a magnifying glass. While you won't actually be able to read the words, you

will get an overall idea of how it looks on the page. When you are through viewing, click on the **Close** button to return to the regular screen.

2. To run a spell check, click on **Tools**, click on **Spelling**, and begin the spell check process.

3. Proofread your resumé carefully. To print, click on **File** and click on **Print**. To print more than one copy, click on **Copies** and type in the number you want; then enter. Click on **OK**. *As a word of caution, print just one copy the first time to make sure everything looks good. Then you can print more.*

4. To save your document to a floppy disk, click on **File**, click on **Save**, and type the path name as **a:\resume**; then enter.

5. To exit you must close your document by clicking on **File**, click on **Close**, click on **File**, and click on **Exit**.

DIRECTIONS FOR RESUMÉ NO. 10
MICROSOFT WORD 6.0 (WINDOWS)

GENERAL SETUP

1. From a clear screen, make sure you are in the Page Layout Mode with your Standard Bar, Format Bar, and Ruler Bar visible—like this:

Standard Bar
Format Bar
Ruler Bar

   If they are not visible, click on **View** and then click on **Page Layout**. Then click on **View** and click on **Ruler**.

2. Click on **File**, click on **Page Setup**, click on **Margins**, click on the down arrow key next to top margin until it reaches .5; then click on the down arrow key next to bottom margin until it reaches .5; then click on **OK**.

3. Click on **File**, click on **Page Setup**, click on **Layout**, click on **Vertical Alignment**, click on **Center**, and click on **OK**.

4. Click on **Format**, click on **Tabs**, and click on **Clear All**. With your cursor in the **Tab Stop Position Box**, type **3**; then enter. With your cursor again in the **Tab Stop Position Box**, type **3.25**; then enter.

MAIN HEADING SETUP

1. Click on the **Center Justification Button** in your Format Bar.

2. Click on **Font** in your Format Bar and scroll down the list until you get to **Times New Roman**, then click on that choice. Click on the **Point Size** button in your Format Bar where it says **12 pt**. From the pull-down list of choices, click on **12**. Then click on **b (Bold)** in your Format Bar.

3. Now type your name in all capitals. Then click on **b (Bold)** in your Format Bar to turn it off. Enter twice.

4. Type your street address; then enter. Type your city, state, and zip code; then enter. Type your area code and phone number; then enter twice.

5. Click on the **Left Justification Button** in your Format Bar.

6. To create the horizontal line, click on **View**, click on **Toolbars**, click on **Borders**, and click on **OK**. The first box in the Borders Toolbar is the Line Style Option Box. Click on the **down arrow in the Line Style Option Box** and from the pull–down list, select the line style you desire. To make the line appear, click on the **second box in the Borders Toolbar (Top Border)** and your line will be inserted.

7. Then enter three times to continue with next section.

CAREER OBJECTIVE SETUP

1. Click on **b (Bold)** in your Format Bar. In all capitals type **CAREER OBJECTIVE:**. Then click on **b (Bold)** in your Format Bar to turn it off.

2. Tab and type your career objective letting it word wrap at the end of the line. When you are through, enter three times.

3. To make your objective statement properly aligned, select it (highlight), click on **Format**, click on **Paragraph**, click on the up arrow next to Indentation until it reaches **3**, enter and click on **OK**.

QUALIFICATIONS SETUP

1. Click on **b (Bold)** in your Format Bar. In all capitals type **QUALIFICATIONS:**.

2. Tab. Click on **Insert**, click on **Symbol**, click on the down arrow next to the **Font Dialog Box**, and click on **Wingdings**. Click on the symbol you'd like to use as a bullet. Then click on **Insert** and click on **Close**. Type your first qualification letting it word wrap if it takes more than one line; enter once.

3. To properly align any text that occupies more than one line, select it (highlight), click on **Format**, click on **Paragraph**, click on the up arrow next to Indentation until it reaces **3**, enter and click on **OK**.

4. Repeat Step 2 until all qualifications have been listed. Then enter three times to continue with the next section.

SKILLS SETUP

1. Click on **b (Bold)** in your Format Bar. In all capitals type **SKILLS:**. Then click on **b (Bold)** in your Format Bar to turn it off.

2. Tab. Click on **Insert**, click on **Symbol**, click on the down arrow next to the **Font Dialog Box**, and click on **Wingdings**.

Click on the symbol you'd like to use as a bullet. Then click on **Insert** and click on **Close**. Type your first skill; enter once.

3. Repeat Step 2 until all skills have been listed. Then enter three times to continue with the next section.

EDUCATION SETUP

1. Click on **b (Bold)** in your Format Bar. In all capitals type **EDU-CATION:**.

2. Tab, click on *i* **(Italics)** in your Format Bar, and begin with your most recent education by typing the name of the school in all capitals. Click on **b (Bold)** and *i* **(Italics)** in your Format Bar to turn them off. Enter once.

3. Tab and type the street address. Enter once.

4. Tab and type the city, state, and zip code of your school; then enter once.

5. Tab, click on **b (Bold)** in your Format Bar, type your course of study or degree received and the date; click on **b (Bold)** in your Format Bar to turn it off; then enter twice.

6. Repeat Steps 2–5 for any other schools you want to list. Then enter three times to begin the next section.

EXPERIENCE SETUP

1. Click on **b (Bold)** in your Format Bar. In all capitals type **EXPE-RIENCE:**.

2. Tab, click on *i* **(Italics)** in your Format Bar, and begin with your most recent experience by typing the name of the company in all capitals. Click on **b (Bold)** and *i* **(Italics)** in your Format Bar to turn them off; then enter once.

3. Tab and type the street address; then enter once.

4. Tab and type the city, state, and zip code of the company; then enter once.

5. Tab, click on **b (Bold)** in your Format Bar, and type your job title followed by the dates of your employment in parentheses. Click on **b (Bold)** in your Format Bar to turn it off; then enter twice.

6. Repeat Steps 2–5 until all experience has been listed. Enter three times to continue with the last section.

REFERENCE SETUP

1. Click on **b (Bold)** in your Format Bar. In all capitals type **REFERENCES:**. Then click on **b (Bold)** in your Format Bar to turn it off. Tab and type Available upon Request.

   DO NOT ENTER AFTER THE LAST LINE.

FINAL REVIEW

1. Hit your **Page Up Key** to take you to the top of your page. Click on the button in your Format Bar that looks like a magnifying glass. While you won't actually be able to read the words, you will get an overall idea of how it looks on the page. When you are through viewing, click on the **Close** button to return to the regular screen.

2. To run a spell check, click on **Tools**, click on **Spelling**, and begin the spell check process.

3. Proofread your resumé carefully. To print, click on **File** and click on **Print**. To print more than one copy, click on **Copies** and type in the number you want; then enter. Click on **OK**. *As a word of caution, print just one copy the first time to make sure everything looks good. Then you can print more.*

4. To save your document to a floppy disk, click on **File**, click on **Save**, and type the path name as **a:\resume**; then enter.

5. To exit you must close your document by clicking on **File**, click on **Close**, click on **File**, and click on **Exit**.

Notes

APPENDIX ***D*** **TYPING YOUR REFERENCE SHEET**

*B*elow you will find specific directions for typing your reference sheet using WordPerfect 6.1 (Windows), WordPerfect 6.0 (DOS), and Microsoft Word 6.0 (Windows).

References should be centered on the page, both vertically and horizontally. To center, begin typing at the left of your screen using the defult 1-inch top, bottom, and side margins.

DIRECTIONS FOR TYPING REFERENCE SHEET NO. 1 WORDPERFECT 6.1 (WINDOWS)

GENERAL SETUP

1. From a clear screen, make sure you are in the Page Mode, with your Tool Bar, Power Bar, Ruler Bar, Status Bar, and Graphics visible—like this:

Tool Bar
Power Bar

If they are not visible, click on **View** and then click on **Page Mode**. Then click on **View** and click on **Tool Bar**. Then click on **View** and click on **Power Bar**, click on **View** and click on **Ruler Bar**. Then click on **View** and click on **Graphics**.

2. Click on **Format**, click on **Margins**, click on the down arrow key next to top margin until it reaches .5; then click on the down arrow key next to bottom margin until it reaches .5; then click on **OK**.

3. Click on **Format**, click on **Page**, click on **Center**, click on **Current Page**, and click on **OK**.

HEADING SETUP

1. Looking at your Power Bar, click on the justification button where it says **Left▾**. Click on **Center**.

2. Click on the **Font** button in your Power Bar where it says **Courier**, scroll down the list until you get to **Times New Roman**, then click on that choice. Click on the **Point Size** button in the Power Bar where it says **12 pt.** From the pull-down list of choices, click on 14. Then click on **b (Bold)** in your Tool

Bar. Now type your name in all capitals. Then click on **Point Size** and click on **12**.

3. Enter three times.

BODY SETUP

1. Click on **u (Underline)** in your Tool Bar and type **Work References**. Then click on **b (Bold)** and **u (Underline)** in your Tool Bar to turn them off. Enter twice.

2. Type your first work reference starting with the person's name; then enter. Type their title; then enter. Type their company name; then enter. Type the company's street address; then enter. Type the company's city, state, and zip code; then enter. Type the company's area code and phone number with the appropriate extension; then enter twice.

3. Repeat Step 2 until all work references have been listed. Then enter three times to begin the next section.

4. Click on **b (Bold)** and **u (Underline)** in your Tool Bar and type **Educational References**. Then click on **b (Bold)** and **u (Underline)** in your Tool Bar to turn them off. Enter twice.

5. Type your first educational reference starting with the person's name; then enter. Type their title; then enter. Type their school's name; then enter. Type the school's street address; then enter. Type the school's city, state, and zip code; then enter. Type the school's area code and phone number; then enter twice.

6. Repeat Step 5 until all educational references have been listed. Then enter three times to begin the next section.

7. Click on **b (Bold)** and **u (Underline)** in your Tool Bar and type **Personal References**. Then click on **b (Bold)** and **u (Underline)** in your Tool Bar to turn them off. Enter twice.

8. Type your first personal reference starting with the person's name; then enter. Type the person's home street address; then enter. Type the person's home city, state, and zip code; then enter. Type the person's home area code and phone number; then enter twice.

9. Repeat Step 8 until all personal references have been listed. **DO NOT ENTER AFTER THE LAST LINE.**

FINAL REVIEW

1. Hit your **Page Up Key** to take you to the top of your page. Click on the button in your Tool Bar that looks like a magnifying

glass. While you won't actually be able to read the words, you will get an overall idea of how it looks on the page. When you are through viewing, click on the magnifying glass button to return to the regular screen.

2. To run a spell check, click on **Tools**, click on **Spell Check**, and begin the spell check process.

3. Proofread your reference sheet carefully. To print, click on **File** and click on **Print**. To print more than one copy, click on **Number of Copies** and type in the number you want; then enter. Click on **Print**. *As a word of caution, print just one copy the first time to make sure everything looks good. Then you can print more.*

4. To save your document to a floppy disk, click on **File**, click on **Save**, and type the path name as **a:\referenc**; then enter.

5. To exit you must close your document by clicking on **File**, click on **Close,** click on **File,** and click on **Exit.**

DIRECTIONS FOR TYPING REFERENCE SHEET NO. 2
WORDPERFECT 6.1 (WINDOWS)

GENERAL SETUP

1. From a clear screen, make sure you are in the Page Mode, with your Tool Bar, Power Bar, Ruler Bar, Status Bar, and Graphics visible—like this:

Tool Bar
Power Bar

If they are not visible, click on **View** and then click on **Page Mode**. Then click on **View** and click on **Tool Bar**. Then click on **View** and click on **Power Bar**, click on **View** and click on **Ruler Bar**. Then click on **View** and click on **Graphics**.

2. Click on **Format**, click on **Margins**, click on the down arrow key next to top margin until it reaches .5; then click on the down arrow key next to bottom margin until it reaches .5; then click on **OK**.

3. Click on **Format**, click on **Page**, click on **Center**, click on **Current Page**, and click on **OK**.

HEADING SETUP

1. Looking at your Power Bar, click on the justification button where it says **Left**. Click on **Center**.

2. Click on the **Font** button in your Power Bar where it says **Courier**, scroll down the list until you get to **Times New Roman**, then click on that choice. Click on the **Point Size** button in the Power Bar where it says **12 pt**. From the pull-down list of choices, click on 14. Then click on **b (Bold)** in your Tool Bar. Now type your name in all capitals. Then click on **Point Size** and click on **12**.

3. Enter three times.

BODY SETUP

1. Type your first work reference starting with the person's name; then enter. Type their title; then enter. Type their company name; then enter. Type the company's street address;

then enter. Type the company's city, state, and zip code; then enter. Type the company's area code and phone number with the appropriate extension; then enter twice.

2. Repeat Step 1 until all work references have been listed.

3. Type your first educational reference starting with the person's name; then enter. Type their title; then enter. Type their school's name; then enter. Type the school's street address; then enter. Type the school's city, state, and zip code; then enter. Type the school's area code and phone number; then enter twice.

4. Repeat Step 3 until all work references have been listed.

5. Type your first personal reference starting with the person's name; then enter. Type the person's home street address; then enter. Type the person's home city, state, and zip code; then enter. Type the person's home area code and phone number; then enter twice.

6. Repeat Step 5 until all personal references have been listed.
   DO NOT ENTER AFTER THE LAST LINE.

FINAL REVIEW

1. Hit your **Page Up Key** to take you to the top of your page. Click on the button in your Tool Bar that looks like a magnifying glass. While you won't actually be able to read the words, you will get an overall idea of how it looks on the page. When you are through viewing, click on the magnifying glass button to return to the regular screen.

2. To run a spell check, click on **Tools**, click on **Spell Check**, and begin the spell check process.

3. Proofread your reference sheet carefully. To print, click on **File** and click on **Print**. To print more than one copy, click on **Number of Copies** and type in the number you want; then enter. Click on **Print**. *As a word of caution, print just one copy the first time to make sure everything looks good. Then you can print more.*

4. To save your document to a floppy disk, click on **File**, click on **Save**, and type the path name as **a:\referenc**; then enter.

5. To exit you must close your document by clicking on **File**, click on **Close**, click on **File**, and click on **Exit**.

DIRECTIONS FOR TYPING REFERENCE SHEET NO. 1
WORDPERFECT 6.0 (DOS)

GENERAL SETUP

1. From a clear screen, make sure you are in the **Graphics Mode**, with your **Ribbon Bar** and **Fonts Button Bar** visible—like this:

Menu Bar
Ribbon Bar
Fonts Button Bar

If the top of your screen looks different from the example above:

   a.   Click on **View** and then click on **Graphics Mode**.

   b.   Click on **View** and click on **Ribbon**.

   c.   Click on **View** and click on **Button Bar Setup**.

   d.   Click on **Select** and highlight **FONTS**; then enter.

2. Click on **Layout**, click on **Margins**, click on the down arrow key next to top margin until it reaches .5; then click on the down arrow key next to bottom margin until it reaches .5; then click on **OK**.

3. Click on **Layout**, click on **Page**, click on **2 (Center Current Page)**, click on **OK**.

HEADING SETUP

1. Click on the **Justification Button** in your ribbon bar. Double click on **Center**.

2. Click on the **Font Button** in your ribbon bar and scroll the pull–down list until you get to **Dutch 801 Roman**; then double click on that choice.

3. Click on the **Point Size Button** in your ribbon bar. Scroll the pull–down list and double click on **14**.

4. Click on **Bold** in your button bar. Now type your name in all capitals.

5. Click on **Point Size** and double click on **12**. Enter three times.

BODY SETUP

1. Click on **Underline** in your button bar and type **Work References**. Then click on **Bold** and **Underline** in your button bar to turn them off. Enter twice.

2. Type your first work reference starting with the person's name; then enter. Type their title; then enter. Type their company name; then enter. Type the company's street address; then enter. Type the company's city, state, and zip code; then enter. Type the company's area code and phone number with the appropriate extension; then enter twice.

3. Repeat Step 2 until all work references have been listed. Then enter three times to begin the next section.

4. Click on **Bold** and **Underline** in your button bar and type **Educational References**. Then click on **Bold** and **Underline** in your button bar to turn them off. Enter twice.

5. Type your first educational reference starting with the person's name; then enter. Type the title; then enter. Type the school's name; then enter. Type the school's street address; then enter. Type the school's city, state, and zip code; then enter. Type the school's area code and phone number; then enter twice.

6. Repeat Step 5 until all educational references have been listed. Then enter three times to begin the next section.

7. Click on **Bold** and **Underline** in your button bar and type **Personal References**. Then click on **Bold** and **Underline** in your button bar to turn them off. Enter twice.

8. Type your first personal reference starting with the person's name; then enter. Type the person's home street address; then enter. Type the person's home city, state, and zip code; then enter. Type the person's home area code and phone number; then enter twice.

9. Repeat Step 8 until all personal references have been listed. **DO NOT ENTER AFTER THE LAST LINE.**

FINAL REVIEW

1. Hit your **Page Up Key** to take you to the top of your page. Click on **File** and click on **Print Preview**. If you don't see the entire page, click on **View** and click on **Full Page**. While you won't actually be able to read the words, you will get an overall idea of how it looks on the page. When you are through viewing, click on **Close** to return to the regular screen.

2. To run a spell check, click on **Tools**, click on **Writing Tools**, click on **Speller**, click on **Document**, and begin the spell check process.

3. Proofread your reference sheet carefully. To print, click on **File** and click on **Print**. To print more than one copy, click on **Number of Copies** and type in the number you want; then enter. Click on **Print**. *As a word of caution, print just one copy the first time to make sure everything looks good. Then you can print more.*

4. To save your document to a floppy disk, click on **File**, click on **Save**, and type the path name as **a:\referenc**; then enter.

5. To exit you must close your document by clicking on **File**, click on **Close**, click on **File**, and click on **Exit**.

DIRECTIONS FOR TYPING REFERENCE SHEET No. 2
WORDPERFECT 6.0 (DOS)

GENERAL SETUP

1. From a clear screen, make sure you are in the **Graphics Mode**, with your **Ribbon Bar** and **Fonts Button Bar** visible—like this:

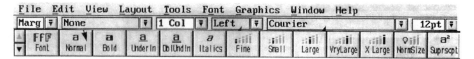

Menu Bar
Ribbon Bar
Fonts Button Bar

If the top of your screen looks different from the example above:

   a. Click on **View** and then click on **Graphics Mode.**

   b. Click on **View** and click on **Ribbon.**

   c. Click on **View** and click on **Button Bar Setup.**

   d. Click on **Select** and highlight **FONTS**; then enter.

2. Click on **Layout**, click on **Margins**, click on the down arrow key next to top margin until it reaches .5; then click on the down arrow key next to bottom margin until it reaches .5; then click on **OK**.

3. Click on **Layout**, click on **Page**, click on **2 (Center Current Page)**, click on **OK**.

HEADING SETUP

1. Click on the **Justification Button** in your ribbon bar and double click on **Center**.

2. Click on the **Font Button** in your ribbon bar and scroll the pull–down list until you get to **Dutch 801 Roman**; then double click on that choice.

3. Click on the **Point Size Button** in your ribbon bar. Scroll the pull–down list and double click **14**.

4. Click on **Bold** in your button bar. Now type your name in all capitals.

5. Click on **Point Size** and double click on **12**.

6. Enter three times.

BODY SETUP

1. Type your first work reference starting with the person's name; then enter. Type their title; then enter. Type their company name; then enter. Type the company's street address; then enter. Type the company's city, state, and zip code; then enter. Type the company's area code and phone number with the appropriate extension; then enter twice.

2. Repeat Step 1 until all work references have been listed.

3. Type your first educational reference starting with the person's name; then enter. Type the title; then enter. Type the school's name; then enter. Type the school's street address; then enter. Type the school's city, state, and zip code; then enter. Type the school's area code and phone number; then enter twice.

4. Repeat Step 3 until all work references have been listed.

5. Type your first personal reference starting with the person's name; then enter. Type the person's home street address; then enter. Type the person's home city, state, and zip code; then enter. Type the person's home area code and phone number; then enter twice.

6. Repeat Step 5 until all personal references have been listed.
   DO NOT ENTER AFTER THE LAST LINE.

FINAL REVIEW

1. Hit your **Page Up Key** to take you to the top of your page. Click on **File** and click on **Print Preview**. If you don't see the entire page, click on **View** and click on **Full Page**. While you won't actually be able to read the words, you will get an overall idea of how it looks on the page. When you are through viewing, click on **Close** to return to the regular screen.

2. To run a spell check, click on **Tools**, click on **Writing Tools**, click on **Speller**, click on **Document**, and begin the spell check process.

3. Proofread your reference sheet carefully. To print, click on **File** and click on **Print**. To print more than one copy, click on **Number of Copies** and type in the number you want; then enter. Click on **Print**. *As a word of caution, print just one copy the first time to make sure everything looks good. Then you can print more.*

4. To save your document to a floppy disk, click on **File**, click on **Save**, and type the path name as **a:\referenc**; then enter.

5. To exit you must close your document by clicking on **File**, click on **Close**, click on **File**, and click on **Exit**.

DIRECTIONS FOR TYPING REFERENCE SHEET NO. 1
MICROSOFT WORD 6.0 (WINDOWS)

GENERAL SETUP

1. From a clear screen, make sure you are in the Page Layout Mode, with your Standard Bar, Format Bar, and Ruler Bar visible—like this:

Standard Bar
Format Bar
Ruler Bar

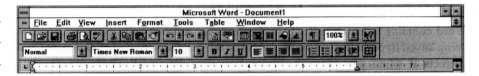

   If they are not visible, click on **View** and then click on **Page Layout**. Then click on **View** and click on **Ruler**.

2. Click on **File**, click on **Page Setup**, click on **Margins**, click on the down arrow key next to top margin until it reaches .5; then click on the down arrow key next to bottom margin until it reaches .5; then click on **OK**.

3. Click on **File**, click on **Page Setup**, click on **Layout**, Click on **Vertical Alignment**, click on **Center**, and click on **OK**.

HEADING SETUP

1. Click on the **Center Justification Button** in your Format Bar.

2. Click on the **Font Button** in your Ribbon Bar and scroll the pull-down list until you get to **Times New Roman**, then click on that choice. Click on the **Point Size** button in the Ribbon Bar where it says **12 pt.** From the pull-down list of choices, click on **14**. Then click on **b (Bold)** in your Format Bar.

3. Now type your name in all capitals. Then click on **Point Size** and click on **12**.

4. Enter three times.

BODY SETUP

1. Click on **u (Underline)** in your Format Bar and type **Work References**. Then click on **b (Bold)** and **u (Underline)** in your Format Bar to turn them off. Enter twice.

2. Type your first work reference starting with the person's name; then enter. Type their title; then enter. Type their company

name; then enter. Type the company's street address; then enter. Type the company's city, state, and zip code; then enter. Type the company's area code and phone number with the appropriate extension; then enter twice.

3. Repeat Step 2 until all work references have been listed. Then enter three times to begin the next section.

4. Click on **b (Bold)** and **u (Underline)** in your Format Bar and type **Educational References**. Then click on **b (Bold)** and **u (Underline)** in your Format Bar to turn them off. Enter twice.

5. Type your first educational reference starting with the person's name; then enter. Type the title; then enter. Type the school's name; then enter. Type the school's street address; then enter. Type the school's city, state, and zip code; then enter. Type the school's area code and phone number; then enter twice.

6. Repeat Step 5 until all educational references have been listed. Then enter three times to begin the next section.

7. Click on **b (Bold)** and **u (Underline)** in your Format Bar and type **Personal References**. Then click on **b (Bold)** and **u (Underline)** in your Format Bar to turn them off. Enter twice.

8. Type your first personal reference starting with the person's name; then enter. Type the person's home street address; then enter. Type the person's home city, state, and zip code; then enter. Type the person's home area code and phone number; then enter twice.

9. Repeat Step 8 until all personal references have been listed. **DO NOT ENTER AFTER THE LAST LINE.**

FINAL REVIEW

1. Hit your **Page Up Key** to take you to the top of your page. Click on the button in your Format Bar that looks like a magnifying glass. While you won't actually be able to read the words, you will get an overall idea of how it looks on the page. When you are through viewing, click on the **Close** button to return to the regular screen.

2. To run a spell check, click on **Tools**, click on **Spelling**, and begin the spell check process.

3. Proofread your reference sheet carefully. To print, click on **File** and click on **Print**. To print more than one copy, click on **Copies** and type in the number you want; then enter. Click on

OK. *As a word of caution, print just one copy the first time to make sure everything looks good. Then you can print more.*

4. To save your document to a floppy disk, click on **File**, click on **Save**, and type the path name as **a:\referenc**; then enter.

5. To exit you must close your document by clicking on **File**, click on **Close**, click on **File**, and click on **Exit**.

> ## DIRECTIONS FOR TYPING REFERENCE SHEET No. 2
> ## MICROSOFT WORD 6.0 (WINDOWS)

GENERAL SETUP

1. From a clear screen, make sure you are in the Page Layout Mode, with your Standard Bar, Format Bar, and Ruler Bar visible—like this:

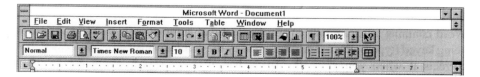

Standard Bar
Format Bar
Ruler Bar

  If they are not visible, click on **View** and then click on **Page Layout**. Then click on **View** and click on **Ruler**.

2. Click on **File**, click on **Page Setup**, click on **Margins**, click on the down arrow key next to top margin until it reaches .5; then click on the down arrow key next to bottom margin until it reaches .5; then click on **OK**.

3. Click on **File**, click on **Page Setup**, click on **Layout**, Click on **Vertical Alignment**, click on **Center**, and click on **OK**.

HEADING SETUP

1. Click on the **Center Justification Button** in your Format Bar.

2. Click on the **Font Button** in your Ribbon Bar and scroll the pull–down list until you get to **Times New Roman**, then click on that choice. Click on the **Point Size** button in the Ribbon Bar where it says **12 pt.** From the pull-down list of choices, click on 14. Then click on **b (Bold)** in your Format Bar.

3. Now type your name in all capitals. Then click on **Point Size** and click on **12**.

4. Enter three times.

BODY SETUP

1. Type your first work reference starting with the person's name; then enter. Type the title; then enter. Type the company name; then enter. Type the company's street address; then enter. Type the company's city, state, and zip code; then

enter. Type the company's area code and phone number with the appropriate extension; then enter twice.

2. Repeat Step 1 until all work references have been listed.

3. Type your first educational reference starting with the person's name; then enter. Type the title; then enter. Type the school's name; then enter. Type the school's street address; then enter. Type the school's city, state, and zip code; then enter. Type the school's area code and phone number; then enter twice.

4. Repeat Step 3 until all work references have been listed.

5. Type your first personal reference starting with the person's name; then enter. Type the person's home street address; then enter. Type the person's home city, state, and zip code; then enter. Type the person's home area code and phone number; then enter twice.

6. Repeat Step 5 until all personal references have been listed.
    DO NOT ENTER AFTER THE LAST LINE.

FINAL REVIEW

1. Hit your **Page Up Key** to take you to the top of your page. Click on the button in your Format Bar that looks like a magnifying glass. While you won't actually be able to read the words, you will get an overall idea of how it looks on the page. When you are through viewing, click on the **Close** button to return to the regular screen.

2. To run a spell check, click on **Tools**, click on **Spelling**, and begin the spell check process.

3. Proofread your reference sheet carefully. To print, click on **File** and click on **Print**. To print more than one copy, click on **Copies** and type in the number you want; then enter. Click on **OK**. *As a word of caution, print just one copy the first time to make sure everything looks good. Then you can print more.*

4. To save your document to a floppy disk, click on **File**, click on **Save**, and type the path name as **a:\referenc**; then enter.

5. To exit you must close your document by clicking on **File**, click on **Close**, click on **File**, and click on **Exit**.

Notes

APPENDIX **E** TYPING YOUR COVER LETTER

*B*elow you will find specific directions for typing your cover letter using WordPerfect 6.1 (Windows). You can save yourself a lot of time if you are able to use WordPerfect's features to create both primary and secondary files and then to merge them together.

You are going to create a basic form letter that will accompany any resumé you mail out in response to a job opening. This is called your primary file. Then you will create a secondary file consisting only of names and addresses related to specific job openings. Through WordPerfect, you can merge the two files together. In other words, the computer puts the address and salutation in the right places in your letter.

You can also customize each and every letter to a specific want ad by using keyboard commands when creating your initial primary file document. By doing so, you can quickly prepare several letters for mailing, and no one will know that the cover letter is basically a form letter.

STEPS FOR CREATING A PRIMARY FILE USING WORDPERFECT 6.1 (WINDOWS)

GENERAL SETUP

1. From a clear screen, make sure you are in the Page Mode, with your Tool Bar, Power Bar, Ruler Bar, Status Bar, and Graphics visible – like this:

Tool Bar
Power Bar

If they are not visible, click on **View** and then click on **Page Mode**. Then click on **View** and click on **Tool Bar**. Then click on **View** and click on **Power Bar**, click on **View** and click on **Ruler Bar**. Then click on **View** and click on **Graphics.**

2. Click on **Format**, click on **Line**, click on **Tab Set**, click on **Absolute**, click on **Clear**, click on the box opposite **Position** and type **4.25;** and enter.

3. Click on **Tools**, click on **Merge**, click on **Form**, click on **New Document** in the dialog box, and click on **OK**. In the **Create Form File** dialog box, click on **None**; then click on **OK**.

4. A new Merge Button Bar will appear below your ruler bar.

5. Hit your enter key six times, tab, and type your street address. Then enter.

6. Tab and type your city, state, and zip code; then enter.

You have no idea when this letter will actually be merged for mailing, so you need to give a Date Command so the appropriate date will automatically be placed in your letter when you are ready to merge the files. To do this:

7. Tab; click on the **Date** button. The word DATE will appear in red on your screen.

8. Hit your enter key five times. Now you are going to create a separate field for each possible line in the inside address. Under most circumstances, you will not need more than five lines for your inside address. However, the exact space needed for an inside address will vary. Therefore, as you create each field you will type a ? that will allow the computer to automatically take out any extra space related to a particular inside address of less than five lines. To create a field for each line of any inside address, follow these steps:

   a. Click on the **Insert Field** button. This message will appear: *No field Names or Records were found.* Click on **OK**. An Insert Field Names or Numbers Prompt Box will appear. Type **1?,** click on **Insert** and then enter. You should see **Field(1?)** on your screen where eventually the first line of your inside address will be merged. Notice that the Dialog Box is still open in the upper right corner of your screen. Click your mouse inside the white area box to reposition your cursor there.

   b. Type **2?,** click on **Insert** and then enter. You should see **Field(2?)** on your screen where eventually the second line of your inside address will be merged. Notice that the Dialog Box is still open in the upper right corner of your screen. Click your mouse inside the white area box to reposition your cursor there.

   c. Type **3?,** click on **Insert** and then enter. You should see **Field(3?)** on your screen where eventually the third line of your inside address will be merged. Notice that the Dialog Box is still open in the upper right corner of your screen. Click your mouse inside the white area box to reposition your cursor there.

   d. Type **4?,** click on **Insert** and then enter. You should see **Field(4?)** on your screen where eventually the fourth line of your inside address will be merged. Notice that the Dialog Box is still open in the upper right corner of your screen. Click your mouse inside the white area box to reposition your cursor there.

e. Type **5?,** click on **Insert** and then enter. You should see **Field(5?)** on your screen where eventually the fifth line of your inside address will be merged. Now click on **Close** in the Dialog Box.

f. Enter twice so that there will be a double space between the inside address and the salutation.

Because you do not know to whom this letter eventually will be sent, you need to give a keyboard command where the appropriate salutation will appear after merging. If you want to use mixed punctuation, meaning you will type a colon after the salutation and a comma after the complimentary closing, then type a colon after the keyboard command.

7. Click on the **Keyboard** button. An Insert Merge Code Prompt Box will appear. Type **Salutation**; then enter. This process will return you to your document, and you should see the word **KEYBOARD** (Salutation) on the spot where your salutation will eventually go. Hit enter twice.

8. Now you are ready to type the body of your letter. Because you are typing in modified block style (your return address, date, complimentary closing, and signature line begin at the center), you have the choice of indenting or blocking your paragraphs. Double–space between each paragraph.

9. At any point in the letter where you might want to type something geared toward a specific ad, insert a keyboard command to hold that spot so that later you can type your message. **Refer to Step 7 above to create a Keyboard Command.** For example, the position you desire and the name of the newspaper from which you got the ad might require you to insert a keyboard command.

10. Enter twice after the last line of the body of your letter. Then hit the tab key to take you to the center. Type your **complimentary closing.** Follow it with a comma if you used a colon in your salutation. Then hit the enter key four more times, tab to the center, and type **your name.** Hit the enter key twice and type **Enclosure.** (You will always enclose a resumé with your letter.)

FINAL REVIEW

1. Hit your **Page Up Key** to take you to the top of your page. Click on the button in your Tool Bar that looks like a magnifying glass. While you won't actually be able to read the words, you will get an overall idea of how it looks on the page. When you are through viewing, click on the magnifying glass button to return to the regular screen.

2. To run a spell check, click on **Tools**, click on **Spell Check**, and begin the spell check process.

3. Proofread your letter carefully.

4. To save your document to a floppy disk, click on **File**, click on **Save**, and type the path name as **a:\covltr.pf**; then enter. The .pf extension represents primary file.

5. To exit you must close your document by clicking on **File**, click on **Close**, click on **File**, and click on **Exit**.

You can follow the same procedures to create a primary file for your letter of application. Name the file **a:appltr.pf.** Then take the list of company names from the phone book or other source and create a secondary file to be merged with the letter.

STEPS FOR CREATING A SECONDARY FILE USING WORDPERFECT 6.1 (WINDOWS)

A secondary file is just a list of companies to which you want to send your cover letter and resumé. The addresses are from the want ads you cut out from the newspapers. To create this file, follow these steps:

1. Start at the top of a clear screen. Click on **Tools**, click on **Merge**, click on **Data**, click on **New Document Window**, click on **OK**.

2. A Create Data File Dialog Box will appear. Your cursor will be blinking inside the Name a Field Box. Type **Inside Address** and click on **OK**.

3. Next a Number of Files Dialog Box will appear. Click on the up arrow until it reaches **five;** then click on **OK**.

4. A Quick Data Entry Box will appear. Your cursor will be blinking in the top box. Type the first line of your first inside address. Then click on **Next Field**. Type the second line of your inside address and click on **Next Field**. Continue in this

manner until all the lines of just your first inside address have been created. Proofread carefully; then click on **New Record**.

5. You will see what you just created partially peaking out from behind the Dialog Box you are currently working with. Continue this process following the directions in Step 4 until all of your inside addresses have been created.

6. Then click on **Close**. Your screen will automatically prompt you to save. Answer **Yes** and name this file **a:\covlist.sf**; then enter. The .sf extension represents secondary file.

7. To exit, you must close your document by clicking on **File**, click on **Close**, click on **File**, and click on **Exit**.

Once you have merged your primary and secondary files, this secondary file of addresses will never be used again. As a result, each time you create a new secondary file, you begin with a clear screen. When you have finished, you follow Step 6 to save the file and again name it **a:covlist.sf.** Because you saved your last list under the same name, the computer will automatically replace your old list with this new one. Continue in this manner each week as you create a new secondary file.

If you want to create a secondary file to be merged with your letter of application, save it under the name **a:\applist.sf**.

MERGING PRIMARY AND SECONDARY FILES USING WORDPERFECT 6.1 (WINDOWS)

Below are specific directions for merging your primary file cover letter and secondary file of addresses. It is absolutely essential that you have no errors of any kind in either your primary or secondary file. Begin the merge process by following these steps:

1. From a clear screen, click on **Tools**, click on **Merge**, and click on **Merge**. In the Perform Merge Box, your cursor will be blinking in the Form File Box. Type **a:\covltr.pf** and enter. In the Data File Box, type **a:\covlist.sf** and enter. Then click on **OK**.

2. Wait a moment. Your first letter will appear on the screen with the cursor resting at the point of your first keyboard command. Your computer expects you to type in the salutation. Type in the appropriate salutation based on your inside address and then click on the **Continue** button.

3. Your cursor will automatically go to the spot of the next keyboard command you created, which might be the name of

the newspaper you found your ad in. Type in the newspaper's name and then click on the **Continue** button.

4. Follow through with this process until all the keyboard commands for all your letters have been completed.

5. When you have finished replacing the keyboard commands with the words you want, hit the home key three times and the up arrow key to take you quickly to the top of the screen. Now examine each letter to verify that it meets the needs of the particular want ad. If you want to make any additions or changes to a particular letter, make them. In this way, you customize your form letter to fit each want ad.

6. Get ready to print out all your letters. Make sure the paper in your printer is properly aligned. Click on **File**, click on **Print**, click on **Text Quality** and select **H (high)**. Then click on **Graphics Quality** and select **H (high)**. Click on **Number of Copies** and type in **2**. Click on **Print**. You will print two copies of each letter—one to send and one to keep with your Activity Log.

7. While your letters are printing, save this entire document to your disk. Click on **File**, click on **Save**, and name this document **a:\sept10**. (Note that this name contains the date on which you merged and sent your letters, in this case, September 10. Including the date in your file name enables you to refer to the letters later if necessary.)

8. To exit, click on **File**, click on **Close**, click on **File**, and click on **Exit**.

9. Staple your want ad to each of the respective letters, and fill out an Activity Log for that company. Put these letters in a file folder. Then sign the duplicate letter, place it on top of your resumé, fold, and place in the addressed envelope (See Appendix F).

*B*elow you will find specific directions for typing your cover letter using WordPerfect 6.0 (DOS). You can save yourself a lot of time if you are able to use WordPerfect's features to create both primary and secondary files and then to merge them together.

You are going to create a basic form letter that will accompany any resume you mail out in response to a job opening. This is called your primary file. Then you will create a secondary file consisting only of names and addresses related to specific job openings. Through WordPerfect, you can merge the two files together. In other words, the computer puts the address and salutation in the right spot in your letter.

You can also customize each and every letter to a specific want ad by using keyboard commands when creating your initial primary file document. By doing so, you can quickly prepare several letters for mailing, and no one will know that the cover letter is basically a form letter.

STEPS FOR CREATING A PRIMARY FILE USING WORDPERFECT 6.0 (DOS)

GENERAL SETUP

1. From a clear screen, make sure you are in the **Graphics Mode**, with your **Ribbon Bar** and **Fonts Button Bar** visible—like this:

Menu Bar
Ribbon Bar
Fonts Button Bar

   If the top of your screen looks different from the example above:

   a. Click on **View** and then click on **Graphics Mode.**

   b. Click on **View** and click on **Ribbon.**

   c. Click on **View** and click on **Button Bar Setup.**

   d. Click on **Select** and highlight **FONTS**; then enter.

2. Click on **Layout**, click on **Line**, click on **Tab Set**, click on **Absolute**, click on **Clear All**, click on **Set Tab**, type **4.25** and enter. Click on **OK.**

3. Hit your enter key six times, tab, and type your street address. Then enter.

4. Tab and type your city, state, and zip code; then enter.

You have no idea when this letter will actually be merged for mailing, so you need to give a keyboard command enabling you to key in the appropriate date when you are ready to merge the files.

5. Tab; click on **Tools**, click on **Merge**, click on **Define**, and click on **Keyboard**. A Keyboard Prompt Box will appear. Type **Current Date**; then click on **OK**. This process will return you to your document, and you should see the word **Keyboard** (Current Date) on the spot where your date will eventually go.

6. Hit your enter key five times. Again you are going to create a separate field for each possible line in the inside address. Under most circumstances, you will not need more than five lines for your inside address. However, the exact space needed for an inside address will vary. Therefore, to create a field for each line of any inside address, follow these steps:

   a. Click on **Tools**, click on **Merge**, click on **Define**, and click on **Field**. A Field Prompt Box will appear. Type **1?** and then click on **OK**. This process will return you to your document, and you should see **Field(1?)** on your screen where eventually the first line of your inside address will be merged. Hit enter once. You typed a question mark after the number 1 so that the computer will adjust the spacing for an inside address if you are using fewer than five lines.

   b. Click on **Tools**, click on **Merge**, click on **Define**, and click on **Field**. A Field Prompt Box will appear. Type **2?** and then click on **OK**. Hit enter once.

   c. Click on **Tools**, click on **Merge**, click on **Define**, and click on **Field**. A Field Prompt Box will appear. Type **3?** and then click on **OK**. Hit enter once.

   d. Click on **Tools**, click on **Merge**, click on **Define**, and click on **Field**. A Field Prompt Box will appear. Type **4?** and then click on **OK**. Hit enter once.

   e. Click on **Tools**, click on **Merge**, click on **Define**, and click on **Field**. A Field Prompt Box will appear. Type **5?** and then click on **OK**.

    f.   Now enter twice so that there will be a double space between the inside address and the salutation.

Because you do not know to whom this letter eventually will be sent, you need to give a keyboard command where the appropriate salutation will appear after merging. If you want to use mixed punctuation, meaning you will type a colon after the salutation and a comma after the complimentary closing, then type a colon after the keyboard command.

7.   Click on **Tools**, click on **Merge**, click on **Define**, and click on **Keyboard**. A Keyboard Prompt Box will appear. Type **Salutation**; then click on **OK**. This process will return you to your document, and you should see the word **Keyboard** (Salutation) on the spot where your salutation will eventually go. Hit enter twice.

8.   Now you are ready to type the body of your letter. Because you are typing in modified block style (your return address, date, complimentary closing, and signature line begin at the center), you have the choice of indenting or blocking your paragraphs. Double space between each paragraph. At any point in the letter where you might want to type something geared toward a specific ad, insert a keyboard command to hold that spot so that later you can type your message.

Refer to Step 7 above to create a keyboard command.

For example, the position you desire and the name of the newspaper from which you got the ad might require you to insert a keyboard command.

9.   Enter twice after the last line of the body of your letter. Then hit the tab key to take you to the center. Type your **complimentary closing**. Follow it with a comma if you used a colon in your salutation. Then hit the enter key four more times, tab to the center, and type **your name**. Hit the enter key twice and type **Enclosure**. (You will always enclose a resumé with your letter.)

FINAL REVIEW

1.   Hit your **Page Up Key** to take you to the top of your page. Click on **File** and click on **Print Preview**. If you don't see the entire page, click on **View** and click on **Full Page**. While you won't actually be able to read the words, you will get an overall idea of how it looks on the page. When you are through viewing, click on **Close** to return to the regular screen.

2. To run a spell check, click on **Tools**, click on **Writing Tools**, click on **Speller**, click on **Document**, and begin the spell check process.

3. Proofread your letter carefully.

4. To save your document to a floppy disk, click on **File**, click on **Save**, and type the path name as **a:\covltr.pf**; then enter. The .pf extension represents primary file.

5. To exit you must close your document by clicking on **File**, click on **Close**, click on **File**, and click on **Exit**.

You can follow the same procedures to create a primary file for your letter of application. Name the file **a:appltr.pf.** Then take the list of company names from the phone book or other source, and create a secondary file to be merged with the letter.

STEPS FOR CREATING A SECONDARY FILE USING WORDPERFECT 6.0 (DOS)

A secondary file is just a list of companies to which you want to send your cover letter and resumé. The addresses are from the want ads you cut out from the newspapers. To create this file, follow these steps:

1. Start at the top of a clear screen. Click on **Tools**, click on **Merge**, click on **Define**, click on **2 (Data Text)**.

2. Type the first line of your inside address and then immediately hit **F9**, which automatically returns you to the next line. (Do not space before hitting F9.) Your screen shows what you typed, followed by (*end field*). In other words, you have told the computer that this line is to be inserted into your letter at (*Field*)1.

3. Type the second line of the inside address and immediately hit **F9**.

   The least amount of space an inside address takes is two lines. Therefore, when you have finished creating the field where the last line of the inside address will be merged, skip to Step 7.

4. Type the third line of the inside address and immediately hit **F9**.

5. Type the fourth line of the inside address and immediately hit **F9**.

6. Type the fifth line of the inside address and immediately hit **F9**.

7. Now you need to tell the computer that this is the end of the first complete address in your secondary file. The completed address is called a record. To indicate the end of your first record, hit **Shift+F9** and hit **2 (End Record)**.

8. A double line will appear on your screen indicating a page break. With your cursor resting immediately below that double line, repeat Steps 2–7 for each of the addresses to which you want to send a letter.

9. When you are done, proofread carefully each line of each address. Then save this entire document to your disk. Click on **File**, click on **Save**, and type the path name as **a:\covlist.sf**; then enter. The .sf extension represents secondary file.

10. To exit, you must close your document by clicking on **File**, click on **Close**, click on **File**, and click on **Exit**.

Once you have merged your primary and secondary files, this secondary file of addresses will never be used again. As a result, each time you create a new secondary file, you begin with a clear screen. When you have finished, you follow the Step 9 to save the file and again name it **a:covlist.sf.** Because you save your last list under the same name, the computer will automatically replace your old list with this new one. Continue in this manner each week as you create a new secondary file.

If you want to create a secondary file to be merged with your letter of application, save it under the name **a:\applist.sf.**

MERGING PRIMARY AND SECONDARY FILES USING WORDPERFECT 6.0 (DOS)

Below are specific directions for merging your primary file cover letter and secondary file of addresses. It is absolutely essential that you have no errors of any kind in either your primary or secondary file. Begin the merge process by following these steps:

1. From a clear screen, click on **Tools**, click on **Merge**, and click on **Run**. In the Form File Box, type **a:\covltr.pf** and enter. In the Data File Box, type **a:\covlist.sf** and enter. Then click on **Merge**.

2. Wait a moment. Your first letter will appear on the screen with the cursor resting at the point of your first keyboard command. Your computer expects you to type in the appropriate

date. Do so, and then immediately hit **F9** to move your cursor to the next keyboard command, which is at the salutation. Type in the appropriate salutation based on your inside address, and then immediately hit **F9**. Continue in the same manner throughout all the letters.

3. When you have finished replacing the keyboard commands with the words you want, hit the home key three times and the up arrow key to take you quickly to the top of the screen. Now examine each letter to verify that it meets the needs of the particular want ad. If you want to make any additions or changes to a particular letter, make them. In this way, you customize your form letter to fit each want ad.

4. Get ready to print out all your letters. Make sure the paper in your printer is properly aligned. Click on **File**, click on **Print**, click on **Text Quality** and select **H (high)**. Then click on **Graphics Quality** and select **H (high)**. Click on **Number of Copies** and type in **2**. Click on **Print**. You will print two copies of each letter—one to send and one to keep with your Activity Log.

5. While your letters are printing, save this entire document to your disk. Click on **File**, click on **Save**, and name this document **a:\sept10**. (Note that this name contains the date on which you merged and sent your letters, in this case, September 10. Including the date in your file name enables you to refer to the letters later if necessary.)

6. To exit, click on **File**, click on **Close**, click on **File**, and click on **Exit**.

7. Staple your want ad to each of the respective letters, and fill out an Activity Log for that company. Put these letters in a file folder. Then sign the duplicate letter, place it on top of your resumé, fold, and place in the addressed envelope (See Appendix F).

*B*elow you will find specific directions for typing your cover letter using Microsoft Word 6.0 (Windows). You can save yourself a lot of time if you are able to use Word's features to create both your main document (letter) and your data source document (list of addresses) and then merge them together. In other words, the computer puts the address and salutation in the right spot in your letter.

You can also customize each and every letter to a specific want ad by using the Fill–In command when creating your initial main document. By doing so, you can quickly prepare several letters for mailing, and no one will know that the cover letter is basically a form letter.

STEPS FOR CREATING A MAIN DOCUMENT USING MICROSOFT WORD 6.0 (WINDOWS)

GENERAL SETUP

1. From a clear screen, make sure you are in the Page Layout mode with your Standard Bar, Format Bar, and Ruler Bar visible—like this:

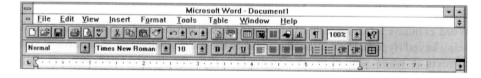

Standard Bar
Format Bar
Ruler Bar

   If they are not visible, click on **View** and then click on **Page Layout**. Then click on **View** and click on **Ruler**.

2. Click on **Format**, click on **Tabs**, and click on **Clear All**. With your cursor in the **Tab Stop Position Box**, type **4.25**; then enter.

3. We are going to create the main document first and then the data source.

MAIN DOCUMENT

1. At a clear document screen, choose **Tools** and then **Mail Merge**.

2. At the Mail Merge Helper dialog box, choose **Create** (below Main Document).

3. At the drop–down list that displays, choose **Form Letters**.

4. At the question asking if you want to use the active document window or a new document, choose **Active Window**.

5. At the Mail Merge Helper dialog box, choose **Get Data** (below Data Source).

6. At the drop–down list that displays, choose **Create Data Source**.

7. At the Create Data Source dialog box, the fields provided by Word are shown in the Field Names in Header Row. These fields are needed for the data source except *Country, Home Phone, and Work Phone.*

8. To remove the *Country* field name, click on the down arrow on the vertical scroll bar for the Field Names in Header Row list box, then click on **Remove Field Name.**

9. To remove the *Home Phone* field name, click on **Remove Field Name**.

10. To remove the *Work Phone* field name, click on **Remove Field Name**. Click on **OK**.

11. At the Save Data Source dialog box, type **a:\listds**, then click on **OK**.

12. At the dialog box containing the warning that the data source contains no data, click on **Edit Main Document**. This will return you to your regular screen so you can start to create your letter.

13. At the clear document screen with the Merge toolbar displayed below the Formatting toolbar, begin to type your letter as follows:

    a. Hit your enter key six times, tab, and type your street address. Then enter.

    b. Tab and type your city, state, and zip code; then enter.

14. You have no idea when this letter will actually be merged for mailing, so you need to give a Fill–In Command for the date. To do this:

    a. Tab; press **ALT+F9** (this turns on the display of fields).

    b. Click on the **Insert Word Field** button on the Merge toolbar.

    c. At the drop–down menu that displays, click on **Fill–In**.

   d. At the Insert Word Field: Fill–in dialog box, type **Insert Date**.

   e. Click on **OK**. At the Word dialog box with *Insert Date* displayed in the upper-left corner, click on **OK**.

15. Enter five times. Now you are going to create a separate field for each line in the inside address.

   a. Click on the **Insert Merge Field** button on the Merge toolbar (first button from the left).

   b. From the drop–down menu that displays, click on **Title**.

   c. Press the space bar once, then repeat Step A only this time click on **First Name**.

   d. Press the space bar once, then repeat Step A only this time click on **Last Name**; then enter once.

   e. Repeat Step A only this time click on **Job Title**; then enter once.

   f. Repeat Step A only this time click on **Company**; then enter once.

   g. Repeat Step A only this time click on **Address1**; then enter once.

   h. Repeat Step A only this time click on **Address2**; then enter once.

   i. Repeat Step A only this time click on **City**; type a comma, and press the space bar once.

   j. Repeat Step A only this time click on **State** and press the space bar twice.

   k. Repeat Step A only this time click on **Postal Code**; then enter twice.

16. Repeat Steps 14b, 14c, and 14d (only this time you will type **Salutation**). Click on **OK**. At the Word dialog box with *Salutation* displayed in the upper left corner, click on **OK**. Then type a **colon**; enter twice.

17. Now you are ready to type the body of your letter. Because you are typing in modified block style (your return address, date, complimentary closing, and signature line begin at the center), you have the choice of indenting or blocking your paragraphs. Double–space between each paragraph.

18. At any point in the letter where you might want to type something geared toward a specific ad, insert a Fill–In command to hold that spot so that later you can type your message. **Refer to Steps 14b, 14c, 14d, 14e**. For example, the position you desire and the name of the newspaper from which you got the ad might require you to insert a Fill–In command.

19. Enter twice after the last line of the body of your letter. Then hit the tab key to take you to the center. Type your **complimentary closing**. Follow it with a comma. Then hit the enter key four more times, tab to the center, and type **your name**. Hit the enter key twice and type **Enclosure**. (You will always enclose a resumé with your letter).

20. After carefully proofreading your letter, save it by clicking on **File**, click on **Save**, and name this **a:\covltrmd**. Then click on **File** and click on **Close**.

STEPS FOR CREATING DATA SOURCE DOCUMENT USING MICROSOFT WORD 6.0 (WINDOWS)

1. At a clear screen, click on **Tools** and then click on **Mail Merge**.

2. At the Mail Merge Helper dialog box, choose **Create**, then from the drop–down list that displays, choose **Form Letters**.

3. At the dialog box asking if you want to use the active document or a new document window, choose **Active Window**.

4. Choose **Get Data**, then from the drop–down list that displays, choose **Open Data Source**. Click on **a:\listds**; then click on **OK**. When the dialog box appears that says "Word found no merge files in your main document", click on **Cancel**. Then click on **Edit** under Data Source. The name of your document **a:\listds** will appear. Click on it.

5. At the Data Form dialog box, begin to key in the information requested in each want ad for the inside address. Hit enter after each field has been keyed. After entering all of the information for the first record, click on **Add New**. This saves the information and displays a blank Data Form dialog box.

6. Repeat Step 5 until all of the inside address information for all of your want ads has been created.

7. After creating the last record for the data source, choose **View Source**.

8. At the data source document, choose **File**, then **Save**

STEPS FOR MERGING USING MICROSOFT WORD 6.0 (WINDOWS)

---

1. Open **a:\covltrmd**

2. Click on the **Merge to New Document** button on the Merge toolbar (fifth button from the right).

3. As Word merges the main document with the first record in the data source, the Word dialog box with **Insert Date** in the upper left corner displays in the document screen. Key the date, then click on **OK**.

4. The Word dialog box with *Salutation* in the upper left corner displays in the document screen. Key in the appropriate salutation for the first record; then click on **OK**.

5. Continue in this manner until all of the Fill–In command data has been entered.

6. Word then completes the merge and all of your letters will be displayed on the screen.

7. Hit the Home Key three times and the up arrow key to take you quickly to the top of the screen. Now examine each letter to verify that it meets the needs of the particular want ad. If you want to make any additions or changes to a particular letter, make them. In this way, you customize your form letter to fit each want ad.

8. Get ready to print out all your letters. Make sure the paper in your printer is properly aligned. Click on **File**, click on **Print**, click on **Copies** and type in **2**. Click on **OK**. You will print two copies of each letter—one to send and one to keep for your Activity Log.

9. While your letters are printing, save this entire document to your disk. Click on **File**, click on **Save**, and name this document **a:\sept10**. (Note that this name contains the date on which you merged and sent your letters, in this case, September 10. Including the date in your file name enables you to refer to the letters later if necessary.)

10. To exit, click on **File**, click on **Close**, click on **File**, and click on **Exit**.

11. Staple your want ad to each of the respective letters, and fill out an Activity Log for that company. Put these letters in a file folder. Then sign the duplicate letter, place it on top of your resumé, fold, and place in the addressed envelope. (See Appendix F.)

Notes

*F*ollowing are examples of envelopes typed to the guidelines of the U.S. Postal Service. However, it is wise to check periodically with your local post office to obtain updates or changes in this procedure. In addition, the post office has excellent free informational pamphlets that may help you.

Typing an Envelope on a Typewriter

Notice that everything is typed in all capitals with no punctuation. The return address begins two lines down and three spaces in from the upper left corner of the envelope. The address to which the letter is being sent begins 14 or 15 lines from the top of the envelope and approximately five spaces to the left of the center point of the the envelope. The center of a large envelope is 57 on a typewriter using elite type size. If you backspace five times, you are at 52. However, because 51 is the natural center point on a typewriter using elite size, just remember to start typing your address at 51.

If you know to whom the letter is going, put his or her name first—followed by the company name on the second line as shown on page 342. Otherwise, use an attention line as shown in the other example on page 342.

PREPARING AN ENVELOPE MERGE FILE USING WORDPERFECT 6.1 (WINDOWS)

WordPerfect allows you to create a separate envelope form file which may be merged with the data file you created and named **a:\covlist.sf** following the directions in Appendix E. The envelope file simply contains the fields to be included in the envelope. Once the envelope file is created and saved with a **.pf** extension, it may be merged with any data file providing the field names match the names used in the data file.[1]

TO CREATE AN ENVELOPE FILE

1. At a clear screen, click on **Format**, click on **Envelope**, click on **Return Address**, and type your name and address in all capital letters with no punctuation. Click on **Append to Document**.

---

[1]You only create the **env.pf** once. From then on as you create a new secondary file of addresses each week that coincide with your want ads, all you have to do is follow the steps to merge.

MR GORDON GROSS
1914 STANHOPE
GROSSE POINTE WOODS MI 48236

GENERAL MOTORS CORPORATION
ATTENTION HUMAN RESOURCES DEPARTMENT
12890 VAN DYKE AVENUE
WARREN MI 48089

MR GORDON GROSS
1914 STANHOPE
GROSSE POINTE WOODS MI 48236

MRS NANCY JOHNSON
GENERAL MOTORS CORPORATION
12890 VAN DYKE AVENUE
WARREN MI 48089

2. Press **Shift+F9**, click on **Form File**, click on **Use File in Active Window**, click on **OK**.

3. With your cursor in the Associate Data File box, type **a:\covlist.sf**; then click on **OK**.

4. Click on **Insert Field**. Your first address from your data file will appear. Click on the first line of that address, click on **Insert**, and then enter once. Click on the second line of that address, click on **Insert**, and then enter once. Click on the third line of that address, click on **Insert**, and then enter once. Click on the fourth line of that address, click on **Insert**, and then enter once. Click on the fifth line of that address, and click on **Insert**.

TO MERGE AN ENVELOPE FILE WITH YOUR SECONDARY FILE OF ADDRESSES

1. Click on **Tools**, click on **Merge**, and click on **Perform Merge**.

2. In the Form File Dialog Box, type **a:\env.pf**; then enter.

3. In the Data File Dialog Box, type **a:\covlist.sf**; then enter.

4. Click on **OK** and the merge will occur.

5. All of your envelopes will appear on your screen separated by page breaks (double lines).

6. Give the command to print, either each page individually as you feed one envelope at a time or the full document if you can stack your envelopes in your printer.

PREPARING AN ENVELOPE MERGE FILE USING WORDPERFECT 6.0 (DOS)

WordPerfect allows you to create a separate envelope form file which may be merged with the data file you created and named **a:\covlist.sf** following the directions in Appendix E. The envelope file simply contains the fields to be included in the envelope. Once the envelope file is created and saved with a **.pf** extension, it may be merged with any data file providing the field names match the names used in the data file.[2]

---

[2]You only create the **env.pf** once. From then on as you create a new secondary file of addresses each week that coincide with your want ads, all you have to do is follow the steps to merge listed above.

TO CREATE AN ENVELOPE FILE

1. From a clear screen, click on **Layout**, click on **Envelope**, and click on **3** (save return address as default).

2. Click on **4** (return address) and type your name and address in all capitals with no punctuation. Press **F7** when done.

3. Click on **5** (addressee) and press **Shift+F9**. Click on **Form File**.

4. When the new menu choices appear, click on **Field** and type 1?; then enter twice. Press **Shift+F9** again, click on **Field** and type 2?; then enter twice. Press **Shift+F9**, click on **Field** and type 3?; then enter twice. Press **Shift+F9**, click on **Field** and type 4?; then enter twice. Press **Shift+F9**, click on **Field** and type 5?; then enter once. Hit **F7** and then click on **Insert**.

5. Now click on **File**, click on **Save**, and name this **a:\env.pf**. Then close your document by clicking on **File** and clicking on **Close**.

TO MERGE AN ENVELOPE FILE WITH YOUR SECONDARY FILE OF ADDRESSES

1. At a clear screen, press **Ctrl+F9**, click on **Merge**, type the form file name **a:\env.pf** and enter. Type the data file name **a:\covlist.sf** and enter. Click on **Merge.**

2. All of your envelopes will appear on your screen separated by page breaks (double lines).

3. Give the command to print, either each page individually as you feed one envelope at a time or the full document if you can stack your envelopes in your printer.

PREPARING AN ENVELOPE MERGE FILE USING MICROSOFT WORD 6.0 (WINDOWS)

An envelope can be created that contains fields that are then merged with your data source. In this way, you can quickly prepare envelopes. Follow these steps:

1. At a clear screen, click on **Tools** and then **Mail Merge**.

2. At the Mail Merge Helper dialog box, click on **Create** (below Main Document).

3. At the drop–down list that displays, click on **Envelopes**.

4. At the question asking if you want to use the active document window or a new document, click on **Active Window**.

5. At the Mail Merge Helper dialog box, click on **Get Data** (below Data Source).

6. At the drop–down list that displays, click on **Open Data Source**.

7. At the Open Data Source dialog box, select **a:\listds** from the list, then click on **OK**.

8. At the Word dialog box telling you that Word needs to set up your main document, click on **Set Up Main Document**.

9. At the Envelope Options dialog box with the Envelope Options tab selected, make sure the correct envelope size is displayed, then click on **OK**.

10. At the Envelope Address dialog box, click on **Insert Merge Field**, then click on **Title** from the drop–down list.

11. Press the space bar once, then click on **Insert Merge Field** and click on **First Name** from the drop–down list.

12. Continue in this manner until all the fields in the Sample Envelope Address section of the dialog box have been entered. Then click on **OK**.

13. At the Mail Merge Helper dialog box, click on **Merge**.

14. At the Merge dialog box, click on **Merge To** option and click on **Printer**. Then click on **Merge**. Insert your envelopes into your printer.

APPENDIX **G** TESTING PROCEDURES

*O*ften you will be asked to take one or more tests before you are interviewed for the position. These could be skill tests, general intelligence tests, or a personality analysis (sometimes referred to as a personanalysis). Preparedness will be your key to success!

The best way to prepare for these tests is to follow all of the advice given you so far and get a good night's sleep the night before. Remember, you are well prepared to tackle any tests that may be administered—so try to relax.

When applying for an office position, you can generally expect to take tests in the following subjects:

- Five minute typing timed writing

- Spelling

- Math

- Punctuation

- Word processing

- Composition

- Shorthand

1. Five-Minute Typing Timed Writing. You will be given a few minutes to warm up on material different from that used for the actual test. You will then be asked to take a timing. Try to relax and concentrate when taking the timing.

   Try to find out what type of equipment you will be tested on at the time you arrange for the interview. If testing on a computer, ask if you are allowed to use the backspace key to correct errors as you type without having it count against you.

2. Spelling Test. To prepare for the spelling test, study the list of most commonly misspelled words found on back inside cover.

3. Math Test. The math test will be very basic and shouldn't cause any concern. You may be asked to do some simple calculations, such as: If the total bill is $387.65, figure the amount due if the company offers a 2 percent discount when the bill is paid within 10 days.

4. Punctuation Test.   The punctuation test may be one where you are asked to punctuate simple sentences correctly. On the other hand, you may be given an unarranged letter with all kinds of errors. You may be asked to type the letter in correct letter format, making all necessary changes, including spelling, punctuation, capitalization, and number transcription.

5. Word Processing Test.   If given a word processing test, be sure to ask if you can use your command template or command sheet. Many companies administer a computer test that asks you to make changes to an existing document. You are given only one chance to perform each function. Your command will be marked either right or wrong, and you will be instructed to proceed to the next step. Before beginning a computer test, ask whether you will have the opportunity to make a correction without being penalized if you give a command and then realize it is the wrong one. An alternative test consists of text on paper that you are asked to format using a word processing program.

6. Composition Test.   You may also be asked to compose a letter based on a particular scenario and type it.

7. Shorthand Test.   For shorthand, you will be given dictation of tape for warm up. Then you will be asked to take down some letters, probably dictated at 80 wpm, and the transcribe them into good letter format.

You can also expect to take a physical examination after being offered a job. Probably included in that exam will be a drug and alcohol analysis.

Most employment agencies thoroughly test for the positions they need to fill. These agencies would be a good place to start your job search so that you can practice and boost your confidence. If you have any shortcomings, you will learn what they are so that you can improve in those areas.

■ SAMPLE TESTS

Most companies or employment agencies are computerizing the majority of their tests. The type and number of tests administered for office positions varies widely.

Generally with employment agencies, however, you are asked to fill out several questionnaires, indicating your qualifications with various office machines, computer and telephone systems, software programs, and skills. Then you are asked to indicate in which areas you would like to be tested. Obviously, the more tests you take and pass, the more employable and better paid you will be. So it is to your advantage to plan to spend two to three hours and take as many tests as possible for which you feel qualified.

Of course you will be nervous, but try to relax. Concentrate. Reading and following directions are just as important as the test itself. Below are descriptions of common tests representative of those you might encounter in your job search. For each category, I have demonstrated only one type of test administered by an employment agency.

THREE-MINUTE TIMED TYPING TEST

You will be given a three-minute timed typing test from straight copy material on a computer. You will have the choice of taking this test with word wrap on or word wrap off. If you select word wrap off, you will have to enter a hard return at the end of each line of text. This is much slower, so choose word wrap on. You can also type with the insert key on or the typeover key on. Again choose insert on so that if you make a mistake, you can hit the backspace key and retype. Remember, however, that backspacing during a timing really slows you down. But, too many errors will negatively affect your score. Therefore, approach the test with the primary goal of accuracy with a reasonable amount of speed. The higher your speed and accuracy, the more placeable you become.

You will be given three minutes to warm up. You may use material supplied by the agency or use your own material. If you don't need the full three minutes to warm up, you hit the ESC key to stop the warm-up session. Then you will be instructed to begin the timing. The material usually is one long paragraph, and you do not have to indent to begin. The directions say that if you finish the material before the three-minute period expires, you should hit the ESC key to stop the timer. At that point, your test is scored. You will not be told about the results until you have completed all tests. If you don't meet the agency's minimum requirements, however, the computer immediately instructs you to take the alternate test.

PRODUCTION TYPING TEST

You will be given a short memo and rough draft letter with revision marks. You will be instructed to take five minutes to proofread both documents, searching for any grammatical, punctuation, spelling, or capitalization errors. You are to write on the test copy. If you finish before the five minutes have expired, hit the ESC key and begin the test. You will be given 15 minutes to type both documents. Begin the memo document only, and hit ESC when you are finished. At that point, your memo will be scored. If you fail, you will be instructed to type the alternate memo immediately. If you pass, you will be instructed to continue with the letter portion of the test. Again, once you have finished, hit ESC and wait for your test to be scored. If you fail that portion, you will be instructed to take the alternate test immediately. As with the timed typing test, you will not learn of your actual score until you have completed the entire testing process.

Below is a sample production typing test shown in rough draft format with revision marks. It is followed by a list of standard revisions marks.

SAMPLE ROUGH DRAFT PRODUCTION TEST

Type the following letter in correct format. The letter is to Mark Stanfield, ABC Corporation, 2020 Hodges, Lansing, MI 48901. The subject concerns his refund request. Please send this letter special delivery. The letter is from Mike Johnson.

¶ We are very happy to send you your money. We behind stand our
refund
merchandise and are happy only when our customers are happy.
stet
¶ Just fill out the enclosed refund-request form and mail it to us
in the postpaid envelope. You will receive your refund within ten
days after we receive the completed form.

REVISION MARKS

Capitalize ≡ or cap	Insert Apostrophe ∨	Lowercase lc or /
Close Up ⌣	Insert Quotation Marks ᵛ ᵛ	Paragraph ¶
Delete ℓ	Move Right ⊐	Spell Out ◯ sp
Insert ∧	Move Left ⊏	Transpose ⌒⌣ or tr
Insert Comma ⌄	Move Down Lower ⌊ ⌋	Let It Stand stet
Insert Period ⊙	Move Up ⌐ ¬	Underline ___
Insert Space , or /		

SHORTHAND TEST

You will be given the choice of trying the 70 word-per-minute (wpm) test or the 80 wpm test. Again, a warm up period is provided. The testing material will be general with no particularly difficult words. When the three-minute dictation period ends, you will be instructed to transcribe your notes in paragraph form, inserting all punctuation, capitalization, and correct spelling. A point will be deducted for each error you make. As with the other tests, if you fail, you are instructed immediately to take the alternate test.

LOTUS TEST

The Lotus test evaluates your data entry skills and knowledge of Lotus concepts. Reading and following directions are crucial in this test. You are given only one chance to execute an instruction. If you hit the wrong key, you will hear a beep, be marked wrong, told what you should have hit, told to make that change, and told to continue.

The short practice exercise may indicate what the test itself is like. You will be shown a spreadsheet with column and row labels already inserted. You will be asked to widen all the columns globally and asked to center the label headings for each column.

The test will begin like the practice exercise. You will be asked to widen the columns globally and to center the label headings. Next, you will be given information to enter in each cell.

In many companies, this type of test might constitute a beginning-level competency test. In an intermediate-level test, you might be expected to create and enter the appropriate formulas to achieve the desired results in the spreadsheet. An advanced-level test might include everything in the first two tests and require you to do one or more of the following things: create a graph from the spreadsheet information, fix titles, create a window, look up information, or sort.

WORD PROCESSING TEST

You will have the option of taking the test for WordPerfect 6.0 for DOS, 6.1 for Windows, or Word 6.0 for Windows. You may use the agency's handbook or your own handbook and template. Again, reading and following directions are essential because you are given only one opportunity to do each required task. If you make a wrong command, you will hear a beep, will be marked wrong, will be told what you should have done, and then will be told to continue.

For this test, you may be asked if you want to take the beginning, intermediate, or advanced test. Several versions at each level are available, and you can take one or all. In an advanced test, for example, your choices might be columns, tables, or macros/merge. For the macros test, you see a screen with the date in the upper left-hand corner and the cursor resting approximately five lines below. There is a macro called a:add, which you are asked to invoke. Just hit the appropriate command, **Alt+F10**, type **a:add,** and enter. The macros test might be that simple. But more realistic is the test in which you will be given information and told to create a macro.

For the merging portion of the test, you will be shown a screen with the date in the upper left-hand corner and the cursor positioned about five lines below the date. You must create Field 1 and leave a space; create Field 2 and leave a space; and create Field 3 and enter a hard return. The create Field 4 and enter a hard return. Create Field 5. Save this as **a:jones.let** and answer **N** (no) when asked if you want to exit WordPerfect. From a clear screen, type **Mr.** and end that field; type **John** and end that field; type **Smith** and end that field; type **12345 Main Street** and end that field; and type **Detroit, MI 44489** and end that field. End that record. You will be given similar information to create a second record. After typing the second record, save it as **a:jones.lis** and again answer **N** (no) when asked to exit WordPerfect. Finally you will be instructed to merge a:jones: let with a:jones:lis.

OTHER TYPES OF TESTS

Spelling tests consist of approximately 25 words. You will be asked to put a check mark in front of any words that are misspelled. Sometimes agencies provide copy in rough draft form with revision marks and instruct applicants to correct all errors, including spelling.

GRAMMAR TESTS

Grammar tests consist of sentences in which you are asked to choose the correct word. For example:

1. His objections to our program _____ trivial.
   a. seems
   b. seem

2. Neither of the men achieved _____ objective.
   a. his
   b. their

3. Jack and _____ can handle the job ourselves.
   a me
   b. I

4. With the help of my colleagues, I _____ answered your questions satisfactorily.
   a. should of
   b. should have

5. Ms. Porter was _____ proud of her department.
   a. real
   b. really

6. _____ answering our letter promptly would be appreciated.
   a. You
   b. Your

7. Mr. Murphy is the person _____ is going to lunch.
   a. whom
   b. that
   c. who

8. Because of _____ involvement, our company cannot vote on the issue.
   a. it's
   b. its

9. _____ is enough work here to keep us busy for the next six months.
   a. They're
   b. There
   c. Their

10. There are times when accuracy is _____ more important than speed.
    a. most
    b. more

Another test encompassing word processing, transcription, proofreading, and letter format follows. While the dictating machine cassette tape is not provided, you will have a chance to view the answer key to see the level of difficulty.

Objectives: To show the applicant's ability to format correctly a letter containing all the special features that could appear in a business situation.

To demonstrate the applicant's ability to transcribe from a dictating machine.

To demonstrate the applicant's expertise in using WordPerfect or Microsoft Word as a word processing tool, including the spell check and thesaurus features.

Today's Date

The Ford Motor Company
Attention Media Department
21133 Michigan Avenue
Dearborn, MI 48121

Ladies and Gentlemen:

FORD MUSTANG FALL ADVERTISING CAMPAIGN

As you requested this morning, I am enclosing the anticipated budget figures for the Ford Mustang account for our fall advertising blitz. These figures reflect the addition of two full-time support staff personnel to **(were asked to use a thesaurus to select a different word than dictated: expedite, hasten, hurry, quicken, speed)** and ease the workload.

Please review this proposal with your department's employees as soon as possible. Your reaction would be appreciated by Friday, October 1, 1996.

Sincerely yours,

Linda Gibraltar
Media Consultant

xx

Enclosure

To establish the applicant's ability to insert correct punctuation, capitalization, number transcription, and paragraphs.

To measure the applicant's production typing speed.

Directions: You will be timed. Using all available features of WordPerfect 6.1 or Microsoft Word, transcribe the business letter from the cassette tape given to you. Use correct format and insert necessary punctuation and paragraphs. Print letter when finished.[1]

Another type of test for punctuation skills follows. You may refer to the answer key with corrections in boldface print.

Objectives: To test the applicant's spelling ability.

To evaluate the applicant's knowledge of punctuation, capitalization, and number usage.

Directions: Correct any errors you see in the following sentences.

1. We have thirty secretaries working at our off-site building.

2. She began to work for us on September 3rd 1996.

3. 18 employees are in that department.

4. Ms Kantor our boss lives in an exclusive apartment building.

5. We must reduce 4 kinds of pollution soil air water and noise.

6. Although winter has been over for weeks we still have snow.

7. The title of the article is What Your Dollar Does for You.

8. Our personnel department is has two openings and would like to fill them as soon as possible.

9. Their Finance Committee will meet Tuesday July 3 1995 at ten o'clock and we would like you to attend.

10. Please submit you quote for under 500 dollars for two full color ads.

11. I want to enlarge my business and have taken a thirty day option on a building that will provide the space for the expansion.

[1]See example of test result on page 354.

12. I am taking a three months vacation next year.

13. The price of the booklet is $.20.

1. We have **30** secretaries working at our off-site building.

2. She began to work for us on September **3,** 1996.

3. **Eighteen** employees are in that department.

4. Ms. Kantor, our boss, lives in an exclusive apartment building.

5. We must reduce **four** kinds of pollution—soil, air, water, and noise.

6. Although winter has been over for weeks, we still have snow.

7. The title of the article is "What Your Dollar Does for You."

8. Our **P**ersonnel **D**epartment has two openings and would like to fill them as soon as possible.

9. Their **f**inance committee will meet Tuesday, July 3, 1995, at **10** o'clock; and we would like you to attend.

11. I want to enlarge my business and have taken a **30**-day option on a building that will provide the space for the expansion.

12. I am taking a three months' vacation next year.

13. The price of the booklet is **20 cents.**

Notes

USING THE INTERNET TO FACILITATE YOUR JOB SEARCH

Check your library for these books and magazines on using the Internet:

- *The Complete Idiot's Guide to the Internet,* 1994

- *Curious About the Internet,* 1995

- *The Essential Internet Information Guide,* 1995

- *The Internet for Everyone: A Guide for Users and Providers,* 1995

- *The Internet Troubleshooter: Help for the Logged-on and Lost,* 1994

- *The Internet via Mosaic and World Wide Web,* 1994

- *Internet World* Magazine

- *The Windows Internet Tour Guide: Cruising the Internet the Easy Way,* 1994

- *Wired* Magazine

- *The World Wide Web Unleashed,* 1994

The following Web sites will help you begin your career exploration. However, new sites are added daily and some site addresses might change. Just keep searching because the site may still exist at a new address.

- **Bss Job Listings** (http://rescomp.stanford.edu/jobs-bbs.html)

  This is a compilation of employment resources on the Web. It gives Web addresses and phone numbers but does not provide access links.

- **Career Magazine** (http://www.careermag.com/careermag/)

  This is an excellent resource to tap into for all of your career exploration and job search needs. It contains job listings downloaded from other Internet employment services, links to other career sites, a career forum discussion group, news and articles, a resumé bank, and employer profiles.

- **Career Planning Services and Resources** (http://www. wpi.edu/Depts/Library/jobguide/career.html)

  This includes career service centers and assistance with job search issues.

- **Careers On-Line from the University of Minnesota** (http://www.disserv.stu.umn.edu/TC/Grants?COL/)

This lists Web employment services and other resources for people with disabilities.

- **The Catapult** (http://www.wm.edu/catapult/catapult.html)

  This site will catapult you to hundreds of different career and job campaign sites. It includes a Career Resources Library.

- **Employment Opportunities and Job Resources on the Internet** (a.k.a. Riley Guide) (Http://www.wpi.edu/~mfriley/jobguide.html)

  This provides links to career and job resources from many disciplines. It also contains information on using the Internet as a job source, and more.

- **Employment Resources on the Internet** (http://www.cs.purdue.edu/homes/swlodin/jobs.html)

  This provides links to hundreds of employment home pages all over the world.

- **E-Span's Interactive Employment Network** (http://www.espan.com)

  You can post your resumé at this site, search for jobs, and access career and salary information.

- **Fedworld** (http://www.fedworld.gov)

  This site gives information about the federal government, including job listings.

- **Graduate Employers** (http://www.gold.net/arcadia/horizons/employers/)

  This site gives information on job openings with firms that seek to fill entry-level positions with college graduates.

- **Huber Commercial Site Directories** (http://www.huber.com/Home/commercial.html)

  This site provides links to hundreds of businesses' home pages.

- **Internet Job Surfer** (http://rpinfo.its.rpi.edu:80/dept/cdc/jobsurfer.html)

  This links you to more than 80 Internet job and career sites listed alphabetically.

- **Job Search and Employment Opportunities**
  (http://asa.ugl.lib.umich.edu/chdocs/employment/)

  This site gives an annotated list of employment-related Web resources.

- **MecklerWeb Home Page**
  (http:/www.mecklerweb.com/home.htm)

  This site provides information about the Internet and includes a Career Web that contains some job listings.

- **NETworth Navigator**
  (http://networth.galt.com/www/home/navigator.html)

  This site has a section entitled "The Insider: Public Companies" that links you to the home pages of more than 400 companies.

- **On-Line Career Center** (http://www.occ.com/occ/)

  This site allows you to search jobs, add your resumé, research employers, gain career assistance, and much more.

- **Open Market's Commercial Sites Index**
  (http://www.directory.net/)

  This site lists and provides quick access to hundreds of companies' home pages.

- **Resources for International Opportunities**
  (http://www.wpi.edu/Depts/Library/jobguide/internat.html)

  This site lists sites of job announcements for countries other than the United States or Canada.

BIBLIOGRAPHY

Ancona, Paula. "Total Quality Management Focuses on One Problem at a Time." *The Detroit News*, September 19, 1994, p. 19F.

Ancona, Paula. "Coping with Life in a Downsized Work Place." *The Detroit News,* May 9, 1994, p. 18F.

Ancona, Paula. "Save It, Toss It, Or Do It, But Keep a Clear Desk." *The Detroit News,* January 17, 1994, p. 16F.

Ancona, Paula. "Workplace: Female Executives Confront Different Set of Perceptions as They Move Up." *The Detroit News,* December 6, 1993, p. 18F.

Beatty, Richard H. *The Perfect Cover Letter.* New York: John Wiley & Sons, 1989.

Benson, Tracey E. "Quality and Teamwork." *Industry Week,* April 6, 1992, p. 66.

Boxton, Debra. *Lions Don't Need to Roar.* New York: Warner Books, 1992.

Boyett, Joseph H., and Henry P. Conn. *Workplace 2000.* New York: Penguin Books, 1991.

Calman, Janice. "How to Manage a Tough Boss." *The Detroit News,* December 13, 1993, pp. 8–9F.

Career Services and Placement. *Placement Manual.* Lansing: Michigan State University, Cass Recruitment Publications. 1995–96.

Cassady, Ellen, and Karen Nussbaum. *9 to 5: The Working Woman's Guide to Office Survival.* New York: Penguin Books, 1983.

Chapman, Elwood. N. *Plan B: Protecting Your Career from the Winds of Change.* Los Altos, CA: Crisp Publications, 1988.

Galagan, Patricia A. "How to Get Your TQM Training on Track." *Nation's Business,* October 1992, pp. 24–28.

Good, C. Edward. *Does Your Resumé Wear Apron Springs?* Charlottesville, VA: Blue Jeans Press, 1989.

Greenfield, Joan. "Careers: You Can't Be Productive at Work if You Are Dead on Your Feet." *The Detroit News,* July 24, 1995, p. 11F.

Greenfield, Joan. "How to Prepare for Job Reference Checks." *The Detroit News,* February 27, 1995, p. 12F.

Greenfield, Joan. "Relax—Stress Can Become Manageable." *The Detroit News,* January 17, 1994, p. 16F.

Greenfield, Joan, and Harvey Mackay. "Sharkproof Offers a Repellent to Fight Career Dissatisfaction." *The Detroit News,* June 20, 1994, p. 13F.

Grove, Andrew S. "Pumping up Your Staff's Productivity." *Working Woman,* August 1992, p. 22.

Hein, Pat and Susan Golant. *Hardball for Women.* Los Angeles: Lowell House, 1992.

Holton, Ed. "The Critical First Year on the Job." *CPC Annual.* Bethlehem, PA: College Placement Council, 1992–93.

HR Magazine on Human Resource Management 37, no. 6 (June 1992); 37, no. 11 (November 1992); 38 no. 1 (January 1993).

Inside WordPerfect 4, no. 7 (July 1993), The Cobb Group, p. 13.

Joyner, Tammy. "Power Lunch." *The Detroit News,* July 11, 1994. p. 14F.

Joyner, Tammy. "How To Avoid Burnout on the Job." *The Detroit News,* May 9, 1994, pp. 10–11F.

Joyner, Tammy. "How to Work Your Way Out of the Dog House." *The Detroit News,* March 28, 1994. pp. 10–11F.

Kanarek, Lisa. "10 Ways to Get More out of Your Time at the Office." *The Secretary* 54, no. 1 (January 1994), p. 12–13.

Kennedy, Marily N. Moats. "10 Reasons People Get Fired." *Business Week Careers,* pp. 39–41.

Krannich, Ronald L., and Caryl Rae Krannich. *Salary Success.* Woodbridge, VA: Impact Publications, 1990.

Kulfan, Ted. "Right Approach in a Career Can Make All the Difference." *The Detroit News,* August 14, 1994, p. 14F.

Medley, H. Anthony. *Sweaty Palms.* Berkeley, CA: Ten Speed Press, 1992.

Mundell, Charles. "How to Handle Ilegal Interview Questions." *CPC Annual.* Bethlehem, PA: College Placement Council, 1992–93.

Petrocelli, William, and Barbara Kate Repa. *Sexual Harassment on the Job.* Berkeley, CA: Nolo Press, 1992.

Price, Sara. *Today's Professional Secretary,* 4th ed. Shawnee Mission, KS: The Business Woman's Training Institute, 1987.

Sabo, Sandra R. "Team Spirit." *The Secretary* 54, no. 1, (January 1994), pp. 14–17.

Schmidt, Peggy. *Making It On Your First Job.* Princeton, NJ: Peterson's Guides, 1991.

Schoeppel, Cynthia. "Tips on Checking up on a Potential Employer." *The Detroit News,* February 27, 1995, p. 12F.

Seebacher, Noreen. "Casual Dress Rules." *The Detroit News,* August 22, 1994, pp. 8–9F.

Serja, Tricia. "Tired Old Excuses Are No Substitute for Good Time Management Skills." *The Detroit News,* February 27, 1995, p. 13F.

Springston, Jeff, and Joann Keyton. "The Resumé: Advertising Your Ability to Do the Job." *CPC Annual.* Bethlehem, PA: College Placement Council, 1992–93.

36th Edition CPC Annual. Special Two-year College Edition, Bethlehem, PA: College Placement, 1992–93.

Thomson, Roger. "No Easy Answers." *Nation's Business,* July 1989, p. 38.

Walberg, Marvin. "Searching for a Job Is Selling Yourself." *The Detroit News,* February 27, 1995, p. 13F.

Waldrop, Dawn. "Your Professional Best." *The Secretary,* April 1994, pp. 16–18.

Yate, Martin. *Knock 'Em Dead.* Holbrook, MA: Bob Adams, Inc., 1992.